After the Fact

After the Fact

THE ART OF HISTORICAL DETECTION

SIXTH EDITION

Volume I

James West Davidson

Mark Hamilton Lytle
Bard College

McGraw Hill

Connect
Learn
Succeed™

Published by McGraw-Hill, an imprint of The McGraw-Hill Companies, Inc., 1221 Avenue of the Americas, New York, NY 10020. Copyright © 2010, 2005, 2000, 1992. All rights reserved. No part of this publication may be reproduced or distributed in any form or by any means, or stored in a database or retrieval system, without the prior written consent of The McGraw-Hill Companies, Inc., including, but not limited to, in any network or other electronic storage or transmission, or broadcast for distance learning.

This book is printed on acid-free paper.

3 4 5 6 7 8 9 0 DOC/DOC 0

ISBN: 978-0-07-729268-3
MHID: 0-07-729268-5

Editor in Chief: *Michael Ryan*
Publisher: *Chris Freitag*
Sponsoring Editor: *Matthew Busbridge*
Marketing Manager: *Pam Cooper*
Developmental Editor: *Denise Wright*
Managing Editor: *Nicole Bridge*
Production Editor: *David Blatty*
Manuscript Editor: *Andrea McCarrick*
Design Manager and Cover Designer: *Laurie Entringer*
Photo Research: *Sarah Evertson*
Production Supervisor: *Rich DeVitto*
Composition: *10.5/12 Janson by Laserwords*
Printing: *45# New Era Matte Plus, R.R. Donnelley & Sons*

Cover Images: Shawnee Village pot effigy courtesy of Arkansas Department of Parks and Tourism, Hampson Archaeological Museum; Upper Nodena rendering and the photograph of the pot effigy courtesy of Angie Payne, Center for Advanced Spatial Technologies, University of Arkansas.

Credits: The credits section for this book begins on page 203 and is considered an extension of the copyright page.

Library of Congress Cataloging-in-Publication Data

Davidson, James West.
  After the fact : the art of historical detection / James West Davidson, Mark Lytle.—6th ed.
    p. cm.
  Includes bibliographical references and index.
  ISBN-13: 978-0-07-729268-3 (v. 1 : acid-free paper)
  ISBN-10: 0-07-729268-5 (v. 1 : acid-free paper)
  1. United States—Historiography. 2. United States—History. I. Lytle, Mark H. II. Title.
  E175.D38 2009
  973—dc22
                                                 2009029656

The Internet addresses listed in the text were accurate at the time of publication. The inclusion of a Web site does not indicate an endorsement by the authors or McGraw-Hill, and McGraw-Hill does not guarantee the accuracy of the information presented at these sites.

www.mhhe.com

About the Authors

JAMES WEST DAVIDSON received his PhD from Yale University. A historian who has pursued a full-time writing career, he is the author of numerous books, among them *The Logic of Millennial Thought: Eighteenth-Century New England* and *Great Heart: The History of a Labrador Adventure* (with John Rugge). He is coeditor, with Michael Stoff, of the Oxford New Narratives in American History, in which his own most recent book appears, *"They Say": Ida B. Wells and the Reconstruction of Race*.

MARK H. LYTLE, a PhD from Yale University, is Professor of History and Chair of the Environmental Studies Program at Bard College. He has served two years as Mary Ball Washington Professor of American History at University College Dublin, in Ireland. His publications include *The Origins of the Iranian-American Alliance, 1941–1953, America's Uncivil Wars: The Sixties Era from Elvis to the Fall of Richard Nixon,* and most recently, *The Gentle Subversive: Rachel Carson, Silent Spring, and the Rise of the Environmental Movement*. He recently coedited a joint issue of the journals *Diplomatic History* and *Environmental History* dedicated to the field of environmental diplomacy.

Contents

Preface

We began this book more than a quarter century ago with an introduction—still there, if you turn the page—which compares the process of doing history to deciphering the tales hidden in the tree rings of a newly felled hemlock. The dust jacket to the first edition even included an authors' photo of the two of us in front of such a stump, looking very young, very hirsute, and vaguely disreputable. (This was the 1970s, by way of historical context.)

The sixth edition finds us quantitatively less hirsute, but the book certainly has gained foliage, having accumulated nearly as much of a history as the old hemlock in our introduction. The first edition of *After the Fact* contained thirteen chapters; the recent fifth edition boasted seventeen, not counting an additional three chapters that have been retired over the years. History may be the past, but its writing moves ahead. We decided that for this edition, we needed to focus on pruning and shaping as well as adding and revising.

We went over each of the existing chapters with an eye to streamlining the narrative, making it more accessible, and eliminating unnecessary detail, without compromising our portrayal of the often messy process of historical detection. The result is that most chapters are shorter and, we believe, more engaging and readable. As in previous editions, we have added two new chapters, as well as rewritten an old one, but the total number remains at seventeen. They progress in chronological order through American history.

"Contact," our new Chapter 1, uses the De Soto expedition of 1539–1543 to examine the difficulties of reconstructing the contested ground of first contact, and the need to take a broader ecological perspective. The progress made by archaeologists over the past few decades allows us to see better some of the remarkable transformations sparked by the De Soto *entrada*, as well as the meeting of Europeans and first Americans more generally. This chapter replaces our previous essay on ecological history, "The Invisible Pioneers." While the new chapter incorporates some material from the original chapter, it also demonstrates how new scholarship has turned other parts of the story nearly upside down.

"Sitting-In," our new Chapter 15, uses the early years of the civil rights struggle to examine how and why broad social movements emerge when and where they do. The lunch-counter demonstrations at Greensboro in 1960 appeared to be a spontaneous event, which then spread like wildfire. Why did the sit-ins in Greensboro trigger this outburst of activism when earlier demonstrations did not? Was Greensboro really spontaneous, as many observers and historians first thought? And does the response to it support the notion that discontinuity rather than continuity defines the process of change over time?

"The Madness of John Brown," Chapter 7, still asks the same question: "Was John Brown insane?" But it employs dynamic psychology rather than psychoanalytic theory to reach a similar conclusion. In times of political upheaval "it's hard to tell who's mad."

Finally, we have included a new feature periodically throughout the text, "Past and Present." In it we make connections between the topics on which we practice detective work from the past with present-day issues or themes worthy of further examination.

Besides streamlining and adding new material, we have made our interactive Web site the place where ancillary materials are now available. The Primary Source Investigator (PSI), previously supplied on CD-ROM, is redesigned and now online. There you will find additional documents and images, as well as chapters from previous editions, including "The 'Noble Savage' and the Artist's Canvas," "Huey Generis," "Instant Watergate," and "The Body in Question." The Research and Writing Center, also found on PSI, will assist students in a range of skills, from time management to conducting their own research and producing quality papers.

Meantime, we owe thanks to those who helped with revisions to this edition. For reviews of this book and for assistance on one or both of our new chapters, we would like to thank Amelia Dees-Killette, Coastal Carolina Community College; Andrew Eugene Barnes, Arizona State University; Angela M. Payne, University of Arkansas; Angela T. Thompson, East Carolina University; Ann F. Ramenofsky, University of New Mexico; Carmen V. Harris, University of South Carolina-Upstate; Kenneth Millen-Penn, Fairmont State University; Mario A. Perez, Crafton Hills College; Marlon Mowdy, Hampton Archaeological Museum State Park, Wilson, Arkansas; Martin B. Cohen (retired), George Mason University; Nancy Mitchell, North Carolina State University; Natalie Graham, University of Florida; Raymond Nathan Wilson, University of Tulsa; W. Frederick Limp, University of Arkansas.

We also have benefited from the assistance of the editorial team at McGraw-Hill, including Nicole Bridge and Denise Wright. As always, we appreciate the enthusiasm of our readers and are pleased to receive any advice, corrections, or comments on this new edition.

Introduction

This book began as an attempt to bring more life to the reading and learning of history. As practicing historians, we have been troubled by a growing disinterest in or even animosity toward the study of the past. How is it that when we and other historians have found so much that excites curiosity, other people find history irrelevant and boring? Perhaps, we thought, if lay readers and students understood better how historians go about their work—how they examine evidence, how they pose questions, and how they reach answers—history would engage them as it does us.

As often happens, it took a mundane event to focus and clarify our preoccupations. One day while working on another project, we went outside to watch a neighboring farmer cut down a large old hemlock that had become diseased. As his saw cut deeper into the tree, we joked that it had now bit into history as far back as the Depression. *"Depression?"* grunted our friend. "I thought you fellas were historians. I'm deep enough now so's Hoover wasn't even a gleam in his father's eye."

With the tree down, the three of us examined the stump. Our woodcutter surprised us with what he saw.

"Here's when my folks moved into this place," he said, pointing to a ring. "1922."

"How do you know without counting the rings?" we asked.

"Oh, *well*," he said, as if the answer were obvious. "Look at the core, here. The rings are all bunched up tight. I bet there's sixty or seventy—and all within a couple inches. Those came when the place was still forest. Then, you notice, the rings start getting fatter all of a sudden. That's when my dad cleared behind the house—in '22—and the tree started getting a lot more light. And look further out, here—see how the rings set together again for a couple years? That's from loopers."

"Loopers?" we asked cautiously.

"Sure—*loopers*. You know. The ones with only front legs and back." His hand imitated a looping, hopping crawl across the log. "Inchworms. They damn near killed the tree. That was sometime after the war—'49 or '50." As his fingers traced back and forth among the concentric circles, he spoke of other events from years gone by. Before we returned home, we had learned a good deal about past doings in the area.

Now it occurs to us that our neighbor had a pretty good knack for putting together history. The evidence of the past, like the tree rings, comes easily enough to hand. But we still need to be taught how to see it, read it, and explain it before it can be turned into a story. Even more to the point, the explanations and interpretations *behind* the story often turn out to be as interesting as the story itself. After all, the fascination in our neighbor's account came from the way he traced his tale out of those silent tree rings.

Unfortunately, most readers first encounter history in schoolbooks, and these omit the explanations and interpretations—the detective work, if you will. Textbooks, by their nature, seek to summarize knowledge. They have little space for looking at how that knowledge was gained. Yet the challenge of doing history, not just reading it, is what attracts so many historians. Couldn't some of that challenge be communicated in a concrete way? That was our first goal.

We also felt that the writing of history has suffered in recent years because some historians have been overly eager to convert their discipline into an unadulterated social science. Undeniably, history would lose much of its claim to contemporary relevance without the methods and theories it has borrowed from anthropology, psychology, political science, economics, sociology, and other fields. Indeed, such theories make an important contribution to these pages. Yet history is rooted in the narrative tradition. As much as it seeks to generalize from past events, as do the sciences, it also remains dedicated to capturing the uniqueness of a situation. When historians neglect the literary aspect of their discipline—when they forget that good history begins with a good story—they risk losing that wider audience that all great historians have addressed. They end up, sadly, talking to themselves.

Our second goal, then, was to discuss the methods of American historians in a way that would give proper due to both the humanistic and scientific sides of history. In taking this approach, we have tried to examine many of the methodologies that allow historians to unearth new evidence or to shed new light on old issues. At the same time, we selected topics that we felt were inherently interesting as stories.

Thus our book employs what might be called an apprentice approach to history rather than the synthetic approach of textbooks. A textbook strives to be comprehensive and broad. It presents its findings in as rational and programmatic a manner as possible. By contrast, apprentices learn through a much less formal process; they learn their profession from artisans who take their daily trade as it comes through the front door. A customer orders a pewter pot? Very well, the artisan proceeds to fashion the pot and in doing so shows the apprentice how to pour the mold. A client needs some engraving done? Then the apprentice receives a first lesson in etching. The apprentice method of teaching communicates a broad range of knowledge over the long run by focusing on specific situations.

So also this book. Our discussion of methods is set in the context of specific problems historians have encountered over the years. In piecing the individual stories together, we try to pause as an artisan might and point out problems of evidence, historical perspective, or logical inference. Sometimes we focus on problems that all historians must face, whatever their subjects. These problems include such matters as the selection of evidence, historical perspective, the analysis of a document, and the use of broader historical theory. In other cases, we explore problems that are not encountered by all historians but are characteristic of specific historical fields; these include the use of photographic evidence, questions of psychohistory, problems encountered analyzing oral interviews, the value of decision-making models in political history, and so on. In each case, we have tried to provide the reader with a sense of vicarious participation—the savor of doing history as well as of reading it.

Given our approach, the ultimate success of this book can be best measured in functional terms—how well it works for the apprentices and artisans. We hope that the artisans, our fellow historians, will find the volume's implicit as well as explicit definitions of good history worth considering. In choosing our examples, we have naturally gravitated toward the work of those historians we most respect. At the same time, we have drawn upon our own original research in many of the topics discussed; we hope those findings also may be of use to scholars.

As for the apprentices, we admit to being only modest proselytizers. We recognize that of all the people who read this book, only a few will go on to become professional historians. We do hope, however, that even casual readers will come to appreciate the complexity and excitement that go into the study of the past. History is not something that is simply brought out of the archives, dusted off, and displayed as "the way things really were." It is a painstaking construction, held together only with the help of assumptions, hypotheses, and inferences. Readers of history who push dutifully onward, unaware of all the backstage work, miss the essence of the discipline. They miss the opportunity to question and to judge their reading critically. Most of all, they miss the chance to learn how enjoyable it can be to go out and do a bit of digging themselves.

After the Fact

PROLOGUE

The Strange Death
of Silas Deane

The rumors floating around London pointed to suicide. But "what really happened" to Silas Deane could not be discovered unless historians rejected the notion that they were merely couriers between the past and present.

The writing of history is one of the most familiar ways of organizing human knowledge. And yet, if familiarity has not always bred contempt, it has at least encouraged a good deal of misunderstanding. All of us meet history at a tender age when tales of the past easily blend with heroic myths of the culture. In Golden Books, Abe Lincoln looms every bit as large as Paul Bunyan, while George Washington's cherry tree gets chopped down yearly with almost as much ritual as St. Nick's Christmas tree goes up. Despite this long familiarity, or perhaps because of it, most students absorb the required facts about the past without any real conception of what history is. Even worse, most think they do know what it is and never get around to discovering what they missed.

"History is what happened in the past." That statement is the everyday view of the matter. It supposes that historians must return to the past through the surviving records and bring it back to the present to display as "what really happened." The everyday view recognizes that this task is often difficult. But historians are said to succeed if they bring back the facts without distorting them or forcing a new perspective on them. In effect, historians are seen as couriers between the past and present. Like all good messengers, they are expected simply to deliver their information without adding to it.

This everyday view of history is profoundly misleading. In order to demonstrate how it is misleading, we would like to examine in detail an event that "happened in the past"—the death of Silas Deane. Deane does not appear in most American history texts, and rightly so. He served as a distinctly second-rank diplomat for the United States during the years of the American Revolution. Yet the story of Deane's death is an excellent example of an event that cannot be understood merely by transporting it, courier-like, to the present. In short, it illustrates the important difference between "what happened in the past" and what history really is.

AN UNTIMELY DEATH

Silas Deane's career began with one of those rags-to-riches stories so much appreciated in American folklore. In fact, Deane might have made a lasting place for himself in the history texts, except that his career ended with an equally dramatic riches-to-rags story.

He began life as the son of a humble blacksmith in Groton, Connecticut. The blacksmith had aspirations for his boy and sent him to Yale College, where Silas was quick to take advantage of his opportunities. After studying law, Deane opened a practice near Hartford; he then continued his climb up the social ladder by marrying a well-to-do widow, whose inheritance included the business of her late husband, a merchant. Conveniently, Deane became a merchant. After his first wife died, he married the granddaughter of a former governor of Connecticut.

Not content to remain a prospering businessman, Deane entered politics. He served on Connecticut's Committee of Correspondence and later as a delegate to the first and second Continental Congresses, where he attracted the attention of prominent leaders, including Benjamin Franklin, Robert Morris, and John Jay. In 1776 Congress sent Deane to France as the first American to represent the united colonies abroad. His mission was to purchase badly needed military supplies for the Revolutionary cause. A few months later, Benjamin Franklin and Arthur Lee joined him in an attempt to arrange a formal treaty of alliance with France. The American commissioners concluded the alliance in March 1778.

Deane worked hard to progress from the son of a blacksmith all the way to Minister Plenipotentiary from the United States to the Court of France. Most observers described him as ambitious: someone who thoroughly enjoyed fame, honor, and wealth. "You know his ambition—" wrote John Adams to one correspondent, "his desire of making a Fortune. . . . You also know his Art and Enterprise. Such Characters are often useful, altho always to be carefully watched and contracted, specially in such a government as ours." One man in particular suspected Deane enough to watch him: Arthur Lee, the third member of the American mission. Lee accused Deane of taking unfair advantage of his official position to make a private fortune—as much as £50,000, some said. Deane stoutly denied the accusations, and Congress engaged in a heated debate over his conduct. In 1778 it voted to recall its Minister Plenipotentiary, although none of the charges had been conclusively proved.

Deane embroiled himself in further controversy in 1781, having written friends to recommend that America sue for peace and patch up the quarrel with England. His letters were intercepted, and copies of them turned up in

Drawn from the life by Du Simitier in Philadelphia.   *Engraved by B. L. Prevost at Paris.*

"You know his ambition—his desire of making a Fortune. . . . You also know his Art and Enterprise. Such Characters are often useful, altho always to be carefully watched and contracted, specially in such a government as ours."—John Adams on Silas Deane.

a New York Tory newspaper just after Cornwallis surrendered to Washington at Yorktown. For Deane, the timing could not have been worse. With American victory complete, anyone advocating that the United States rejoin Britain was considered as much a traitor as Benedict Arnold. So Deane suddenly found himself adrift. He could not return to America, for no one would have him. Nor could he go to England without confirming his reputation as a traitor. And he could not stay in France, where he had injudiciously accused Louis XVI of aiding the Americans for purely selfish reasons. Rejected on all sides, Deane took refuge in Flanders.

The next few years of his life were spent unhappily. Without friends and with little money, he continued in Flanders until 1783, when the controversy had died down enough for him to move to England. There he lived in obscurity, took to drink, and wound up boarding at the house of an unsavory prostitute. The only friend who remained faithful to him was Edward Bancroft, another Connecticut Yankee who, as a boy, had been Deane's pupil and later his personal secretary during the Paris negotiations for the alliance.

The only friend who remained faithful was Edward Bancroft, a spy for the Americans who had known Deane in Paris.

Although Bancroft's position as a secretary seemed innocent enough, members of the Continental Congress knew that Bancroft was also acting as a spy for the Americans, using his connections in England to secure information about the British ministry's war plans. With the war concluded, Bancroft was back in London. Out of kindness, he provided Deane with living money from time to time.

Finally, Deane decided he could no longer live in London and in 1789 booked passage on a ship sailing for the United States. When Thomas Jefferson heard the news, he wrote his friend James Madison: "Silas Deane is coming over to finish his days in America, not having one sou to subsist on elsewhere. He is a wretched monument of the consequences of a departure from right."

The rest of the sad story could be gotten from the obituaries. Deane boarded the *Boston Packet* in mid-September, and it sailed out of London down the Thames River to the Atlantic. A storm came up, however, and on September 19 the ship lost both its anchors and beat a course for safer shelter, to wait out the storm. On September 22, while walking the quarterdeck with the ship's captain, Deane suddenly "complain'd of a dizziness in his head, and an oppression at his stomach." The captain immediately put him to bed. Deane's condition worsened; twice he tried to say something, but no one was able to make out his words. A "drowsiness and insensibility continually incroached upon his faculties," and only four hours after the first signs of illness he breathed his last.

Such, in outline, was the rise and fall of the ambitious Silas Deane. The story itself seems pretty clear, although certainly people might interpret it in different ways. Thomas Jefferson thought Deane's unhappy career demonstrated "the consequences of a departure from right," whereas one English newspaper more sympathetically attributed his downfall to the mistake of "placing confidence in his [American] Compatriots, and doing them service before he had got his compensation, of which no well-bred Politician was before him ever guilty." Yet either way, the basic story remains the same— the same, that is, until the historian begins putting together a more complete account of Deane's life. Then some of the basic facts become clouded.

For example, a researcher familiar with the correspondence of Americans in Europe during 1789 would realize that a rumor had been making its way around London in the weeks following Deane's death. According to certain people, Deane had become depressed by his poverty, ill health, and low reputation, and consequently had committed suicide. John Cutting, a New England merchant and friend of Jefferson, mentioned the rumor that Deane "had predetermin'd to take a sufficient quantity of Laudanum [a form of opium] to ensure his dissolution" before the boat could sail for America. John Quincy Adams heard that "every probability" of the situation suggested Deane's death was "voluntary and self-administered." And Tom Paine, the famous pamphleteer, also reported the gossip: "Cutting told me he took poison."

At this point we face a substantial problem. Obviously, historians cannot rest content with the facts that come most easily to hand. They must search the odd corners of libraries and letter collections in order to put together a complete story. But how do historians know when their research is "complete"? How do they know to search one collection of letters rather than another? These questions point up the misconception at the heart of the everyday view of history. History is not "what happened in the past"; rather, it is the act of selecting, analyzing, and writing about the past. It is something that is done, that is constructed, rather than an inert body of data that lies scattered through the archives.

The distinction is important. It allows us to recognize the confusion in the question of whether a history of something is "complete." If history were merely "what happened in the past," there would never be a "complete" history of Silas Deane—or even a complete history of the last day of his life. The past holds an infinite number of facts about those last days, and they could never all be included in a historical account.

The truth is, no historian would want to include all the facts. Here, for example, is a list of items from the past that might form part of a history of Silas Deane. Which ones should be included?

> Deane is sent to Paris to help conclude a treaty of alliance.
> Arthur Lee accuses him of cheating his country to make a private profit.
> Deane writes letters that make him unpopular in America.
> He goes into exile and nearly starves.
> Helped out by a gentleman friend, he buys passage on a ship for America as his last chance to redeem himself.
> He takes ill and dies before the ship can leave; rumors suggest he may have committed suicide.

*   *   *

> Ben Franklin and Arthur Lee are members of the delegation to Paris.
> Edward Bancroft is Deane's private secretary and an American spy.
> Men who know Deane say he is talented but ambitious and ought to be watched.

*   *   *

> Before Deane leaves, he visits an American artist, John Trumbull.
> The *Boston Packet* is delayed for several days by a storm.
> On the last day of his life, Deane gets out of bed in the morning.

He puts on his clothes and buckles his shoes.
He eats breakfast.
When he takes ill, he tries to speak twice.
He is buried several days later.

Even this short list demonstrates the impossibility of including all the facts. For behind each one lie hundreds more. You might mention that Deane put on his clothes and ate breakfast, but consider also: What color were his clothes? When did he get up that morning? What did he have for breakfast? When did he leave the table? All these things "happened in the past," but only a comparatively small number of them can appear in a history of Silas Deane.

Readers may object that we are placing too much emphasis on this process of selection. Surely, a certain amount of good judgment will suggest which facts are important. Who needs to know what color Deane's clothes were or when he got up from the breakfast table?

Admittedly, this objection has some merit, as the list of facts about Deane demonstrates. The list is divided into three groups, roughly according to the way common sense might rank them in importance. The first group contains facts that every historian would be likely to include. The second group contains less important information, which could either be included or left out. (It might be useful, for instance, to know who Arthur Lee and Edward Bancroft were, but not essential.) The last group contains information that appears to be either too detailed or else unnecessary. Deane may have visited John Trumbull, but then he surely visited other people as well. Why include any of that? Knowing that the *Boston Packet* was delayed by a storm reveals little about Silas Deane. And readers will assume without being told that Deane rose in the morning, put on his clothes, and had breakfast.

But if common sense helps select evidence, it also produces a good deal of pedestrian history. The fact is, the straightforward account of Silas Deane we have just presented has actually managed to miss the most fascinating parts of the story.

Fortunately, one enterprising historian named Julian Boyd was not satisfied with the traditional account of the matter. He examined the known facts of Deane's career and put them together in ways that common sense had not suggested. Take, for example, two items on our list: (1) Deane was down on his luck and left in desperation for America; and (2) he visited John Trumbull. One fact is from the "important" items on the list and the other from items that seem incidental. How do they fit together?

To answer that, we have to know the source of information about the visit to Trumbull's, which is the letter from John Cutting informing Jefferson of Deane's rumored suicide.

A subscription had been made here chiefly by Americans to defray the expense of getting [Deane] out of this country. . . . Dr. Bancroft with great humanity and equal discretion undertook the management of the man and his business. Accordingly his passage was engaged, comfortable cloaths and stores for his voyage were laid in, and apparently without much reluctance he embarked. . . . I happen'd to see him a few days since at the lodging of Mr. Trumbull and thought I had never seen him look better.

We are now in a better position to see how our two items fit together. And as Julian Boyd has pointed out, they don't fit. According to the first, Deane was depressed, dejected, almost starving. According to the second, he had "never looked better." Alert historians begin to get nervous when they see contradictions like that, so they hunt around a little more. And Julian Boyd found, among the collection of papers published by the Connecticut and New York historical societies, that Deane had been writing letters of his own.

One went to his brother-in-law in America, who had agreed to help pay Deane's transportation over and to receive him when he arrived—something that nobody had been willing to do for years. Other letters reveal that Deane had plans for what he would do when he finally returned home. He had seen models in England of the new steam engines, which he hoped might operate gristmills in America. He had talked to friends about getting a canal built from Lake Champlain in New York to the St. Lawrence River in order to promote trade. As early as 1785 Deane had been at work drumming up support for his canal project. He had even laboriously calculated the cost of the canal's

Was Deane really depressed enough to commit suicide? Or looking forward to a chance to clear his name?

construction ("Suppose a labourer to dig and remove six feet deep and eight feet square in one day. . . . 2,933 days of labour will dig one mile in length, twenty feet wide and eight feet deep.") Obviously, Deane looked forward to a promising future.

Lastly, Deane appeared to believe that the controversy surrounding his French mission had finally died down. As he wrote an American friend,

It is now almost ten years since I have solicited for an impartial inquiry [into the dispute over my conduct] . . . that justice might be done to my fortune and my character. . . . You can sufficiently imagine, without my attempting to describe, what I must have suffered on every account during so long a period of anxiety and distress. I hope that it is now drawing to a close.

Other letters went to George Washington and John Jay, reiterating Deane's innocence.

All this information makes the two items on our list even more puzzling. If Deane was depressed and discouraged, why was he so enthusiastic about coming back to build canals and gristmills? If he really believed that his time of "anxiety and distress" was "drawing to a close," why did he commit suicide? Of course, Deane might have been subject to dramatic shifts in mood. Perhaps hope for the future alternated with despair about his chances for success. Perhaps a sudden fit of depression caused him to take his life.

But another piece of "unimportant" information, way down in the third group of our list, makes this hypothesis difficult to accept. After Deane's ship left London, it was delayed offshore for more than a week. Suppose Deane did decide to commit suicide by taking an overdose of laudanum. Where did he get the drug? Surely not by walking up to the ship's surgeon and asking for it. He must have purchased it in London, before he left. Yet he remained on shipboard for more than a week. If Deane bought the laudanum during a temporary "fit" of depression, why did he wait a week before taking it? And if his depression was not just a sudden fit, how do we explain the optimistic letters to America?

This close look at three apparently unrelated facts indicates that perhaps there is more to Deane's story than meets the eye. It would be well, then, to reserve judgment about our first reconstruction of Silas Deane's career and try to find as much information about the man as possible—whether or not it seems relevant at first. That means investigating not only Deane himself but also his friends and associates, such as Ben Franklin, Arthur Lee, and Edward Bancroft. Since it is impossible in this prologue to look closely at all of Deane's acquaintances, for purpose of example we will take only one: his friend Bancroft.

SILAS DEANE'S FRIEND

Edward Bancroft was born in Westfield, Massachusetts, where his step-father presided over a respectable tavern, the Bunch of Grapes. Bancroft was a clever fellow, and his father soon apprenticed him to a physician. Like many boys before him, Edward did not fancy his position and so ran away to sea. Unlike many boys, he managed to make the most of his situation. His ship landed in Barbados, and there Bancroft signed on as the surgeon for a plantation in Surinam, also known as Guiana. The plantation owner, Paul Wentworth, liked the young man and let him use his private library for study. In addition, Bancroft met another doctor who taught him much about the area's exotic tropical plants and animals. When Bancroft returned to New England in 1766 and continued on to London the following year, he knew enough about Surinam's wildlife to publish a book entitled *An Essay on the Natural History of Guiana in South America*. It was well received by knowledgeable scholars and, among other things, established that an electric eel's shock was caused by electricity, a fact not previously recognized.

A young American bright enough to publish a book at age twenty-five and to experiment with electric eels attracted the attention of another electrical experimenter then in London, Ben Franklin. Franklin befriended Bancroft and introduced him to many influential colleagues, not only learned philosophers but also the politicians with whom Franklin worked as colonial agent for Pennsylvania. A second trip to Surinam produced more research on plants used in making color dyes, research so successful that Bancroft soon found himself elected to the prestigious Royal Society of Medicine. At the same time, Franklin led Bancroft into the political arena, both public and private. On the public side, Bancroft published a favorable review of Thomas Jefferson's pamphlet *A Summary View of the Rights of British America;* privately, he joined Franklin and other investors in an attempt to gain a charter for land along the banks of the Ohio River.

Up to this point we have been able to sketch Bancroft's career without once mentioning the name of Silas Deane. Common sense would suggest that the information about Bancroft's early travels, his scientific studies, his friends in Surinam, tell us little about Deane, and that the story ought to begin with a certain letter Bancroft received from Deane in June 1776. (Common sense is again wrong, but we must wait a little to discover why.)

The letter, which came to Bancroft in 1776, informed him that his old friend Silas Deane was coming to France as a merchant engaged in private business. Would Bancroft be interested in crossing over from England to meet Deane at Calais to catch up on news for old time's sake? An invitation like that would very likely have attracted Bancroft's curiosity. He did know Deane, who had been his teacher in 1758, but not very well. Why would Deane now write and suggest a meeting? Bancroft may have guessed the rest, or he may have known it from other contacts; in any case, he wrote his "old friend" that he would make all possible haste for Calais.

The truth of the matter, as we know, was that Deane had come to France to secure military supplies for the colonies. Franklin, who was back in Philadelphia, had suggested to Congress's Committee of Secret Correspondence that Deane contact Bancroft as a good source of information about British war plans. Bancroft could easily continue his friendship with English officials, because he did not have the reputation of being a hotheaded American patriot. So Deane met Bancroft at Calais in July, and the two concluded their arrangements. Bancroft would be Deane's "private secretary" when needed in Paris and a spy for the Americans when in England.

It turned out that Deane's arrangement worked well—perhaps a little too well. Legally, Deane was permitted to collect a commission on all the supplies he purchased for Congress, but he went beyond that. He and Bancroft used their official connections in France to conduct a highly profitable private trade of their own. Deane, for instance, sometimes sent ships from France without declaring whether they were loaded with private or public goods. Then if the ships arrived safely, he would declare that the cargo was private, his own. But if the English navy captured the goods on the high seas, he labeled it government merchandise and the public absorbed the loss.

Deane used Bancroft to take advantage of his official position in other ways. Both men speculated in the London insurance markets, which were the eighteenth-century equivalent of gambling parlors. Anyone who wished could take out "insurance" against a particular event that might happen in the future. An insurer, for example, might quote odds on the chances of France going to war with England within the year. The insured would pay whatever premium he wished, say £1,000, and if France did go to war and the odds had been five-to-one against it, the insured would receive £5,000. Wagers were made on almost any public event: which armies would win which battles, which politicians would fall from power, and even whether a particular lord would die before the year was out.

Obviously, someone who had access to inside information—someone who knew in advance, for instance, that France was going to war with England—could win a fortune. That was exactly what Bancroft and Deane decided to do. Deane was in charge of concluding the French alliance, and he knew that if he succeeded, Britain would be forced to declare war on France. Bancroft hurried across to London as soon as the treaty

Deane and Bancroft both made money from inside information, by gambling on the London insurance markets.

had been concluded and took out the proper insurance before the news went public. The profits shared by the two men from this and similar ventures amounted to approximately £10,000. Like most gamblers, however, Deane also lost wagers. In the end, he netted little for his troubles.

Historians know these facts because they now have access to the papers of Deane, Bancroft, and others. Acquaintances of the two men lacked this advantage, but they suspected shady dealings anyway. Arthur Lee publicly accused Deane and Bancroft of playing the London insurance game. (Deane shot back that Lee was doing the same thing.) And the moralistic John Adams found Bancroft's conduct distasteful. Bancroft, according to Adams, was

> a meddler in stocks as well as reviews, and frequently went into the alley, and into the deepest and darkest retirements and recesses of the brokers and jobbers . . . and found amusement as well, perhaps, as profit, by listening to all the news and anecdotes, true or false, that were there whispered or more boldly pronounced. . . . This man had with him in France, a woman with whom he lives, and who by the French was called La Femme de Monsieur Bancroft. At tables he would season his foods with such enormous quantities of cayenne pepper which assisted by generous burgundy would set his tongue a running in the most licentious way both at table and after dinner.

Yet for all Bancroft's dubious habits, and for all the suspicions of men like Lee and Adams, there was one thing that almost no one at the time suspected, and that not even historians discovered until the records of certain British officials were opened to the public more than a century later. Edward Bancroft was a double agent.

At the end of July 1776, after he had arranged to be Deane's secretary, Bancroft returned to England and met with Paul Wentworth, his friend from Surinam, who was then working in London for Britain's intelligence organization. Immediately Wentworth realized how valuable Bancroft would be as a spy and introduced him to two secretaries of state. They in turn persuaded Bancroft to submit reports on the American negotiations in France. For his services, he received a lifetime pension of £200 a year—a figure the British were only too happy to pay for such good information. So quick was Bancroft's reporting that the secretaries of state knew about the American mission to France even before the United States Congress could confirm that Deane had arrived safely!

Eventually, Bancroft discovered that he could pass his information directly to the British ambassador at the French court. To do so, he wrote innocent letters on the subject of "gallantry" and signed them "B. Edwards." On the same paper would go another note written in invisible ink, to appear only when the letter was dipped in a special developer held by Lord Stormont, the British ambassador. Bancroft left his letters every Tuesday morning in a sealed bottle in a hole near the trunk of a tree on the south terrace of the Tuileries, the royal palace. Lord Stormont's secretary would put any return information near another tree on the same terrace. With this system in operation, Stormont could receive intelligence without having to wait for it to filter back from England.

Did any Americans suspect Bancroft of double-dealing? Arthur Lee once claimed he had evidence to charge Bancroft with treason, but he never produced it. In any case, Lee had a reputation for suspecting everybody of everything. Franklin, for his part, shared lodgings with Deane and Bancroft during their stays in Paris. He had reason to guess that someone close to the American mission was leaking secrets—especially when Lord Stormont and the British newspapers made embarrassingly accurate accusations about French aid. The French wished to keep their assistance secret in order to avoid war with England as long as possible, but of course Franklin knew America would fare better with France fighting, so he did little to stop the leaks. "If I was sure," he remarked, "that my valet de place was a spy, as he probably is, I think I should not discharge him for that, if in other respects I liked him." So the French would tell Franklin he really ought to guard his papers more closely, and Franklin would say yes, yes, he really would have to do something about that; and the secrets continued to leak. Perhaps Franklin suspected Deane and Bancroft of playing the London insurance markets, but there is no evidence that he knew Bancroft was a double agent.

What about Deane, who was closer to Bancroft than anyone else? We have no proof that he shared the double agent's secret, but his alliance with Bancroft in other intrigues tells against him. Furthermore, one published leak pointed to a source so close to the American commissioners that Franklin began to investigate. As Julian Boyd has pointed out, Deane immediately directed suspicion toward a man he knew perfectly well was not a spy. We can only conclude he did so to help throw suspicion away from Bancroft. Very likely, if Bancroft was willing to help Deane play his games with the London insurers, Deane was willing to assist Bancroft in his game with British intelligence.

The Tuileries, much as it appeared when Bancroft and Lord Stormont used the south terrace as a drop for their secret correspondence. The royal palace overlooks a magnificent formal garden that, as a modern observer has noted, "seems so large, so full of surprising hidden corners and unexpected stairways, that its strict ground plan—sixteen carefully spaced and shaped gardens of trees, separated by arrow-straight walks—is not immediately discernable."

Of the two, Bancroft seems to have made out better. While Deane suffered reproach and exile for his conduct, Bancroft returned to England still respected by both the Americans and the British. Not that he had been without narrow escapes. Some of the British ministry (the king especially) did not trust him, and he once came close to being hanged for treason when his superiors rightly suspected that he had associated with John the Painter, an unbalanced fanatic who tried to set England's navy ablaze. But Bancroft left for Paris at the first opportunity, waited until the storm blew over, and returned to London at the end of the war with his lifetime pension raised to £1,000 a year. At the time of Deane's death, he was doing more of his scientific experiments, in hopes that Parliament would grant him a profitable monopoly on a new process for making dyes.

Deane's Death: A Second Look

So we finally arrive, the long way around, back where the story began: September 1789 and Deane's death. But now we have a much larger store of information out of which to construct a narrative. Since writing history involves the acts of analyzing and selecting, let us review the results of our investigation.

We know that Deane was indeed engaged in dubious private ventures, ventures Congress would have condemned as unethical. We also have reason to suspect that Deane knew Bancroft was a spy for the British. Combining that evidence with what we already know about Deane's death, we might theorize that Deane committed suicide because, underneath all his claims to innocence, he knew he was guilty as Congress charged. The additional evidence, in other words, reveals a possible new motive for Deane's suicide.

Yet this theory presents definite problems. In the first place, Deane never admitted any wrongdoing to anyone—not in all the letters he wrote, not in any of his surviving papers. That does not mean he was innocent, nor even that he believed himself innocent. But often it is easier for a person to lie to himself than to his friends. Perhaps Deane actually convinced himself that he was blameless, that he had a right to make a little extra money from his influential position, and that he did no more than anyone would in his situation. Certainly his personal papers point to that conclusion. And if Deane believed himself innocent—correctly or not—would he have any obvious motive for suicide? Furthermore, the theory does not explain the puzzle that started this investigation. If Deane felt guilty enough about his conduct to commit suicide, why did that guilt increase ten years after the fact? If he did feel suddenly guilty, why wait a week aboard ship before taking the fatal dose of laudanum? For that matter, why go up and chat with the captain when death was about to strike?

No, things still do not sit quite right, so we must question the theory. What proof do we have that Deane committed suicide? Rumors about London. Tom Paine heard it from Cutting, the merchant. And Cutting reports in his letter to Jefferson that Deane's suicide was "the suspicion of Dr. Bancroft." How do we know the circumstances of Deane's

Since writing history involves the acts of analyzing and selecting, we need to review the results of our investigation.

death? The captain made a report, but for some reason it was not preserved. The one account that did survive was written by Bancroft, at the request of a friend. Then there were the anonymous obituaries in the newspapers. Who wrote them? Very likely Bancroft composed at least one; certainly, he was known as Silas Deane's closest friend and would have been consulted by any interested parties. There are a lot of strings here, which, when pulled hard enough, all run back to the affable Dr. Bancroft. What do we know about his situation in 1789?

We know Bancroft is dependent on a pension of £1,000 a year, given him for his faithful service as a British spy. We know he is hoping Parliament will grant him a monopoly for making color dyes. Suddenly his old associate Deane, who has been leading a dissolute life in London, decides to return to America, vindicate himself to his former friends, and start a new life. Put yourself in Bancroft's place. Would you be just a little nervous about that idea? Here is a man down on his luck, now picking up and going to America to clear his reputation. What would Deane do to clear it? Tell everything he knew about his life in Paris? Submit his record books to Congress, as he had been asked to do so many years before? If Deane knew Bancroft was a double agent, would he say so? And if Deane's records mentioned the affair of John the Painter (as indeed they did), what would happen if knowledge of Bancroft's role in the plot reached England? Ten years earlier, Bancroft would have been hanged. True, the angry feelings of the war had faded, but even if he were spared death, would Parliament grant a monopoly on color dyes to a known traitor? Would Parliament continue the £1,000 pension? It was one thing to have Deane living in London, where Bancroft could watch him; it would be quite another to have him all the way across the Atlantic Ocean, ready to tell—who knows what?

Admit it: if you were Bancroft, wouldn't you be just a little nervous?

We are forced to consider, however reluctantly, that Deane was not expecting to die as he walked the deck of the *Boston Packet*. Yet if Bancroft did murder Deane, how? He was not aboard ship when death came and had not seen Deane for more than a week. That is a good alibi, but then, Bancroft was a clever man. We know (once again from the letters of John Cutting) that Bancroft was the person who "with great humanity and equal discretion undertook the management of the man and [the] business" of getting Deane ready to leave for America. Bancroft himself wrote Jefferson that he had been visiting Deane often "to assist him with advice, medicins, and money for his subsistence." If Deane were a laudanum addict, as Bancroft hinted to Cutting, might not the good doctor who helped with "medicins" also have procured the laudanum? And having done that, might he not easily slip some other deadly chemical into the mixture, knowing full well that Deane would not use it until he was on shipboard and safely off to America? That conclusion is only conjecture. We have no direct evidence to suggest that this scenario is what really happened.

But we do know one other fact for sure; and in light of our latest theory, it is an interesting one. Undeniably, Edward Bancroft was an expert on poisons.

He did not advertise that knowledge, of course; few people in London at the time of Deane's death would have been likely to remember the fact. But twenty years earlier, the historian may recall, Bancroft wrote a book on the natural history of Guiana. At that time he not only investigated electric eels and color dyes, but also the poisons of the area, particularly curare (or "Woorara" as Bancroft called it). He investigated it so well, in fact, that when he returned to England he brought samples of curare with him, which (he announced in the book) he had deposited with the publishers so that any gentleman of "unimpeachable" character might use the samples for scientific study.

Furthermore, Bancroft seemed to be a remarkably good observer not only of the poisons, but also of those who used them. His book described in ample detail the natives' ability to prepare poisons that,

given in the smallest quantities, produce a very slow but inevitable death, particularly a composition which resembles wheat-flour, which they sometimes
use to revenge past injuries, that have been long neglected, and are thought
forgotten. On these occasions they always feign an insensibility of the injury
which they intend to revenge, and even repay it with services and acts of
friendship, until they have destroyed all distrust and apprehension of danger in
the destined victim of the vengeance. When this is effected, they meet at some
festival, and engage him to drink with them, drinking first themselves to obviate suspicion, and afterwards secretly dropping the poison, ready concealed
under their nails, which are usually long, into the drink.

Twenty years later Bancroft was busy at work with the color dyes he had
brought back from Surinam. Had he, by any chance, also held onto any of
those poisons?

Unless new evidence comes to light, we will probably never know for
sure. Historians are generally forced to deal with probabilities, not certainties, and we leave you to draw your own conclusions about the death of Silas
Deane.

What does seem certain is that whatever "really happened" to Deane two
hundred years ago cannot be determined today without the active participation of the historian. Being courier to the past is not enough. For better or
worse, historians inescapably leave an imprint as they go about their business: asking interesting questions about apparently dull facts, seeing connections between subjects that had not seemed related before, shifting and
rearranging evidence until it assumes a coherent pattern. The past is not
history, only the raw materials of it. How those raw materials come to be
fashioned and shaped is the central concern of this book.

Additional Reading

The historian proposing the possibility of foul play on the *Boston Packet* is
Julian Boyd. He makes his case in a series of three articles titled "Silas Deane:
Death by a Kindly Teacher of Treason?" *William and Mary Quarterly*, 3d
ser., 16 (1959): 165–187, 319–342, and 515–550. Edward Bancroft's role as
double agent was not established conclusively until the 1890s. His connections to the British are spelled out in Paul L. Ford, *Edward Bancroft's Narrative of the Objects and Proceedings of Silas Deane* (Brooklyn, NY, 1891). Further
background on Bancroft's youth may be gained, of course, from his lively
Essay on the Natural History of Guiana in South America (London, 1769).

Boyd's case for murder has been questioned by William Stinchcombe
in "A Note on Silas Deane's Death," *William and Mary Quarterly*, 3d ser.,
32 (1975): 619–624. Stinchcombe has suggested that, contrary to Boyd's

suggestion, Deane did not face any really hopeful prospects for success in America. If Deane continued to be down on his luck when he departed for America, then the suicide theory again becomes more probable. For a third opinion, consult D. K. Anderson and G. T. Anderson, "The Death of Silas Deane," *New England Quarterly* 62 (1984): 98–105. The Andersons surveyed several medical authorities and concluded that Deane may well have suffered from chronic tuberculosis and died from a stroke or some other acute attack.

CHAPTER I

Contact

In 1539 Hernando de Soto ventured into North America looking for Indian empires. More than a century passed before other Europeans returned. What went unrecorded in the years following that first contact?

Here is what the conquistador Hernando de Soto prescribed for his final resting place, as set out in his last will and testament: that a chapel be erected within the Church of San Miguel in Jerez de los Caballeros, Spain, where De Soto grew up, at a cost of 2,000 ducats, with an altarpiece featuring the Virgin Mary, Our Lady of the Conception; that his tomb be covered over in fine black broadcloth topped by a red cross of the Order of the Knights of Santiago, and on special occasions a pall of black velvet with the De Soto coat of arms placed on the altar; that a chaplain be hired at a salary of 12,000 *maravedis* to perform five masses every week for the souls of De Soto, his parents, and wife; that thirty masses be said for him on the day his body was interred, and twenty for Our Lady of the Conception, ten for the Holy Ghost, sixty for souls in purgatory and masses for many others as well; that 150,000 *maravedis* be given annually to his wife Isabel for her needs and an equal amount used yearly to marry off "three orphan damsels . . . the poorest that can be found," who would then assist his wife and also serve to burnish the memory of De Soto as a man of charity and substance.

These instructions were written, signed, and witnessed the tenth day of May 1539. Eight days later De Soto departed from Havana, Cuba, at the head of some 600 followers into the unknown lands called La Florida by Spain. The expedition went in search of gold, treasure, fame, and power.

And this is how De Soto actually died and was buried, almost three years and some 3,000 miles later:

His final headquarters lay in the house of an Indian chief, whose people had fled their village upon the expedition's arrival. Walled in by a tall palisade, the village lay near a very large river; the Indians called it Tamaliseu; to the Spanish it was Río del Espíritu Santo. We know it today as the Mississippi, and the settlement's most likely location was near present-day McArthur, Arkansas. But De Soto had no idea where he was, except in the most

Even artists who pay attention to the details of historical dress usually clothe the De Soto expedition in the equipment that they started with. But after several years of trekking through the continent, most members of the expedition were wearing Indian blankets or animal skins to survive.

general terms. The big river, he felt certain, must flow into the great sea—the Gulf of Mexico. But how far away that sea was, who could say?

His expedition was in tatters. It had survived only by commandeering stores of food grown by the Indians, as it had done from the start. After three years of wandering in search of an empire to conquer, most of De Soto's men no longer had the original clothes on their backs. Modern paintings of the expedition show the conquistadors with the armored helmets, vest-like leather jerkins, breeches, and boots. But by April 1542 native substitutes had replaced much of that equipment. From Indian blankets "were made loose coats and cassocks," one member of the expedition reported. "From the deerskins were also made some jerkins, shirts, stockings, and shoes, and from the bear skins some very good cloaks, for water would not go through them." One high-ranking knight was reduced to "wearing a short garment of the blankets of that country, torn on the sides, his flesh showing, no hat, bare-headed, bare-footed, without hose or shoes, a buckler on his back, a sword without a shield, amidst heavy frosts and cold."

The area around the Mississippi where the expedition was encamped seemed as thickly settled as any De Soto had encountered. Immediately he dispatched scouts on horseback south, to seek news of the great sea. Meanwhile, he sent a message to the leader of Quigualtam, a powerful chiefdom across the river. Perhaps because he felt threatened by the dense population, he announced in his message that he was no ordinary human but the son of the sun, a personage to be worshiped. He requested that the ruler of Quigualtam visit him. To another chief who approached the Spanish he showed a mirror, which the Indians had never seen before, angled so that De Soto's face was reflected in it. The mirror image was his spirit, which flitted invisibly among the Indians and returned with news of whatever they were saying. They could not deceive him, he warned.

After a week struggling across swamps and streams, the scouts returned with no reliable information about the great sea. A retreat on foot seemed near impossible; if the expedition built boats, it was not clear how far down-river they would have to float, or if there were any big falls of water to block their way. After all the searching, the hardships, the constant skirmishing, De Soto's "grief was intense on seeing the small prospect he had for reaching the sea. . . . With that thought, he fell sick" and took to bed with a fever. Worse, the chief of Quigualtam answered that he was not accustomed to visit any-one; De Soto should visit *him*. This newcomer was "the son of the sun"? If so, "let him dry up the great river and [then the chief] would believe him."

De Soto raged; if he had not been so ill, he would have led a raiding party to capture the chief. Instead, he ordered a detachment to attack a nearby village, whose leader had also angered him. The Spanish rode down on the settlement, slaying men, women, and children without mercy. Still the rumors persisted that Quigualtam was preparing an attack. "The danger of being lost in that land . . . stared them all in the face."

"The danger of being lost in that land . . . stared them all in the face."

As De Soto's strength ebbed, he gave up his command. The next day he died, "in a land and a time when his illness had very little solace," one associate recalled. Fortune had raised him high, "as she is wont to do with others, so that he might fall from a greater height." Another comrade was even less generous: "The governor, at seeing himself surrounded, and nothing coming about according to his expectation, sickened and died."

The new leader, Luis de Moscoso, decided that the Indians must not learn of De Soto's death—especially given the conquistador's boast that he was the immortal son of the sun. In the dead of night, his men buried his body near a gate to the town. But the Indians knew De Soto was now nowhere to be seen; and they noticed the disturbed earth by the gate. So again under cover of darkness, Moscoso ordered the body dug up and smuggled into a canoe. Wrapped in blankets, weighted down with sand, it was paddled out into the Mississippi and dispatched to a watery grave.

So much for a memorial chapel back in Spain, the red cross atop black broadcloth, the hundreds of masses. Before dying, De Soto was forced to scribble a new will. In executing it, Moscoso gathered the ragged remnants of the expedition and auctioned off their leader's magnificent possessions: four Indian slaves, three horses, and 700 hogs.

There is more later to say about the hogs.

A romanticized view of De Soto's burial as portrayed in *Footprints of Four Centuries: The Story of the American People* (1894).

CONSTRUCTION AND RECONSTRUCTION

In the annals of American history, the death of Hernando de Soto is more widely known than that of Silas Deane. But the two make a useful pair. In fitting together the facts surrounding Deane's death, we came to understand that history is not simply "what happened in the past," but rather a construction of it, fashioned from the raw materials of that past. As De Soto's story will show, we need to take that insight one step further. History is not only constructed; it is continually in need of *re*construction. It needs to be reassembled and rebuilt, over and over again.

Skeptics resist the notion that history has to be refashioned on a regular basis. Objections most often surface in relation to textbooks. As historians, the two of us have written a number of surveys of the American past. (This is the fifth time we have revised *After the Fact*.) When we mention that we are revising a text, the reaction is often puzzlement. What is there to do, other than to add a few pages to bring the story up-to-date? Yes, detective work went into putting the story together. But historians have had decades, even centuries, to piece together topics from the past. Regardless of the construction involved, the past itself has not changed.

But in point of fact, the further back in time historians reach, the greater the need for regular reassessment. Nowhere is this need more apparent than in the story of the first encounters between the civilizations of the western and eastern hemispheres.

Traditionally, American history has been taught as if it begins with first contact. Why that should be is not particularly self-evident. Humans have lived in the Americas at the very least for over 12,000 years. If you extend your arm outward and imagine that the distance from your shoulder to the end of your fingers represents the time humans have inhabited the western hemisphere, Columbus's arrival in 1492 would be located at about the second joint of your index finger. In most American history texts, a description of all the human events taking place before Columbus—from your shoulder to that second finger joint—takes up about 20 pages. The last inch or so of your fingers—the 500 years following 1492—takes up about 980.

Why the imbalance? One reason is that, by and large, contact marks the beginning of recorded history in the Americas, especially North America. For the first time, written sources exist to document events, and we can see in more detail what is going on. Or so it would seem.

Over the past half century, however, historians have come to realize that they have taken far too narrow a view of the situation. Archaeologists have long excavated a wealth of evidence about societies lacking written records. Their efforts have expanded as more sites have been discovered, analyzed, and compared. Archaeologists have also made progress in deciphering Aztec and Mayan systems of writing and have unearthed inscriptions from the earlier Olmec and Zapotec civilizations. Even in North America where no early written languages have been found, archaeologists have reconstructed the daily lives, hunting and farming practices, the structures of villages and societies, and even religious attitudes. They have done so based on evidence from pottery shards, animal bones, grave sites, architectural remains, and even pollen and soil samples.

Equally important, historians have begun to place human culture within a broader natural framework. They have recognized, to put it bluntly, that human history is not merely the history of humans. The traditional topics—politics, war, economics, culture—play out within a larger natural setting that is physical, geographical, biological. *Ecosystem* is the term used to define a region as a network of relationships between organisms and their environment; *ecology*, the discipline that studies such relationships. In those terms, the era of contact set in motion a complex series of ecological interactions that upended the Americas, as Europeans, Africans, and Asians began moving into the hemisphere. The Atlantic and Pacific oceans had long acted as barriers isolating the western hemisphere from ecosystems in the rest of the world. As the oceanic barriers broke down after 1492, the resulting migrations created

The era of contact set in motion a complex series of ecological interactions that transformed the Americas.

frontiers, not only of people but also of plants and animals. Indeed, the plants and animals frequently traveled in advance of human immigrants, and their arrivals transformed existing ecosystems in fundamental ways. Finally, there were also frontiers of microorganisms—frontiers of disease—which spread with astonishing and deadly results.

Stories of first contact, then, are remarkably valuable, immensely complex, and extremely difficult to sort out. De Soto's entry into North America—his *entrada,* it is often called—was key. He and his followers were the first Europeans to encounter native cultures throughout much of the southeastern interior. Furthermore, after De Soto's exploration, Europeans did not return to that interior until the 1670s and 1680s. It was as if a curtain had been briefly lifted with De Soto's arrival, to reveal an astonishing landscape of human, animal, and plant ecologies in the Southeast—only to descend again for well over a century. Historians and archaeologists have thus seized on the accounts of the expedition in order to shed light on what America must have been like not only during the era of contact, but also in the years leading up to it.

ENTRY INTO AN UNKNOWN WORLD

De Soto was born in 1500 in the province of Extremadura, an impoverished region of Spain whose difficult conditions pushed many of its ambitious young men to seek their fortunes overseas. Balboa, the conquistador who in 1513 crossed the Isthmus of Panama and viewed the Pacific Ocean, hailed from Extremadura. So did Hernán Cortés, who marched into Mexico in 1519 and brought down the Aztec empire. De Soto arrived in Castilla del Oro (present-day Panama) when he was only fourteen. With his air of command, he soon received the nickname "the Captain." Through his boldness he became wealthy from the conquest of Panama and Nicaragua, partly by amassing gold and silver, but more from leading slaving raids against the Indians.

By the time De Soto turned thirty, Cortés had found fame and fortune by reducing the Aztecs and looting their treasures. Another Extremaduran, Francisco Pizarro, cast his eye on the more recently discovered Incan civilization in South America. In 1531 De Soto joined Pizarro's tiny army of 168 men, leading a vanguard of mounted horse. Pizarro boldly confronted the monarch Atahualpa, despite the presence of a ceremonial Incan army numbering perhaps 80,000. As the two leaders faced off, De Soto played his own dramatic part. On horseback, he rode directly up to Atahualpa to intimidate him. Horses had become extinct in the Americas thousands of years earlier, so these large creatures at first terrified many Indians. Deliberately, De Soto crowded so close that when his horse snorted, it ruffled the ceremonial fringe Atahualpa wore across his forehead. In an audacious surprise attack of cannon, cavalry, lances, and swords, Pizarro scattered the terrified Incan army while taking its king hostage. Then he demanded an entire roomful of gold and silver as ransom in return for freeing Atahualpa. When Atahualpa complied, Pizarro executed him anyway. De Soto shared in the ransom.

Such conquests only whetted the appetite of "the Captain" for more. De Soto returned to Spain to obtain the blessing of Emperor Charles V to conquer new lands, looking this time to the north. Several expeditions to La Florida had failed spectacularly, but as survivors straggled home, rumors of treasure and riches spread. With the emperor's blessing, De Soto sailed to Cuba. By May of 1539 his ships lay off the coast of Florida, tacking in search of a deep harbor where they could land.

What did those 600 Europeans see, looking onto the bay? A thick wall of red mangroves spread mile after mile, some reaching as high as 70 feet, with intertwined and elevated roots making landing difficult. And very soon "many smokes" appeared "along the whole coast," billowing against the sky. The Indians had spotted the newcomers and were spreading the alarm by signal fires.

Inland from the coast, the environment of the Southeast was little like what we would see today. In our mind's eye we must banish not only the highways, buildings, and bridges, but also less obvious features. Except for Florida, the southeastern part of the continent had many fewer lakes, which in modern times have been created by dams. Though the climate was colder than at present when De Soto arrived—and had been for over a century—the forest had actually evolved in response to a hotter climate that dominated for centuries previously. During those years, prevailing westerly winds dried out the vegetation, which was regularly scoured by lightning fires. In many areas only trees resistant to fire flourished, primarily longleaf pine, slash pine, and loblolly, spreading from the southern end of Chesapeake Bay through much of Florida and westward into present-day Mississippi. Such old-growth vegetation is scarce today.

The balance of wildlife was as different as the trees of the forest. Many animals were much more common, including the predatory wolf and panther. Some birds have since become extinct, including the brightly hued Carolina parakeet (the only parrot native to North America) and the ivory-billed woodpecker, which stood a foot and a half tall.

The land looked different for another reason. What the Europeans viewed as natural, the Indians had shaped and altered in a host of significant ways. Fire was prime among them, because the first inhabitants of the Americas used it for more than making "smokes" to communicate. Cabeza de Vaca, a Spanish explorer who preceded De Soto by a decade, noted that the Ignaces Indians of Texas went about

> with a firebrand, setting fire to the plains and timber so as to drive off the mosquitoes, and also to get lizards and similar things which they eat, to come out of the soil. In the same manner they kill deer, encircling them with fires, and they do it also to deprive the animals of pasture, compelling them to go for food where the Indians want.

In California, where grass seeds were an important food, Indians burned fields annually to remove old stocks and increase the yield. Along the Atlantic Coast, Indians set fires to keep down the scrub brush. The resulting forest was almost parklike, with large, widely spaced trees, few shrubs, and plenty of succulent grasses.

Few European colonists understood the Indians' ecological role. Still, as they penetrated the interior of North America over the next two centuries, they were continually struck by the profusion of wildlife. "The aboundance of Sea-Fish are almost beyond beleeving," noted an early settler of Massachusetts Bay, "and sure I should scarce have beleeved it except I had seene it with mine owne eyes." In Virginia, English settlers fording streams sometimes found that the hooves of their horses killed fish, the rivers were so thick with them. Governor Thomas Dale, in one setting of his net, hauled in 5,000 sturgeon.

As with fish, so with wildfowl. In Virginia the beating wings of ducks, geese, brant, and teal sometimes sounded "like a great storm coming over the water." And the number of passenger pigeons—a bird hunted into extinction by 1914—astounded everyone. The famous naturalist, John James Audubon, in 1813 watched vast flocks darken the sun along the banks of the Ohio River. In "almost solid masses, they darted forward in undulating and angular lines, descended and swept close over the earth with inconceivable velocity, mounted perpendicularly so as to resemble a vast column, and, when high, were seen wheeling and twisting within their continued lines, which then resembled the coils of a gigantic serpent." At night "the pigeons, arriving by thousands, alighted everywhere . . . it was a scene of uproar and confusion. I found it quite useless to speak or even to shout to those persons who were nearest to me."

Similar tales were told of mammals. Red and fallow deer congregated along the Virginia coasts in the hundreds. Gray and black squirrels ate so much of the colonists' grain that eighteenth-century Pennsylvanians killed more than 600,000 squirrels in one year alone. On the prairies, an estimated 50 million bison roamed in herds. Some of the creatures had moved east as far as Kentucky; a few even pushed into Virginia along the Potomac River. Pronghorn antelope may have outnumbered even buffalo. Beavers swelled the streams of eastern forests as well as those of the Rockies, and grizzly bears "were everywhere," reported one mountain man early in the nineteenth century.

Thus the landscapes De Soto and his men entered in 1539 looked different for many reasons, including a changed climate, a greater variety and abundance of species, and Indians shaping the environment.

But when the Europeans entered the Americas, they almost immediately began to change the ecosystems they encountered. Newcomers brought with them plants and animals that were foreign to the Americas, and they took back American species to introduce to their home provinces. Historian Alfred Crosby labeled this ongoing process the Columbian exchange. Many of the introductions to the Americas were deliberate: crops such as wheat or grapes that were favorites at home. Spaniards did not believe they could live without bread and wine. In the Caribbean, Europeans imported lemons, oranges, and figs. Banana trees from the Canary Islands "have multiplied so greatly that it is marvelous to see the great abundance of them on the islands," wrote one chronicler. In return, Europeans brought home American tomatoes, corn, potatoes, peanuts, and beans—crops that over the next few centuries revolutionized agriculture everywhere from Ireland to Italy to China.

Other imports to the Americas were accidental. Seeds arrived in chests of folded clothes or in clods of mud or dung. Many of these European plants spread quickly because American plants had been relatively isolated from competition for thousands of years and were pushed out by hardier European stocks. Some plants spread so widely that today they are commonly taken to be native. "Kentucky" bluegrass originated in Europe. So did the dandelion, the daisy, white clover, ragweed, and plantain. (The last was called "the Englishman's foot" by New England Indians, for it seemed to sprout wherever the new settlers wandered.)

We have already had one glimpse of how European animals unsettled the western hemisphere: De Soto's horse breathing down Atahualpa's neck—literally. The Spanish understood that their horses frightened Indian opponents, and De Soto brought 200 to La Florida. The mounts were likely a small but tough Arabian breed originating along Africa's Barbary Coast, but sea transport was not an easy matter. To keep the animals from panicking and rearing, they were suspended from the ceiling below decks by canvas belts around their bellies, so that their hooves remained several inches above the decking. Once ashore, the horses were mounted by soldiers carrying steel-tipped lances about 15 feet long. Indians on foot could not outrun these lancers; the safest response was to flee to a swamp, where the horses would flounder, or find shelter in canebrake or other thick vegetation.

Horses, not seen before by the Indians, were of greater strategic advantage to De Soto than firearms.

Indian astonishment and fear soon turned to bravery and cunning. One of the first of De Soto's horses to die was a mount shot by Indian bow and arrow. The arrow sped with such strength, it pierced the horse's tightly woven cloth armor and tore through the saddle, the arrow's shaft lodging more than a third of the way into the animal's flesh. In the long run, Indians took possession of stray horses and learned to ride them bareback.* In the short term, though, De Soto and other newcomers used the horse and lance to great tactical advantage.

De Soto also brought a number of large dogs, which the Indians learned to fear. Conquistadors had used dogs in the Caribbean. De Soto's first master there, the governor of Castilla del Oro, sponsored manhunts in which prisoners were set loose and, for sport, hunted down by dogs. In La Florida the dogs would attack their Indian foes in pitched battles or chase after wounded warriors and bring them down. (Some dogs were equipped with spiked or metal collars, to make it difficult for those being attacked to choke them.) Dogs proved useful on the march as well: their keen hearing and sense of smell helped defend the Spanish against surprise attacks.

---

* By the nineteenth century, Comanche riders were so accomplished that in one friendly contest, a unit of the U.S. Cavalry was disgusted to find its finest Kentucky mare beaten by a "miserable sheep of a pony" upon which a Comanche rider was mounted backward so he could mockingly wave (with "hideous grimaces") for his American rival to "come on a little faster!"

At the the time of De Soto's death, the pigs accompanying the expedition numbered more than 700. The animals were an efficient way of providing protein to the expedition, but their importation into North America very likely sparked a chain reaction of unintended consequences.

Finally, De Soto brought along pigs, a most efficient source of calories. When slaughtered, more than 80 percent of the carcass could be consumed, compared with only 50 percent of a cow or sheep. Hogs could be herded on the march, foraging for food as they went. Unlike today's pale domestic pigs, they were black or gray, with long legs and long snouts. They used sharp tusks to defend themselves and multiplied rapidly. In the Caribbean, early explorers sometimes marooned several pigs on a small island, returning a few years later for food after the swine had overrun the land. Inevitably, some pigs escaped into the wild. "This day they lost many pigs," wrote one of De Soto's chroniclers, the current having carried them off while crossing a river. And some Indians snuck into the expedition's camp and poached them for a meal themselves.

INTO THE WOODS

To understand De Soto's impact on the land, historians have tried to trace his route, but the task is not easy. When the Spanish landed in 1539, they understood little of North American geography. Earlier expeditions to La Florida and the Carolina coast in 1514 and 1521 believed these regions to be islands, like Cuba and Hispaniola. Even if we knew where De Soto landed (and that has been vigorously argued over), the descriptions of his overland journey are vague. For example: "Tuesday, the twenty-third of September, the Governor and his army left from Napituca, and arrived at the river of the Deer." No Indian map or manuscript is available to locate Napituca; no record of it survives other than from the expedition. As for the "river of the Deer," that is merely a Spanish invention, so named "because the Indian messengers . . . brought there certain deer."

Occasionally the accounts mention distances: "From [Patofa] to the port of Espiritu Santo . . . a distance of about three hundred and fifty leagues or so." But this information opens up new puzzles, because in Spain, a league might have referred to the *legua legal*, about 2.6 miles, or it might have meant the *legua común*, nearly 3.5 miles. Depending on the measure being used, 350 leagues could be 910 miles or 1,225.

Descriptions of physical features provide clues: the mention of mountains or "rough pine groves, low and very swampy." And although names like Napituca were unknown when Europeans settled in the region a century later, others persisted. Apalachee, the first formidable chiefdom De Soto reached, was also the name of the people later encountered by French settlers near present-day Tallahassee, Florida. The anthropologist John R. Swanton, head of a federal commission to reconstruct De Soto's route in 1936, explicitly assumed that "the Indian tribes encountered by De Soto . . . preserved the same locations down to the late seventeenth and early eighteenth centuries when English and French explorers and traders visited them."

Over the past 300 years, scholars have suggested at least a dozen alternative expedition routes. By the time Swanton's federal commission of 1936 attempted a definitive solution, the confusion was evident.

Swanton's route remained the accepted alternative until the 1980s. Then anthropologist Charles Hudson began a reevaluation, taking advantage of a wealth of archaeological studies underway. At Indian sites Swanton thought might be along De Soto's route, new excavations revealed problems. For Coosa, a prosperous chiefdom the Spanish visited in 1540, archaeologists found Indian settlements at the site Swanton proposed, but none whose remains reached back earlier than the eighteenth century. As scholars gained a better picture of how Indian cultures had grown and spread, by studying the layouts of villages, pottery styles, and other evidence, it became clear that Swanton should not have assumed that an Indian tribe living at a certain location in 1800 must have lived at the same place in 1500.

Of course this makes perfect sense, if we consider the more familiar territory of recorded history. Imagine standing at the shoreline of Manhattan in 1539, the year De Soto arrived off Florida. Then, the island is called Scheyischbi—"the place bordering the ocean"—by the Lenape Indians living there. A hundred years later the settlement is known as New Amsterdam and is ruled by the Dutch. By 1739 it has become New York and is governed by the English. Over 300 years Manhattan was much changed! Yet because so little was known about the southeastern Indians of the sixteenth century, it was all too easy for anthropologists, archaeologists, and historians to assume that if the Cherokees or Apalachees were living at a certain place in 1739, the same groups were living there several centuries earlier. If we have no evidence of change, why not assume things stayed the same? It is perhaps only human nature to make such assumptions.

By 1997 Hudson had in place what he believed was a more accurate accounting of De Soto's wanderings, though he cautioned that he could not identify with absolute certainty virtually any of his suggested sites along the

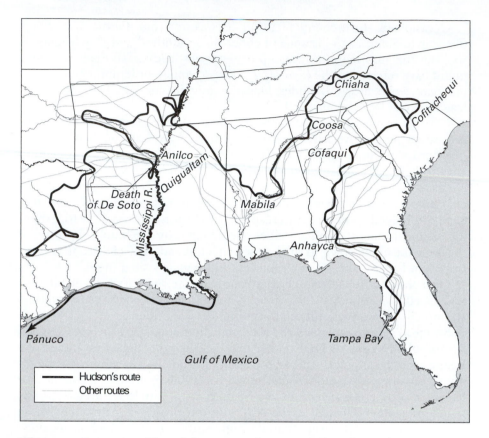

This map gives some idea of the range of routes attributed over the past two centuries to the De Soto expedition. The most recent reconstruction, by anthropologist Charles Hudson, suggests that De Soto landed in Tampa Bay. The remnants of his expedition finally made their way along the Gulf coast to the Spanish settlement of Pànuco.

route. The expedition most likely landed in Tampa Bay on Florida's west coast and, over the summer and fall of 1539, made its way north and west, reaching the Apalachee town of Anhayca. (This site, located at present-day Tallahassee, is one of the few locations that most reconstructions of the journey agree on.)

As the expedition made its way into the interior, relations between the Europeans and native Americans ranged through a mixture of friendship, pretended friendship, suspicion, and outright hostility. De Soto's purpose, after all, was to conquer rich Indian empires, just as Cortés and Pizarro had. The most important questions he asked, once he entered a village, were whether there were any chiefdoms in the region possessing gold, silver, or other treasures, and whether the local chief could supply him with food for 600 people. These were not inquiries likely to encourage trust.

This tiny bell—only 1⅜ inches wide—proved helpful in tracking De Soto's route through the Southeast. Despite the many traces that 600 Europeans must have left during their journey, archaeologists have until recently found few items that can be linked not merely to Europeans, but to Europeans from the sixteenth century. The bell, found in northwest Georgia at the archaeological site known as Little Egypt, is a distinctive sort the Spanish used on sixteenth-century horses such as those De Soto brought. Other European artifacts from a variety of sites include the iron arrowpoint of a crossbow, a horseshoe, a wrought-iron nail, and a sword. Of course, just because an artifact is found in a particular place does not mean that De Soto had been there. Indians could have carried the artifacts to nearby or even distant locations. Still, such pieces of evidence are among the data used by Charles Hudson and others to chart De Soto's approximate route.

In some cases, Indians did bring gifts of corn, squash, or other provisions, as well as clothing or copper ornaments. Other settlements, hostile from the outset, showered the Spanish with arrows and insults. Sometimes whole villages simply fled into the woods until they could gain a better sense of how the newcomers would behave. Often De Soto sent patrols on horse to capture anyone who could be found. Then he would ask his captives to summon the local chief. When asking did not work, he would scour the neighborhood until he found the chief, whom he then held hostage to ensure the expedition's safety as it passed through a region.

The Spanish possessed crossbows and primitive muskets—"arquebuses"—but these weapons provided little advantage in battle. In the time it took to reload either the musket or crossbow, an Indian could shoot six or seven arrows, using a large and powerful bow. A typical specimen was perhaps five feet tall and as thick as a man's wrist. Apalachee archers aimed for cracks in the Spanish armor, and their arrows were shot with such force that they could penetrate a tree to the depth of six inches or pierce a horse entirely.

The Indians seldom announced their intentions toward the strangers. A delegation bearing gifts might come primarily to assess Spanish fortifications and plan attacks. Sometimes an individual pretending to be the chief

In condemning many practices of the conquistadors, the Spanish priest Bartolomé de las Casas included information about De Soto's treatment of noncooperative Indians. This illustration from the German edition of Las Casas's book showed in one grisly scene the many cruelties employed.

would come, in order to protect the real leader. Indian guides might deliberately lead the expedition into swamps or thick canebrake. When De Soto suspected such deceptions, he struck back ruthlessly, chopping off a guide's hand or nose or, worse, throwing him to the dogs. The warriors never flinched, pretending not to mind such punishments. And the chiefs were often disdainful of the Spanish. "To me you are professional vagabonds," one is quoted as saying,

> who wander from place to place, gaining your livelihood by robbing, sacking, and murdering people who have given you no offense. I want no manner of friendship or peace with people such as you. . . . I promise to maintain war upon you so long as you wish to remain in my province, not by fighting in the open, although I could do so, but by ambushing and waylaying you whenever you are off guard.

After De Soto had occupied the town of Anhayca for his winter camp, the Apalachees fled. But they continuously harassed De Soto, ambushing Spaniards when they ventured too far afield and setting fire to the houses where they were staying. In the spring of 1540 De Soto resumed his march toward a richer kingdom to the north named Cofitachequi. Traveling through present-day Georgia, he crossed the Savannah River into what is now South Carolina, demanding 400 Indian porters along the way from another chiefdom. At Cofitachequi, several leaders in dugout canoes met him, including a woman who was a paramount chief, a leader whose authority extended across a broad territory of settlements. Soon after, another woman of importance appeared, whom the Spanish referred to as "La Señora de Cofitachequi." She arrived on a litter shaded by a canopy of white cloth and traveled in a ceremonial canoe "with many trappings and ornaments."

The lady made a gift that pleased De Soto—a "great rope of pearls as large as hazelnuts." He was interested in shiny yellow and white stones as well, he told her, by which he meant gold and silver. The lady commanded that such gifts be brought. But the "yellow" and "white" stones proved to be only bits of copper and mica. As for pearls, La Señora directed him to a mortuary, a sheltered building on stilts in which decomposing bodies of the nobility were kept in boxes. The stench was overpowering, but the mortuary had compensating rewards. In smaller woven-reed baskets were hundreds upon hundreds of pearls. De Soto and his men carried off approximately 200 pounds of them, apparently with the lady's blessing.

Furthermore, the lady offered the expedition half of the village in which to make camp. Cofitachequi was laid out in the same way as many of the towns De Soto would visit, though it was more prosperous and elaborate. A central plaza was anchored by one or more mounds, upon which the village chief lived. Maize corn was central to this Mississippean culture. The cultivation of maize spread throughout much of the Southeast after 800 CE, producing agricultural surpluses that permitted more dense populations. In the centuries before De Soto's arrival, these settlements increasingly united under paramount chieftains whose sphere of influence encompassed many villages. The paramount chief of Cofitachequi may have collected tribute from the flanks of the Carolina mountains all the way to the mouth of the Santee River along the Atlantic—"a hundred leagues, in which, as we saw, she was very well obeyed," wrote one chronicler. Intermediate "great nobles" administered portions of the chiefdom, each of these rulers known as a *mico*. At the lowest level, a lesser noble known as an *orata* was in charge of one or a few villages.

Many expedition members thought De Soto should begin his colony here. The Indians seemed more "civilized" than others they had met—which was to say, they showed a "desire to serve and please" the Spanish. That desire did not last long, as the expedition ate its way through Cofitachequi's food stores. When La Señora decided to flee, De Soto held her hostage until he headed north out of her lands, up the valley of the Wateree and Catawba rivers and crossing over the southern Appalachians—"very rough and lofty mountains." The pattern of encounter regularly repeated itself: greetings, gifts, a tentative peace, then conflict. At Chiaha the flashpoint came when De Soto demanded 30 Indian women as slaves for some of his men (who

This modern reconstruction of Cofitachequi shows the typical structure of a Mississippian village, with its central plaza anchored by two mounds, one being the residence of the village chieftain.

desired them for purposes "more than was proper"). At Coosa, where the paramount chief again appeared on a litter and ordered his people to empty their houses for the Spanish, De Soto put him in chains and the town fled.

But at the end of this second season in the country, he met more than he bargained for in the person of Tascaluza, a paramount chief who lived near present-day Montgomery, Alabama. The Spanish marveled at the stature of the Indians of the region: they were much taller, and Tascaluza "seemed a giant," towering a foot and a half over De Soto. He received the Europeans from a ceremonial seat atop the plaza mound, and De Soto's lieutenant Luis de Moscoso tried the same maneuver De Soto had performed for Pizarro with the Incas, riding horseback around the plaza to intimidate the chief. Tascaluza feigned indifference and even requested a horse to ride himself. He was so tall for the small pony, however, that his legs hung down nearly to the ground.

De Soto met more than he bargained for in the person of Tascaluza, a paramount chief who towered a foot and a half over many of the Spanish.

While De Soto tried displays of horsemanship, Tascaluza offered dances by his people in the plaza, which reminded the Spanish of "the way of the peasants of Spain, in such a manner that it was a pleasure to see." De Soto then asked for Indian porters to carry the Spanish baggage, as well as women for the men. Tascaluza refused and was put in irons, but after expressing his displeasure, he seemed to accept his fate. Four hundred porters materialized; the women De Soto demanded were waiting at the nearby town of Mabila, Tascaluza promised. Messengers from Mabila brought cornbread seasoned with chestnuts.

Mabila proved to be guarded by a stout palisade, and despite a celebration of welcome, the houses on the plaza concealed Indian warriors. Hot words between the Indians and the Spaniards led to a scuffle in which an Indian had his arm chopped off. In an instant Tascaluza's men poured out. De Soto, suspecting a trap, had nevertheless entered the walled village with a dozen or so comrades and found himself surrounded. He barely fought free to the outside, losing some of his men in the process. Meanwhile the Indians killed a number of horses and dragged inside all the baggage that the 400 porters had carried. Defiantly they emptied out clothing, food, supplies, and even the 200 pounds of pearls. The ensuing battle lasted the entire day, with perhaps 5,000 Indians showering the Spanish with arrows from behind their pali-saded village. Eventually De Soto's men surmounted the fence and set fire to the thatched huts, as hand-to-hand combat continued through a haze of smoke and flames. Tascaluza's men urged their chief to flee, and he may have; or he may have been killed—the records do not say. Once the palisade was breached, however, Spanish lancers on horseback provided a decisive advantage. Victory came at a steep cost: 22 killed and another 148 wounded, much clothing gone, winter coming on—and De Soto's men ready to mutiny.

Many wanted to head south toward the gulf and leave La Florida to someone else. But De Soto had no intention of retreating without riches or an empire subdued. It took another year of the same futile struggles: west in the spring of 1541 to the Mississippi River, beyond it into present-day Arkansas and the Ozark Mountains, finally encountering a chiefdom of fierce Indians, the Tula, who fought the Spanish tooth and claw, driving the 350 or so surviving members of the expedition back toward the Mississippi. After enduring the harshest winter yet, with drenching cold rains and drifting snows, De Soto returned to the thickly settled region around Anilco. There, in the spring of 1542, he died.

Even then, the expedition consumed yet another year in a futile quest for an overland route to Mexico. Only during the winter of 1542–1543 did the men return to the Mississippi to build seven boats, in which to take their chances with the big river. When the spring floodwaters rose and floated the boats free, the Indians of Quigualtam were waiting, eager to ambush.

The Indians' canoes were not rustic birchbarks of the sort popular in the modern American imagination. They were massive dugouts, hollowed and shaped from the largest trees available. When Indians first met De Soto on the river in May 1541, the paramount chief brought a fleet of about 200, about 60 to 70 men aboard each craft and a canopy at the stern to shelter its commander. The men were "painted with red ocher and having great plumes of white and many colored feathers on either side [of the canoes] and holding shields in their hands with which they covered the paddlers, while the warriors were standing from prow to stern with their bows and arrows in their hands." With "the feathers, the shields, and banners, and the many men in them, they had the appearance of a beautiful fleet of galleys."

Their fighting abilities made them even more fearsome, as the seven handmade Spanish boats began their escape downriver to "the great sea," each towing a small dugout canoe. Quigualtam sent forth perhaps 100 dugouts, the men singing and hallooing loudly. When Moscoso dispatched four or five Spanish canoes to meet them, some Indians jumped out of their boats into the water—half swimming to the lead Spanish canoe to capsize it, the other half stabilizing their own canoes to prevent the Spanish from doing the same. Eleven Spaniards drowned in the encounter. The larger Spanish boats could not come to their aid because the river's current carried them downstream. For the rest of the day, Quigualtam pursued, raining down a hail of arrows and boasting in song that if the Spanish had risked being "food for birds and dogs on land, in the river they would make them food for the fishes."

So it proceeded down the river. Almost never did the Indians approach close enough for hand-to-hand combat, but they would swarm from shore in their dugouts, a new group taking the place of previous warriors once the Spanish entered a new territory. "This same battle and strife . . . proceeded continuously for ten days and nights," explained one chronicler. He may have exaggerated the extent of the attacks, but by the time the expedition reached the Gulf of Mexico, its men were exhausted from the constant paddling and skirmishing. It took another month and a half to reach the Spanish settlement of Pánuco, Mexico, in the summer of 1543.

The 311 survivors gave thanks to God, and some even began to think they should have stayed and founded a colony. But while a few Spanish expeditions probed the edges of North America over the next hundred years, no Europeans reached the populous interior or the chiefdoms of Quigualtam and Anilco, the many agricultural villages spreading around the Mississippi with their plazas and mounds. It was only in 1682 that the French explorer René-Robert Cavelier, Sieur de La Salle, swept down the broad river in canoes, passing through the same country all the way to the gulf.

Except in La Salle's telling, that same country seemed hardly the same at all. The French saw fewer than a dozen Indian villages along the way. For 200 miles at one stretch, there were none at all, "a solitude unrelieved by the faintest trace of man," wrote the nineteenth-century historian Francis Parkman in recounting the journey. La Salle did record herds of bison wandering where open lands stretched along the river. But where were the villages of the region that spread out "continually through land of

Where were the painted dugout canoes, with sixty warriors to each boat when La Salle paddled down the Mississippi?

open field, very well peopled with large towns," as one of De Soto's men put it? Where were the massed forces of Quigualtam and the other paramount chiefdoms? Where were the fleets of painted dugout canoes with their canopies, their warriors harrying yet another set of newcomers from one bend in the river to the next?

In 1543 thousands of Indians crowded into the territory. In 1682 there seemed to be only a relative handful. And between those two accounts in the historical record, there was silence. Where had all the Indians gone?

THE QUESTION OF NUMBERS

To explain that contrast, historians have to answer basic questions about population. How many Native Americans were living in North America when Europeans first came into it? As we can see from the accounts of De Soto's expedition, hundreds of diverse cultures spread across many areas of the continent. But there are no written records, let alone anything as formal as a census. How can historians even begin to calculate a precontact population?

One method has been to collect, adjust, and average available estimates from early European explorers and settlers. By proceeding region by region, researchers can assemble numbers that provide an approximate total of Indian inhabitants when Europeans arrived. During the early twentieth century, anthropologist James Mooney did just that. His estimates, published in 1928, proposed a precontact North American population of approximately 1.1 million. A decade later, anthropologist Alfred Kroeber reduced the estimate to 1 million or less. (Mooney's figures were "probably mostly too high rather than too low," Kroeber asserted.) These figures were widely accepted for decades, and appeared in many American history texts.

But if we examine Mooney's original notes, preserved at the Smithsonian Institution, a disquieting pattern emerges. Mooney died before he could publish his figures. For unstated reasons, the editor who did publish them often reduced the totals by 5 or 10 percent. In addition, Mooney's numbers were not necessarily what he believed to be the true precontact population—merely a bedrock minimum. In many cases, his preliminary notes show even larger totals, which he cautiously reduced for the final tally.

For example, in 1674 Daniel Gookin, a missionary, tried to calculate the precontact population of New England. To do so, he asked Indian elders to estimate the number of adult males each tribe could have called together for a war in the years before Europeans arrived. The elders' total came to 18,000. Assuming that for every able-bodied male there might have been three or four additional women, children, and old men, Gookin estimated a New England population anywhere from 72,000 to 90,000. His number was noted by a nineteenth-century historian, John Palfrey, but Palfrey lowered it to about 50,000, for reasons never stated. Mooney cut that figure to "about 25,000 or about one-half what the historian Palfrey makes it."

Of course, estimates varied. For the Massachusetts Indians alone, the minister Edward Johnson in 1654 judged that the chiefdom had 30,000 "able men"—a number six times higher than Gookin's claim of 5,000 for that tribe. Mooney laughed off Johnson's number as ridiculously high and also rejected Gookin's ("his usual exaggeration"), instead settling on a figure of 1,000 Massachusetts warriors, which was Gookin's estimate of the adult male population in his own day, half a century after whites had arrived in New England. Mooney did not explain his reasoning; he may have thought Gookin's information about his own times was more accurate than numbers supplied by elderly chiefs about bygone days when their tribes were supposed to have been much more powerful.

Perhaps Gookin's number did reflect "his usual exaggeration." But when such estimates are so imprecise to begin with, we may wonder whether the results are being influenced by unstated assumptions. Why was it that Mooney, Kroeber, and Palfrey virtually always reduced estimates rather than increasing them? Could it have been partly because they viewed Indian societies as primitive and therefore unable to support larger populations? Palfrey made no attempt to hide his disdain for Indian culture. "These people held a low place on the scale of humanity," he wrote. Even though "it was said they would run eighty or a hundred miles in a day," their "lymphatic temperament" led them to sink "under continuous labor."

Alfred Kroeber shunned the racism evident in Palfrey's remarks. Still, he hesitated to accept the high-population estimates of many sixteenth- and seventeenth-century observers. Indian societies in general, he explained, were characterized by "insane, unending, continuously attritional" warfare, which prevented tribes from becoming too large. Kroeber admitted that Indians along the eastern lands of North America grew crops and that the practice of agriculture in general encouraged larger populations. But the Indians along the Atlantic "were agricultural hunters," not really "farmers," he argued. "Every man, or his wife, grew food for his household. The population remaining stationary, excess planting was not practiced, nor would it have led to anything in the way of economic or social benefit nor of increase of numbers."

"The population remaining stationary": here Kroeber's argument was circular—for he possessed no hard information about whether the population was expanding or decreasing. It *must* have remained stationary, he assumed, because Indians were constantly fighting and lacked the skills to expand. But we have already seen that as De Soto's hungry troops made their way through the Southeast, they depended constantly on Indian surpluses. Kroeber seems to have ignored evidence that did not fit his assumptions.

Indeed, the pattern of sharply cutting back older population estimates in New England was repeated elsewhere in the hemisphere. Early-twentieth-century scholars discounted Spanish estimates of 40 to 60 million Indians in Central and South America. "To count is a modern practice," explained one scholar; "the ancient method was to guess; and when numbers are guessed they are always magnified." Those who proposed such hypotheses offered no concrete evidence of exaggeration.

By the mid-1970s, many anthropologists and archaeologists had come to believe that the conservative estimates were seriously flawed. They looked for more accurate methods to calculate population. One involved projecting numbers over a larger region by analyzing smaller areas in detail. In excavating an archaeological site, how many shelters or structures were constructed on a village plaza? How far did the village extend? How broad and deep were deposits of materials indicating a habitation: discarded shells, bones, or other garbage? The mounds on village plazas were usually built up over decades, with new houses being erected over the remains of older ones. A careful analysis of materials can help project population densities on a wider scale.

There is another method of projecting—of moving from the known to the unknown. That is by projecting across time. The practice is known as "upstreaming." As historian Daniel Richter explained,

> Scholars take a cultural pattern for which they do have written documentation or firsthand evidence and project it backward in time—"upstream"—in a period for which no such evidence exists. Thus, if we know that a seventeenth-century Native American group lived in a particular kind of housing, and if a fourteenth-century archaeological site shows a pattern of post molds matching that style of housing, we can be fairly confident that people lived in similar dwellings in that earlier period. With slightly less confidence—but quite responsibly—we can also assume that if this kind of house was home to a particular kind of family group in the seventeenth century, it was so in the fourteenth century as well. Similarly, if we know that women were the people who made ceramic pots in the seventeenth century, we assume that was the case in the first century also. But the further back in time we try to upstream, the less confidence we can have.

Upstreaming is an ingenious and valuable technique. But—to be frank—it is one that is used at least in part out of desperation. With so little evidence, one grabs at any available straw.

> *"Upstreaming" is an ingenious and valuable technique—but also one used at least in part out of desperation.*

And we have already seen one example where upstreaming was not helpful: Swanton's attempt to reconstruct De Soto's route. By upstreaming from settlements in the eighteenth century, he wrongly assumed that the same Indian tribes were living in the same places a century and more earlier. Other archaeologists, especially in the Southwest, have calculated earlier population density from information about nineteenth- and twentieth-century Pueblo Indian dwellings. "It is no accident" that such techniques have been popular in the Southwest, points out archaeologist Ann Ramenofsky, precisely because

> the survival of some aboriginal groups into the twentieth century permits an assumption of spatial continuity between prehistoric and historic populations . . . [I]f the number of people inhabiting a dwelling in the twentieth century is seven, the assumption is that same number occupied a dwelling in the thirteenth century.

That assumption, she pointed out, may underestimate the number of people staying in a room or dwelling. On the other hand, using a count of village sites can sometimes lead to overestimates. Many Indian groups lived in two or three different locations, depending on where game or nuts and fruits were available in different seasons. Three settlements do not necessarily equal three different groups of people.

By the 1970s enough studies had been done to suggest that older estimates of precontact population were markedly low. Rather than a population of 8 to 14 million in North and South America, newer studies suggested anywhere from 57 to 112 million, 5 to 10 million of whom lived north of Mexico. If these figures are correct, when Columbus landed in 1492 on Hispaniola, that island alone was inhabited by as many as 7 or 8 million people, compared with about 6 to 10 million for all of Spain. (England's population at the time was only about 5 million.) The Aztec capital of Tenochtitlán, estimated to have held anywhere from 165,000 to 250,000 inhabitants, was larger than the greatest European cities of the day: Constantinople, Naples, Venice, Milan, and Paris. In fact, more people may have been living in the Americas in 1492 than in western Europe.

For the southeastern regions of North America, more recent studies (including Ramenofsky's) suggest a population decline of as much as 80 percent between De Soto's *entrada* and La Salle's. That drop is immense. De Soto's army disrupted dozens of societies on its march through North America. Several thousand Indians must have died in pitched battles at Mabila and elsewhere along the way. Indians enslaved by the expedition perished from malnutrition and harsh conditions, while other inhabitants starved after the Spanish ate up their food stores. But those tragedies are a drop in the bucket when placed against a population decline of 80 percent over the next hundred years. What happened?

THE MIGRATION OF MICROBES

As De Soto's lieutenants collected pearls from the mortuary at Cofitachequi, one glimpsed a different color flashing in the shadows: "a thing like a green and very good emerald." He brought the object to De Soto. "My Lord," he advised, "do not call anyone; it could be that there might be some precious stone or jewel here." But when the "emerald" was brought into the daylight, it proved to be made only of glass. That was even more of a puzzle. Indians knew nothing of how to make glass. Inside the mortuary, De Soto's men found other beads—even more striking, beads fashioned as rosaries. The conclusion was inescapable: these were Spanish goods.

It did not take long to discover an explanation. Only two days' journey from Cofitachequi, said the Indians, was the ocean—along the Carolina coast. In 1526 an expedition led by Lucas Vázquez de Ayllón had landed at Winyaw Bay and exchanged trade goods there. These beads must be some of them. De Soto's men noticed something else about Cofitachequi. Many of the towns in the area were deserted, with weeds and trees growing up in the plazas. When asked, the Indians said that a great plague had come two years earlier and wiped out many inhabitants.

Did Ayllón unwittingly bring disease along with his glass beads? There is no evidence to prove this. Arguing against the possibility, the epidemic raged only two years earlier, according to the Indians, and Ayllón's visit was twelve years before that. The gap in time would seem too large to make the connection. On the other hand, scholars have come to realize the ravages of European diseases all across the western hemisphere after 1492.

Before 1492 Native Americans had never been exposed to smallpox, measles, malaria, or yellow fever. When their ancestors came to America tens of thousands of years earlier, the migration cut them off from the major disease pools of the world. In order to survive, disease-carrying microorganisms need a population large and dense enough to prevent them from gradually running out of new hosts. Thus large cities or any large groups of people (armies, schools) are prime disease pools. But the hunters who made their way over the Asian land bridge to America migrated in small bands, and the cold climates through which they passed served as a barrier to many disease-carrying microorganisms. As a result, Indians were not subjected to cycles of epidemics like those that drastically reduced populations in Europe and Asia.

Because Europeans and Asians were periodically reexposed to diseases such as smallpox, many developed immunities. For diseases such as measles, protection was acquired during childhood (when the body is better able to build immunity). By the sixteenth century, much of Europe's adult population was protected when outbreaks reappeared.

For unprotected populations, however, such "virgin-soil" epidemics were deadly. When the Pilgrim settlers arrived in New England in 1620, they found cleared agricultural fields and deserted villages, similar to those De Soto encountered around Cofitachequi. The Indian villages near the Pilgrim settlements had experienced mortality

For unprotected populations, "virgin-soil" epidemics of smallpox or other diseases were deadly.

rates as high as 95 percent, and early colonists were often astonished to find pile after pile of unburied bones, picked clean by the wolves and bleached by the sun. The most likely cause was chicken pox European fishermen had brought to American shores four years before the Pilgrims arrived.

More to the point, in De Soto's time Cortés was able to conquer the mighty Aztec empire in large part because smallpox ravaged the capital of Tenochtitlán. When the Spanish entered the conquered city, "the streets, squares, houses, and courts were filled with bodies, so that it was almost impossible to pass. Even Cortés was sick from the stench in his nostrils." Last but not least, scholars have come to realize that in South America De Soto and his commander Francisco Pizarro benefited from the diseases that had decimated Incan settlements a half dozen years earlier. According to one Spanish chronicle, "a great plague of smallpox broke out [around 1524 or 1525], so severe that more than 200,000 died of it, for it spread to all parts

The pustules from smallpox were horrifying and painful. In their own drawings, the Lakota Sioux used a spiral symbol to indicate the intense pain associated with the disease.

of the kingdom." Pizarro achieved his stunning victory because the Incan people had been demoralized by disease and wracked by the civil war that followed the death of their leaders.

Anthropologists like Mooney were aware of such diseases. But they had not calculated how severely such epidemics could reduce total populations. In the Southeast, however, a problem remains. Aside from the reference to disease at Cofitachequi, the De Soto accounts mention Indian sickness only three times in four years. If De Soto was responsible for spreading diseases that led to widespread native depopulation, why is there no mention of them?

To begin with, all diseases have an incubation period before the first visible symptoms appear. Because De Soto was often on the move, such symptoms may have surfaced only after he left an area. In this way, his men may have spread sexually transmitted diseases such as syphilis if they engaged in conduct "more than was proper" in Cofitachequi and other chiefdoms. Smallpox, too, could have been imported: the virus can actually survive in a dried state for several years before emerging.

But Patricia Galloway and Ann Ramenofsky have suggested another avenue of transmission. We have already noted that diseases flourish among dense populations. The same is true of epizootics among animals. Additionally, diseases often make a jump from animals to humans, as happens with modern influenza, which typically starts among Asian farm animals kept in close quarters with humans. And as we have learned, there was a sizable population of hogs following the same route: 700 at one point.

Some, we know, escaped from the Spanish and ran off into the wild. And Indians, the accounts indicate, occasionally stole swine for their own use. "When humans constitute the sole reservoir [of a disease]," note Galloway and Ramenofsky, "the infection tends to have a rapid onset and to last for a short period of time. Infections from nonhuman animals are typically longer-lived and may not ever be expressed in acute observable symptoms in the [animal] reservoir." In other words, the pigs could have appeared healthy while infecting the human population.

Furthermore, pigs are scavengers by nature, eating everything from nuts to mice to garbage to human waste. That would have increased the chance of passing along parasitical diseases, particularly in De Soto's winter camps, where sanitary conditions worsened. Diseases like trichinosis could have been passed along as pigs were butchered and eaten, or by drinking contaminated water. Pigs also could have devastated Indian crops and, by reducing food supply, left weakened human populations that were more prone to disease.

Thus despite the silences of a 140-year gap, scholars have been able to gather the outlines of Indian societies dramatically disrupted. Very likely, additional epidemics spread as Spanish expeditions made landfalls along the edges of the continent in the decades after De Soto. Although it is difficult to pinpoint deaths from disease by examining grave sites, archaeologists have found occasional telltales. The remains of many skeletons all laid on a single bed of sand, for example, suggest a mass burial. Certainly the effects of disease in later centuries illustrate the toll on Native Americans. During the nineteenth century, as fur traders and pioneers crossed the Great Plains, no fewer than twenty-seven epidemics decimated the continent: thirteen of smallpox, five of measles, three of cholera, two of influenza, and one each of diphtheria, scarlet fever, tularemia, and malaria. Loss of life ran anywhere from 50 to 95 percent of the populations affected.

Those cases also demonstrated how disease undermined not just physical health but the foundations of a culture. Virgin-soil epidemics proved most deadly to those between the ages of fifteen and forty. Healthy, in the prime of life, these victims were precisely those individuals who contributed the most to a community's economy, as hunters, farmers, or food gatherers.

Socially, the disruptions were equally severe. Because male warriors were among those hit hardest, hostile neighbors, either white or Indian, were more difficult to resist. The plague-stricken Indians of New England had "their courage much abated," reported one colonist; "their countenance is dejected, and they seem as a people affrighted." Near Charleston, South Carolina, an Indian told a settler that his people had "forgotten most of their traditions since the Establishment of this Colony, they keep their Festivals and can tell but little of the reasons: their Old Men are dead."

AN ECOLOGICAL EDEN?

La Salle's Mississippi River carved its way through a world vastly different from the one De Soto explored 140 years earlier. The plaza and mound cultures had disappeared; Indian population had diminished sharply. The Columbian exchange of Indian and European flora and fauna had been underway for nearly two centuries. Not only had pigs and horses entered the American landscape, Indians along the lower Mississippi served La Salle melons, pomegranates, peaches, pears, and apples—fruits brought to the Americas by Europeans. How these plants made their way to the lower Mississippi by 1682 is not clear; archaeological evidence suggests that Indian traders may have brought them from the orchards of Spanish missions in northern Mexico.

Once again we are reminded that history is about change and that in the era of contact, historians have underestimated the amount of change, assuming Indian societies were relatively stable over long periods of time. The vast majority of recent research suggests that disruption and discontinuity were a central part of the precontact era and that they accelerated after 1492, often in unpredictable ways.

One final example demonstrates the point. It centers not on hogs, a European import, but on the classic American buffalo, master of the continent's open spaces. La Salle reported bison "grazing in herds on the great prairies which then bordered the [Mississippi]," as Francis Parkman put it. As we noted earlier, 50 million bison may have roamed North America, with seventeenth-century colonists spotting some as far east as the Potomac River in Virginia. They were but one example of the abundant wildlife that led some Europeans to portray America as a kind of Eden, a natural paradise full of wild creatures of every sort.

Strange to say, 140 years earlier De Soto's expedition wandered 4,000 miles across the Southeast and well beyond the Mississippi into Arkansas and the Ozarks and never reported seeing a single bison. Buffalo were certainly around: at the westernmost reach of the expedition's travels, the Spanish went looking for "cows" (*bison* had not yet become the accepted term). But the herds were never sighted, only buffalo hides in the western Indian settlements. Where were the herds that La Salle viewed without traveling half as far?

Was it a coincidence that in 1682, after the Indian population had drastically decreased, that the bison population seemed to have increased? A number of ecologists have suggested that precisely because the animal's most dangerous predators—humans—declined, the buffalo population surged. Our model of the region's ecology should not assume a static situation. Bison, too, have a history that must incorporate change!

> *Was it a coincidence that when the Indian population was in drastic decline, the bison population had expanded greatly?*

During the early nineteenth century, Audubon described huge flocks of passenger pigeons that darkened the skies with their numbers. But can we reliably "upstream" such numbers to the precontact era? Recently some ecologists have questioned that assumption.

When we spoke earlier about a land of abundance—the multitudes of fish, beavers, squirrels, and wildfowl encountered by Europeans—the descriptions came from an earlier version of this chapter we wrote in 1985. The latest research on bison suggests that the abundant herds were *not* present in 1492 and that our picture of that era was distorted. In fact, virtually all the evidence we provided of the abundance of wildlife in precontact America depended on a kind of unspoken upstreaming. The colonists recording the abundant sturgeon in the rivers, the huge numbers of wildfowl, beavers, and squirrels, were early settlers, to be sure. But "early" in this case means the seventeenth century, which is still more than a hundred years after Columbus. As for the passenger pigeons darkening the skies, these were described by Audubon in 1813. Was it possible that 300 years *before* Audubon, different conditions applied?

If Indians had been hunting and eating passenger pigeons in 1500, archaeologists would expect to find pigeon bones when excavating older sites. Very few turn up. "What happened was that the impact of European contact altered the ecological dynamics in such a way that the passenger pigeon [population] took off," archaeologist Thomas Neumann has suggested.

North America was so thickly settled by Indians before contact that they kept the pigeon population under control. The massive flocks of 1813 were "outbreak populations—always a symptom of an extraordinarily disrupted ecological system."

Indeed, our species—*Homo sapiens*—had become what ecologists refer to as a keystone predator. Just as a keystone keeps the arch of a doorway in place, human predators at the top of the food chain influenced a host of plants and animals below them. Passenger pigeons, for example, eat mast, the nuts of forest trees that fall to the ground: acorns, beechnuts, hazelnuts, and chestnuts. Audubon described how pigeons could descend on a field like a devouring plague, leaving nothing in their wake. They were such a threat in Canada that the bishop of Quebec formally excommunicated the passenger pigeon in 1703! Since Indians depended on mast for much of their diet, these birds were competing with humans for the same food. So were other animals such as turkeys, raccoons, deer, and squirrels, which also ate mast. Neumann has noted that, unlike passenger pigeons, the bones of these "competitors" show up regularly in settlement excavations. By eating their competitors, Indians ensured that there was more mast to eat as well.

Not only that, Indians hunted in a way that worked to reduce the populations of these species. They hunted pregnant does in the spring, making it harder for young deer to replenish the population. Turkeys, too, were killed before they could lay eggs studies suggest a similar pattern of outbreak populations. In California, during the early 1800s noted the abundance of sea otter, shellfish, grizzly bears, elk, and antelopes. But these populations seem to have ballooned only after earlier epidemics decimated their human predators.

Some archaeologists contest these findings, but the evidence has steadily gained acceptance. If true, the new hypothesis turns our conception of precontact America nearly on its head. The abundant wildlife witnessed by so many European colonists was not a part of America before the dawn of history. It was actually new, the large populations a direct consequence of immigrants arriving from across the Atlantic.

All historians seek in their narratives an appropriate balance between change and continuity. Some institutions persist for centuries and evolve only gradually. But in the contested era of contact, change was dramatic, even catastrophic. In the centuries after 1491, populations throughout the western hemisphere dropped by anywhere from 50 to 90 percent. Ecosystems were altered and uprooted as the Columbian exchange transformed landscapes across the globe. De Soto and his followers provide a remarkable glimpse into the lost worlds of Cofitachequi, Tascaluza, and Apalachee, as well as a window on the uneasy, often violent interactions that sparked those changes.

Inevitably, the reconstruction goes on. Whether we like it or not, history is continually being reinvestigated and reconstructed. What we know about sixteenth-century America—or to be properly humble, what we *think* we know—is different today from what it was twenty years ago. No wonder we need revisions.

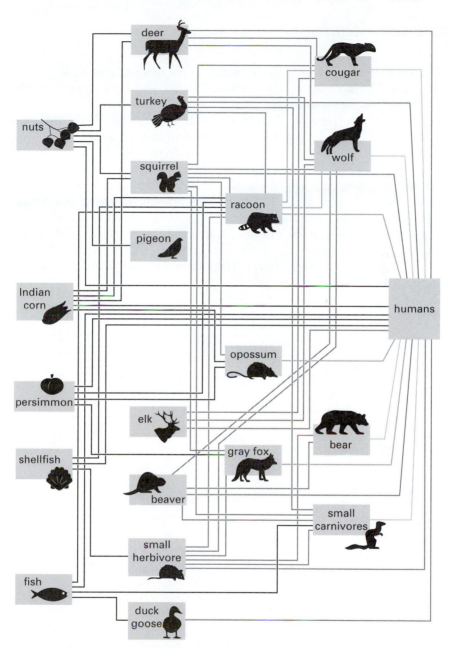

This chart shows humans as keystone predators atop the food chain. Because Indians depended on mast and corn, it was in the their interest to limit the number of competing predators for such food. (Adapted from Thomas Neumann, "The Role of Prehistoric Peoples in Shaping Ecosystems in the Eastern United States," in Charles E. Kay, ed., *Wilderness and Political Ecology: Aboriginal Influences and the Original State of Nature*, Salt Lake City, 2002, p. 156.)

Additional Reading

Charles Hudson, *Knights of Spain, Warriors of the Sun* (Athens, GA, 1997), provides the best account of the DeSoto *entrada* and its encounter with the many Indian chiefdoms of the Southeast. Only four primary—or near-primary—sources recounting the expedition have survived. They are presented in Lawrence A. Clayton, Vernon James Knight Jr., Edward C. Moore, eds., *The De Soto Chronicles: The Expedition of Hernando De Soto to North America in 1539–1543*, 2 vols. (Tuscaloosa, AL, 1993). For a broader survey of Indian cultures on the eve of contact and after, see Charles C. Mann's excellent *1491: New Revelations of the Americas before Columbus* (New York, 2006). Mann's book gives a good sense of the controversies and debates over what we know about the era of contact; as does a collection of essays edited by Patricia Galloway about the De Soto expedition, specifically *The Hernando De Soto Expedition: History, Historiography, and "Discovery" in the Southeast*, new edition (Lincoln, NE, 2005).

CHAPTER 2

Serving Time in Virginia

Pocahontas saved Captain John Smith's life, as everyone knows. Or did she? What we know about the "facts" of the case depends on the perspectives wrapped around those facts.

As has become clear, the historian's simple act of selection always separates "history" from "the past." The reconstruction of an event is clearly different from the event itself. Yet selection is only one in a series of interpretive acts that historians perform as they go about their business. Even during the first stages of research, when the historian is still gathering information, interpretation and analysis are necessary. That is because the significance of any piece of evidence is seldom apparent at first glance. The historian quickly learns that the words *evidence* and *evident* rarely amount to the same thing.

For historians trying to reconstruct an accurate picture of the first English settlements in Virginia, the difficulty of taking any document at face value becomes quickly apparent. The early Virginians were, by and large, an enterprising lot. They gave America its first representative assembly, gave England a new and fashionable vice (tobacco), and helped establish slavery as a labor system in North America. These actions raise perplexing questions for historians. Yet the answers to them cannot be found in the surviving source materials without a good deal of work.

Take, for example, the case of Captain John Smith, a well-known Virginian who was enterprising enough to write history as well as make it. Smith wrote an account of the young colony entitled *A Generall Historie of Virginia*, published in 1624. Much of his history is based on eyewitness, firsthand knowledge. At the vigorous age of twenty-seven, he joined the expedition in 1606 sent by the Virginia Company of London and played a crucial role in directing the affairs of the inexperienced Jamestown colony.

Yet Smith's evidence cannot be accepted without making some basic judgments. Most obvious—is he telling the truth? If we are to believe his own accounts, the captain led a remarkably swashbuckling life. Before joining the Virginia expedition, he had plunged as a soldier of fortune into a string of complicated intrigues in central Europe. There he waged desperate and brave warfare on behalf of the Hungarian nobility before being taken prisoner by the Turks. Once a prisoner, he was made a slave to a young but "noble Gentlewoman" with the romantic name of Charatza Tragabigzanda. The smitten princess "tooke (as it seemed) much compassion" on Smith. But alas, her sadistic brother insulted and taunted the captain so much that Smith lost his temper one day, "beat out [his] braines" with a bat, and made a daring escape, reaching England in time to sign on with the Virginia Company.

In Virginia the adventures came nearly as thick and fast. While the colony's governing council quarreled at Jamestown, Smith went off on an exploring mission. He established the first European contact with many of the Indian tribes around Chesapeake Bay, bought some much-needed corn from them, and was captured by a party of Indians loyal to Powhatan, the principal chief in the region. Facing execution, Smith once again managed to win the affections of a beautiful princess—this one, Powhatan's young daughter Pocahontas.

How much of this romantic adventure do we believe? The tone of Captain Smith's account demonstrates that he was not the sort of man to hide his light under a bushel. (In writing of his adventures, he compared himself with the Roman general Julius Caesar.) Indeed, several nineteenth-century scholars, including Henry Adams, challenged Smith's account of his Indian rescue. Adams pointed out that the Pocahontas story did not appear in Smith's earliest published descriptions of the Virginia colony. Smith probably inserted the story into the *Generall Historie* later, Adams argued, in order to enhance his reputation.

Yet other historians have defended Smith, Philip Barbour among them. Barbour checked Smith's tales against available records in both Hungary and England and found them generally accurate as to names, places, and dates. Smith claimed, for example, that he used an ingenious system of torch signals to coordinate a nighttime attack by his Hungarian friends, "Lord Ebersbaught" and "Baron Kisell." No other records mention Smith's role, but we do know such an attack was launched—led by two Hungarians named Sigismund Eibiswald and Jakob Khissl. Similarly, although the records show no princess named Charatza Tragabigzanda, that may have been Smith's fractured pronunciation of the Greek *koritsi* (girl) *Trapedzoûndos* (from Trebizond). Possibly, when he tried to discover the identity of his new mistress, someone merely replied that she was *koritsi Trapedzoûndos*—a "girl from Trebizond."

Yet even if we grant Smith's honesty, significant problems remain—problems common to all historical evidence. To say that Smith is truthful is only to say that he reported events *as he saw them*. The qualification is not small. Like every observer, Smith viewed events from his own perspective. When he described the customs of the Chesapeake Indians, for instance, he did so as a seventeenth-century Englishman. Behind each observation he made stood a whole set of attitudes and opinions that he took for granted. His descriptions were necessarily limited by the experience and education—or lack of it—that he brought with him.

The seriousness of these limitations becomes clearer if we take a hypothetical example of what might happen if Captain Smith were to set down a history, not of Indian tribal customs, but of a baseball game between the Boston Red Sox and the New York Yankees:

> Not long after, they tooke me to one of their great Counsells, where many of the generalitie were gathered in greater number than ever I had seen before. And they being assembled about a great field of open grass, a score of their greatest men ran out upon the field, adorned each in brightly hued jackets and breeches, with letters cunningly woven upon their Chestes, and wearinge uppon their heades caps of a deep navy blue, with billes, of a sort I know not what. One of their chiefs stood in the midst and would at his pleasure hurl a white ball at another chief, whose attire was of a different colour, and whether by chance or artyfice I know not the ball flew exceeding close to the man yet never injured him, but sometimes he would strike att it with a wooden club and so giveing it a hard blow would throw down his club and run away. Such actions proceeded in like manner at length too tedious to mention, but the generalitie waxed wroth, with greate groaning and shoutinge, and seemed withall much pleased.

Obviously Smith would make a terrible writer for the *New York Post*. (We don't even know if the Yankees won!) But before concluding anything more, compare the description of the baseball game with an account by the real Smith of what happened to him after his capture. (Smith writes in the third person, referring to himself as "he" and "Captain Smith.")

> At last they brought him to Meronocomoco, where was Powhatan their Emperor. . . . Before a fire upon a seat like a bedsted, [Powhatan] sat covered with a great robe, made of Rarowcun skinnes, and all the tayles hanging by. On either hand did sit a young wench of 16 or 18 yeares, and along on each side the house, two rowes of men, and behind them as many women, with all their heads and shoulders painted red; many of their heads bedecked with the white down of Birds; but every one with something: and a great chayne of white beads about their necks. At his entrance before the King, all the people gave a great shout. The Queene of Appamatuck was appointed to bring him water to wash his hands, and another brought him a bunch of feathers, in stead of a Towell to dry them. Having feasted him after their best barbarous manner they could, a long consultation was held, but the conclusion was, two great stones were brought before Powhatan. Then as many as could layd hands on him, dragged him to them, and thereon laid his head, and being ready with their clubs, to beat out his braines, Pocahontas the Kings dearest daughter, when no intreaty could prevaile, got his head in her armes, and laid her owne upon his to save him from death: whereat the Emperour was contented he should live to make him hatchets, and her bells, beads, and copper.

If we had not first read the account of the baseball game, it would not be nearly as obvious just how little Smith has told us about what is going on here. Indeed, anyone who reads any of the captain's writings will be impressed by their wealth of detail. But that is because we, like Smith, are unfamiliar with the rituals of the seventeenth-century Chesapeake Indians.

The Countrey wee now call **Virginia** beginneth at Cape Henry distant from Roanoack 60 miles, where was Sr Walter Raleigh's plantation: and because the people differ very little from them of Powhatan in any thing, I have inserted those figures in this place because of the conveniency.

King Powhatan comands C: Smith to be slaine, his daughter Pokahontas begcs his life his thankfullnes: and how he subiected 39 of their kings, reade heistof

printed by James Reeve

"And being ready with their clubs, to beat out his braines, Pocahontas the Kings dearest daughter . . . got his head in her armes, and laid her owne upon his to save him from death." The tale has been passed down as a romantic rescue, but from Powhatan's point of view, was this event an adoption ceremony designed to cement a political alliance?

Quite naturally—almost instinctively—we adopt Smith's point of view as our own. And that point of view diverts us from asking questions to which Smith does not have the answer. What, after all, is the reason the Indians painted their heads and shoulders red and wore white down on their heads? We know no more than we did about baseball players who were described as wearing bright outfits with letters woven upon their chests.

More to the point, consider the form of Smith's narrative as it has been passed down to us. The good captain is about to die until rescued at the last moment by "the Kings dearest daughter." Does the story have a familiar echo? Indeed—it strongly resembles Smith's being pitied by Princess Tragabigzanda. Equally important, the story has become prominent in our folklore because the nineteenth century delighted in such romantic tales: a pure and noble-born woman saves the life of a brave commoner. Smith tells a story that fits a narrative pattern we love to hear.

But what if we lay aside Smith's narrative perspective and consider the same facts from Powhatan's point of view? That chief led a confederacy of Algonquian Indians spread out around Chesapeake Bay. But his control over the lesser chiefs in the area varied. Some tribal groups resisted paying tribute to him; others at a greater distance showed no allegiance and were rivals.

Into this situation stepped Smith, along with the strange new tribe of white people who had just arrived from across the Atlantic. In hindsight, we see the arrival of Europeans as a momentous event that changed North America radically. But from Powhatan's point of view? Here was simply another new group of people—strange indeed, but people he would have to figure into the balance of his own political equation. Should he treat the newcomers as allies or enemies? Some historians and anthropologists have suggested that Powhatan's behavior toward Smith was a kind of ritualized adoption ceremony and that Smith's supposed execution was a kind of initiation rite in which the captain was being ritually humiliated and subordinated. Once Smith passed the test of bravery in the face of apparent death, Powhatan was willing to adopt him as a vassal. As Smith himself puts it, Powhatan decides his prisoner can "make him hatchets" and "bells, beads, and copper" for Pocahontas.

Was Powhatan's threatened "execution" actually an adoption ceremony?

Powhatan's later actions also suggest that he now considered Smith a chief, or *werowance*, over this new tribe of English allies. Two days later, the chief told Smith "now they were friends" and that Smith should go to Jamestown and send back "two great gunnes, and a gryndstone"—just as other Indian allies supplied Powhatan with tribute. In return, Powhatan would give Smith land and treat him "as his sonne."

This interpretation of Smith's capture and adoption must remain speculative, but it is responsible speculation, informed by historical and anthropological study of the ways of Algonquian Indians. And we would have been blind to the interpretation without having separated Smith's useful information from the narrative perspective in which it came to us.

It is easy enough to see how a point of view is embedded in the facts of someone's narration. But consider for a moment evidence recorded by one of the lowly clerks whose jottings constitute the great bulk of history's raw material. The following excerpts are taken from the records of Virginia's general assembly and the proclamations of the governor:

> We will and require you, Mr. Abraham Persey, Cape Marchant, from this daye forwarde to take notice, that . . . you are bounde to accepte of the Tobacco of the Colony, either for commodities or upon billes, at three shillings the beste and the second sorte at 18d the punde, and this shalbe your sufficient dischardge.

Every man to sett two acres corn (Except Tradesmen following their trades) penalty forfeiture of corn & Tobacco & be a Slave a year to the Colony. No man to take hay to sweat Tobacco because it robs the poor beasts of their fodder and sweating Tobacco does it little good as found by Experience.

In contrast to Smith's descriptions, these excerpts present small bits of information. To understand them, we need a lot more knowledge of what's going on. Whereas Smith attempted to describe the Indian ceremony in some detail because it was new to him, Virginia's general assembly knows all too much about tobacco prices and the planting of corn. Policy is stated without any explanation, just as the box score in the paper lists the single line, "Yankees 10, Red Sox 3." In each case the notations are so terse, the "narratives" so brief, that the novice historian is likely to assume they contain no point of view, only the bare facts.

But the truth is, each statement has a definite point of view that can be summed up as simple questions: (1) Did the Yankees win and if so by how much? (2) Should the price of tobacco be three shillings or eighteen pence or how much? (3) What should colonists use hay for? And so on. These viewpoints are so obvious, they would not bear mentioning—

Even the "bare facts" come attached to a perspective.

except that, unconsciously, we are led to accept them as the only way to think about the facts. Because the obvious perspective often appears irrelevant, we tend to reject the information as not worth our attention.

But suppose a fact is stripped of its point of view. Suppose we ask, in effect, a completely different question of it. Historians looking back on twentieth-century America would probably learn little from baseball box scores, but at least by comparing the standings of the 1950s with those of the 1970s, they would discover that the Giants of New York had become the Giants of San Francisco and that the Brooklyn Dodgers had moved to Los Angeles. If they knew a bit more about the economic implications of major-league baseball franchises, they could infer a relative improvement in the economic and cultural status of the West Coast. Similarly, historians can use the evidence of tobacco prices or corn planting to make inferences about economic and cultural conditions in seventeenth-century Virginia.

Using that approach, historians have taken documents from colonial Virginia, stripped them of their original perspectives, and reconstructed a striking picture of Virginia society. Their research reveals that life in the young colony was more acquisitive, raw, and deadly than most traditional accounts assumed. Between the high ideals of the colony's London investors and the shallow harbors along the Chesapeake, something went wrong. The society that was designed to be a productive and diversified settlement in the wilderness developed into a world in which the single-minded pursuit of one crop—tobacco—made life nasty, brutish, and short. And the colony that had hoped to pattern itself on the traditional customs of England instead found itself establishing something remarkably different: the institution of human slavery.

A Colony on the Edge of Ruin

No English colony found it easy to establish itself along the Atlantic Coast, but for the Virginia colony, the going was particularly rough. In the colony's first ten years, £75,000 was invested to send around 2,000 settlers across the ocean to what Captain Smith described as a "fruitfull and delightsome land" where "heaven and earth never agreed better to frame a place for mans habitation." Yet at the end of that time, the attempt to colonize Virginia could be judged nothing less than an unqualified disaster.

Certainly, most members of the Virginia Company viewed it that way. In 1606 King James had granted a charter to a group of London merchants who became formally known as "The Treasurer and Company of Adventurers and Planters of the City of London for the First Colony in Virginia." The Virginia Company, as it was more commonly called, allowed merchants and gentlemen to "adventure," or invest, money in a joint stock arrangement, pooling their resources to support an expedition to Virginia. The colony would extract the riches of the new country, such as gold or iron, and also cultivate valuable crops, such as grapes (for wine) or mulberry trees (used in making silk). King James, a silkworm buff, even donated some of his own specially bred worms. The proceeds would repay the company's expenses, the "adventurers" would reap handsome profits, the colonists would prosper, and England would gain a strategic foothold in the Americas. So the theory went.

The reality was rather different. After four hard months at sea, only 105 of the original 144 settlers reached Chesapeake Bay in April of 1607. The site chosen at Jamestown for a fort was swampy, its water unhealthy, and the Indians less than friendly. By the end of the first hot and humid summer, 46 more settlers had perished. When the first supply ship delivered 120 new recruits the following January, it found only 38 men still alive.

Part of the failure lay with the colony's system of government. A president led a council of 13 men, but in name only. Council members refused to take direction and continually bickered among themselves. In 1609 a new charter placed centralized control with a governor, but when another 600 settlers set off, a hurricane scattered the fleet and only 400 settlers arrived, leaderless, in September of 1609. Captain Smith, the one old hand who had acted decisively to pull the colony together, was sent packing on the first ship home. And as winter approached, the bickering began anew.

Nobody, it seemed, had planted enough corn to last through the winter. Settlers preferred to barter, bully, or steal supplies from the Indians—just as De Soto had, seventy years before. And the Indians knew that the English depended on them—knew that they could starve out the newcomers simply by moving away. When several soldiers stole off to seek food from the natives, the other settlers discovered their comrades not long after, "slayne with their mowthes stopped full of Breade," killed as a taunt to those who might come seeking food.

As the winter wore on, the store of hogs, hens, goats, sheep, and horses were consumed; the colonists then turned to "doggs Catts Ratts and myce." Conditions became so desperate that one man "did kill his wife, powdered [i.e., salted] her, and had eaten part of her" before leaders discovered his vil-

So thin that they looked like skeletons . . .

lainy and had him executed. By May 1610, when Deputy Governor Thomas Gates and the rest of the original fleet limped in from Bermuda, only 60 settlers had survived the winter, and these were "so Leane thatt they looked Lyke Anotamies Cryeing owtt we are starved We are starved."

Grim as such tales are, we have almost come to expect them in the first years of a new colony. But as the years passed, the colonists seemed to learn little. Ten years after the first landing, yet another governor, Samuel Argall, arrived to find Jamestown hardly more than a slum in the wilderness: "but five or six houses [remaining standing], the Church downe, the [stockade fence] broken, the Bridge in pieces, the Well of fresh water spoiled; the Storehouse they used for the Church; the market-place and streets, and all other spare places planted with Tobacco." Of the 2,000 or so settlers sent since 1607, only 400 remained alive. Even John Rolfe, an optimist among the settlers, could not help taking away with the left hand the praises he bestowed with the right. "Wee found the Colony (God be thanked) in good estate," he wrote home hopefully, "however in buildings, fortyfications, and of boats, much ruyned and greate want." It was not much of a progress report after ten years.

In England, Sir Edwin Sandys was one of the adventurers who watched with distress as the company's efforts went nowhere. Sandys lacked the financial punch of bigger investors such as Thomas Smith, who considered the Virginia enterprise just one venture among many: the East India Company, trading in the Levant, and the Muscovy Company. If Virginia did not pay immediate dividends, they could afford to wait. Sandys and his financially strapped followers pressed for immediate reform, and in 1619 succeeded in electing him treasurer of the company. With real power in his hands for the first time, Sandys set out to reconstruct the failing colony from the bottom up.

BLUEPRINT FOR A VIRGINIA UTOPIA

Sandys knew that to succeed, he would have to attract both new investors to the company and new settlers to the colony. Yet the Virginia Company was deeply in debt, and the colony was literally falling apart. In order to recruit both settlers and investors, Sandys offered the only commodity the company possessed in abundance—land.

In the first years of the colony, Virginia land had remained company land. Settlers who worked it might own shares in the company, but even so, they did not profit directly from their labor. All proceeds went directly into the treasury, to be divided only if there were any profits. There never were. In 1617 the company changed its policy. Old Planters, the settlers who had come to Virginia before the spring of 1616, were each granted 100 acres of land. Freemen received their allotment immediately, while those settlers who were still company servants received their land when their terms of service expired.

Sandys lured new investors with the promise of property too. For every share they purchased, the company granted them 100 acres. More important, Sandys encouraged immigration to the colony by giving investors additional land if they would pay the ship passage of tenant laborers. For every new tenant imported to Virginia, the investor received 50 additional acres. Such land grants were known as "headrights" because the land was apportioned per each "head" imported. Of course, if Old Planters wished to invest in the company, they too would receive 100 acres plus additional 50-acre headrights for every tenant whose passage they paid. Such incentives, Sandys believed, would attract funds to the company while also promoting immigration.

And so private property came to Virginia. This tactic was the much-heralded event that every schoolchild is called upon to recite as the salvation of the colony. "When our people were fed out of the common store and labored jointly together, glad was he could slip away from his labour, or slumber over his taske," noted one settler. But "now for themselves they will doe in a day" what before they "would hardly take so much true paines in a weeke." It is important to understand, however, that the company still had its own common land and stock from which it hoped to profit. Thus a company shareholder had the prospect of making money in two ways: from any goods marketed by company servants working company lands, or directly from his newly granted private lands.

There were other openings for private investment. By 1616 the company had already granted certain merchants a four-year monopoly on providing supplies for the colony. The "magazine," as it was called, sent supply ships to Virginia, where its agent, a man known as the "cape merchant," sold the goods in return for produce. In 1620 the company removed the magazine's monopoly and allowed other investors to send over supply ships.

Sandys and his friends also worked to make the colony a more pleasant place to live. Instead of being governed by martial law, as the colony had since 1609, the company created an assembly with the power to make laws. The laws would be binding so long as the company later approved them. Inhabitants of the various company settlements were to choose two members each as their burgesses, or representatives. When the assembly convened in 1619, it became the first representative body in the English colonies.

Historians have emphasized the significance of this first step in the evolution of American democracy. But the colony's settlers may have considered it equally important that the company had figured out a way to avoid saddling them with high taxes to pay for their government. Again the answer was land, which the company used to pay officials' salaries. The governor received 3,000 acres plus 100 tenants to work them, the treasurer received 1,500 acres and 50 tenants, and so on. Everybody won, or so it seemed. The officers got their salaries without having to "prey upon the people"; the settlers were relieved "of all taxes and public burthens"; and the sharecropping tenants, after splitting the profits with company officials for seven years, got to keep the land they worked. If the company carried out its policy, John Rolfe observed enthusiastically, "then we may truly say in Virginia, we are the most happy people in the world."

In 1619, with the reforms in place, the company moved into high gear. New investors sent scores of tenants over to work their plantations; the company sent servants to tend officers' lands; and lotteries throughout England provided income to recruit ironmongers, vine-tenders, and glass-blowers. The records of the Virginia Company tell a story of immigration on a larger scale than ever before. Historians who do a little searching and counting in company records will find that some 3,570 settlers were sent to join a population that stood, at the beginning of Sandys's program, at around 700.

It would have been an impressive record, except that in 1622, three years later, the colony's population still totaled only about 700 people.

The figures are in the records; you can check the math. What it amounts to is that in 1622, there are about 3,500 Virginians missing. No significant number returned to England; most, after all, could hardly afford passage over. No significant number migrated to other colonies. We can account for the deaths of 347 colonists, slain in an Indian attack of 1622. But that leaves more than 3,000 settlers. There seems to be only one way to do the accounting: those immigrants died.

The figures in the record make it clear: 3,500 Virginians are missing.

Who—or what—was responsible for the deaths of 3,000 Virginians? The magnitude of the failure was so great that the leaders of the company did not care to announce it openly. When the king got word of it, only after the company had virtually bankrupted itself in 1624, he revoked its charter. The historian who confronts the statistical outlines of this horror is forced to ask a few questions. Just what conditions would produce a death rate in the neighborhood of 75 to 80 percent? A figure that high is simply staggering. For comparison, the death rate during the first (and worst) year at the Pilgrims' Plymouth colony stayed a little below 50 percent, and during the severe plague epidemics that swept Britain in the fourteenth century, the death rate probably ranged from 20 to 45 or 50 percent.

Obvious answers suggest themselves. The colony could not sustain the wave of new settlers, especially since Sandys, eager to increase Virginia's population, sent so many people with little or no food to tide them over until they could begin raising their own crops. Housing was inadequate. The company in London repeatedly begged the colony's governors to build temporary "guest houses" for the newcomers, while the governors in return begged the company to send more provisions with recruits.

Disease took its toll. Colonists had discovered early on that Virginia was an unhealthy place to live. For newcomers, the first summer proved so deadly it was called the "seasoning time." Those who survived significantly raised their chances of prospering. But dangers remained year-round, especially for those weakened by the voyage or living on a poor diet. Contaminated wells most likely contributed to outbreaks of typhoid fever, and malaria claimed additional victims.

The obvious answers do much to explain the devastating death rate. Still, even granting the seriousness of typhoid and other diseases, why a death rate higher than the worst plague years? Why, after more than ten years, was the Jamestown colony still not self-sufficient?

Self-sufficiency required that colonists raise their own food, primarily corn. So the historian asks a simple question: how much work did it take to grow corn? A look at the records confirms what might be suspected—that no Virginian in those first years bothered to leave behind a treatise on agriculture. But a search of letters and company records provides bits of data here and there. The Indians, Virginians discovered, spent only a few days a year tending corn, and they often produced surpluses that they traded to the Virginians. A minister in the colony reported that "in the idle hours of one week," he and three other men planted enough corn to last for four months. Other estimates suggested that forty-eight hours' work was enough to plant enough corn for a year. Even allowing for exaggeration, it seems clear that comparatively little effort was needed to grow corn.

Yet if a settler could easily grow corn, and corn was desperately needed to survive, what possible sense is the historian to make of the document we encountered earlier, Governor Argall's proclamation of 1618 requiring "Every man to sett two acres corn (Except Tradesmen following their trades)." That year is not the last time the law appears on the books. It was reentered in the 1620s and periodically up through the 1650s.

It's a puzzle: a law requiring Virginians to plant corn? Everyone is starving, planting and reaping take only a few weeks . . . and the government has to *order* settlers to do it?

Yet the conclusion seems clear: Virginians had to be forced to grow corn. The reason becomes clearer if we reexamine Governor Argall's gloomy description of Jamestown when he stepped off the boat in 1617. The church is down, the palisades pulled apart, the bridge in pieces, the fresh water spoiled. Everything in the description indicates the colony is falling apart, except for one paradoxical feature— the "weeds" in the street. The stock- *Starving colonists have to be forced to grow corn?* ades and buildings may have deteriorated from neglect, but it was not neglect that caused "the market-place and streets, and all other spare places" to be "planted with Tobacco." Unlike corn, tobacco required a great deal of attention to cultivate. It did not spring up in the streets by accident.

What Governor Argall's evidence is telling us, once we strip away the original dull narrative perspective, is that at the same time that settlers were

Virginia's early planters marketed their tobacco to the Dutch as well as the English. This painting on an early-seventeenth-century ceramic tile shows a Dutch smoker attempting the novel accomplishment of blowing smoke through his nose. The new habit of smoking, at once popular and faintly disreputable, led to a demand for Virginia tobacco in Europe that drove up prices and sent enterprising colonists scrambling for laborers to help raise the profitable crop.

willing to let the colony fall apart, they were energetically planting tobacco in all the "spare places" they could find.

Settlers had discovered as early as 1613 that tobacco was marketable. Soon shipments increased dramatically, from 2,500 pounds in 1616 to 18,839 pounds in 1617 and 49,518 pounds in 1618. Some English buyers used tobacco as a medicine, but most purchased it simply for the pleasure of smoking it. Sandys and many other gentlemen looked upon the "noxious weed" as a vice and did everything to discourage its planting. But his protests, as well as the corn laws, had little effect. Tobacco was in Virginia to stay.

VIRGINIA BOOM COUNTRY

The Virginia records are full of statistics like the tobacco export figures: number of pounds shipped, price of the "better sort" of tobacco for the year 1619, number of settlers arriving on the *Bona Nova*. These statistics are the sort of box-score evidence, recorded by pedestrian clerks for pedestrian reasons, day in, day out. Yet once the historian cross-examines the facts for his or her own purposes, they flesh out an astonishing picture of Virginia. Historian Edmund S. Morgan, in his own reconstruction of the situation, aptly labeled Virginia "the first American boom country."

For Virginia was booming. The commodity in demand—tobacco—was not as glamorous as gold or silver, but the social dynamics operated in similar fashion. The lure of making a fortune created an unstable society where wealth changed hands quickly, where an unbalanced economy centered on one get-rich-quick commodity, and where the value of human dignity counted for little.

The shape of this boom-country society becomes clearer if we ask the same basic questions about tobacco that we asked about corn. How much tobacco could one person grow in a year? Could Virginians get rich doing it?

High-quality Virginia tobacco sold for only 1 to 3 shillings during the 1620s. What that price range meant in terms of profits depended, naturally, on how much tobacco a planter could grow in a year. As with corn, the estimates in the records are few and far between. John Rolfe suggested 1,000 plants in one year. William Capps, another settler, estimated 2,000 and also noted that three of his boys, whose labor he equated with one and a half men, produced 3,000 plants. Fortunately, Capps also noted that 2,000 plants made up about 500 "weight" (or pounds) of tobacco, which allows us to convert numbers of plants into number of pounds.

By comparing these figures with other estimates, we can calculate roughly how much money a planter might have received for a crop. The chart below summarizes how many plants or pounds of tobacco one or more workers might have harvested in a year. The numbers in parentheses calculate the number of pounds harvested per worker and the income such a harvest would yield if tobacco were selling at either 1 or 3 shillings a pound.

Tobacco Production and Income Estimates

Number of Workers	One-Year Production			Income	
	Number of Plants	Number of Lbs.	One Man Lbs./Yr.	1s	3s
1 (Rolfe)	1,000		(250)	£12	£37.5
1 (Capps)	2,000	500	(500)	25	75
3 boys (1½ men)	3,000		(500)	25	75
4 men		2,800	(700)	46.5	139.5
6–7 men		3,000–4,000	(540)	27	81

Source: Based on data presented in Edmund Morgan, *American Slavery, American Freedom* (New York, 1975).

These estimates indicate that the amount of tobacco one man could produce ranged from 250 to 700 pounds a year, an understandable variation given that some planters worked harder than others, that some years provided better growing weather, and that, as time passed, Virginians developed ways to turn out bigger crops. Even by John Rolfe's estimate, made fairly early and therefore somewhat low, a man selling 250 pounds at 1 shilling a pound would receive £12 sterling for the year. On the high side, the estimates show a gross of £140 sterling, given good prices. Indeed, one letter tells of a settler who made £200 sterling after the good harvest of 1619. Such windfalls were rare, but considering that an average agricultural worker in England made less than £3 a year, even the lower estimates look good.

They look even better for another reason—namely, because that income was what a planter earned working alone. In a society where servants, tenants, and apprentices were common, if Virginians could get other people to work for them, they could profit spectacularly.

Back to the basic questions. How did an Englishman get others to work for him? He hired them. He made an agreement, a bond indicating what he would give in return for their service and for how long the agreement was to run. The terms varied from servant to servant but fell into several general classes. Most favorable, from the worker's point of view, was the position of tenant. A landowner had fields that needed working; the tenant agreed to work them, usually for a term of four to seven years. In return, the tenant kept half of what he produced. From the landowner's point of view, a servant served the purpose better, since he was paid only room and board, plus his passage from England. In return he gave his master everything he produced. Apprentices, usually called "Duty boys" in Virginia because the ship *Duty* brought many of them over, made up another class of workers. Apprentices served for seven years, then another seven as tenants. Again the master's cost was only transportation over and maintenance once in Virginia.

Little in the way of higher mathematics is required to discover that if it cost a master about £10 to £12 sterling to bring over a servant, and if that master obtained the labor of several such servants for seven years, or even for two or three, he stood to make a tidy fortune. In the good harvest of 1619, one master with six servants managed a profit of £1,000 sterling. That was unusual perhaps, but by no means impossible. And Sandys's headright policies played into the hands of the fortune-makers: every servant imported meant another fifty acres of land that could be used for tobacco.

The lure was too much to resist. Virginians began bending every resource in the colony toward growing tobacco. The historian can now appreciate the significance of Governor Argall's proclamation (page 36) that no hay should be used to "sweat," or cure, tobacco: colonists were diverting hay from livestock that desperately needed it ("it robs the poor beasts of their fodder"), thus upsetting Virginia's

Colonists began bending every resource toward growing tobacco— the boom in Virginia was on.

economy. The scramble for profits extended even to the skilled workers whom Sandys sent over to diversify the colony's exports. The ironmongers deserted in short order, having "turned good honest Tobaccoemongers"; and of similar well-intentioned projects, the report came back to London that "nothinge is done in anie of them but all is vanished into smoke (that is to say into Tobaccoe)." The boom in Virginia was on.

Planters were not the only people trying to make a fortune. The settler who raised tobacco had to get it to market in Europe somehow, had to buy corn if he neglected to raise any himself, and wanted to buy as many of the comforts of life as could be had. Other men stood ready to deal with such planters, and they had a sharp eye to their own profit.

One such settler was Abraham Peirsey, the merchant running the Virginia Company's magazine, or store. And if we now return to the Virginia assembly's order, quoted earlier, requiring Peirsey to accept 3 shillings per pound for the "beste sort" of tobacco, we can begin to understand why the assembly was upset enough to pass the regulation. Peirsey was charging exorbitant prices for his supplies. He collected his fees in tobacco because there was virtually no currency in Virginia. Tobacco had become the economic medium of exchange. If Peirsey counted a pound of the best sort of tobacco as worth only 2 shillings instead of 3, that was as good as raising his prices by 50 percent. As it happened, Peirsey charged two or three times the prices set by the investors in London. Beyond that, he never bothered to pay back the company for its supplies that he sold. Sandys and the other investors never saw a cent of the magazine's profits.

Another hunt through the records indicates what Peirsey was doing with his ill-gotten gain: he plowed it back into the most attractive investment of all, servants. We learn this not because Peirsey comes out and says so, but because the census of 1625 lists him as keeping thirty-nine servants, more than anyone in the colony. At his death in 1628, he left behind "the best Estate that was ever yett knowen in Virginia." When the company finally broke the magazine's monopoly in 1620, other investors moved in. They soon discovered that they could make more money selling alcohol than the necessities of life. So the Virginia boom enriched the merchants of "rotten Wynes" as well as the planters of tobacco, and settlers went hungry, in part, because liquor fetched a better return than food.

Given these conditions in Virginia—given the basic social and economic structures deduced from the historical record—put yourself in the place of most tenants or servants. What would life be like? What were the chances for success?

For servants, the prospect was bad indeed. First, they faced the fierce mortality rate. Chances were that they would not survive the first seasoning summer. Even if they did, their master was out to make a fortune by their labor. Being poor to begin with, they were in no position to protect themselves from abuse. In England the situation was different. Agricultural workers usually offered their services once a year at hiring fairs. Since their contracts lasted only a year, servants could switch to other employers if they became dissatisfied. But going to Virginia required the expense of a long voyage; masters would hire people only if they signed on for four to seven years. Once in Virginia, what could servants do if they became disillusioned? Go home? They had little enough money for the voyage over, even less to get back.

Duty boys, the children, were least in a position to improve their lot. The orphans Sandys hoped to favor by taking them off the London streets faced a hard life in Virginia. They were additionally threatened by a law the Virginia planters put through the assembly, declaring that an apprentice who committed a crime during his service had to begin his term all over again. What constituted a crime, of course, was left up to the governor's council.

One Duty boy, Richard Hatch, appeared before the council because he had commented, in a private house, on the recent execution of a settler for sodomy. Hatch had remarked "that in his consyence" he thought that the settler was "put to death wrongfully." For this offense he was to be "whipt from the forte to the gallows and from thence be whipt back againe, and be sett uppon the Pillory and there to loose one of his eares." Although Hatch had nearly completed his term of service—to Governor George Yeardly—he was ordered to begin his term anew.

Tenants would seem to have been better off, but they too were subject to the demand for labor. If immigrants could pay their passage over but were unable to feed themselves upon arrival, they had little choice but to hire themselves out as servants. And if their masters died before their terms were up, there was virtually always another master ready to jump in and claim them, legally or not. When George Sandys, Sir Edwin's brother, finished his term as colony treasurer, he dragged his tenants with him, even though they had become freemen. "He maketh us serve him whether wee will or noe," complained one, "and how to helpe it we doe not knowe for hee beareth all the sway."

Even independent small planters faced the threat of servitude if their crops failed or if Indian attacks made owning a small, isolated plantation too dangerous. When William Capps, a small planter on the frontier, asked the governor's council to outfit an expedition against hostile tribes in his neighborhood, the council refused. Capps indignantly suggested what was going through the minds of wealthy planters on the council. "Take away one of my men to join the expedition," he imagines them saying,

> there's 2000 Plantes gone, thates 500 waight of Tobacco, yea and what shall this man doe, runne after the Indians? soft, I have perhaps 10, perhaps 15, perhaps 20 men and am able to secure my owne Plantacion; how will they doe that are fewer? let them first be crusht alitle, and then perhaps they will themselves make up the Nomber for their owne safetie. Theis I doubt are the Cogitacions of some of our worthier men.

AND SLAVERY?

This reconstruction of Virginia society, from the Duty boy at the bottom to the planters at the top, indicates that all along the line, labor had become a valuable and desperately sought commodity. Settlers who were not in a position to protect themselves found that the economy put constant pressure on them. Planters bought, sold, and traded servants without their consent and, on occasion, even used them as stakes in gambling games. There had been "many complaints," acknowledged John Rolfe, "against the Governors, Captaines, and Officers in Virginia: for buying and selling men and boies," something that "was held in England a thing most intolerable." One Englishman put the indignity quite succinctly: "My Master Atkins hath sold me for £150 sterling like a damnd slave."

"About the last of August came in a dutch man of warre that sold us twenty Negars." So wrote John Smith in 1619. The illustration is by Howard Pyle, a nineteenth-century artist who prided himself on his research into costume and setting. Yet even here, Pyle's depiction of the first African Americans probably reflects illustrations he saw of the very different slave traffic of the eighteenth and nineteenth centuries. These early arrivals may have been sold as servants, not slaves. Court records indicate that in the 1640s at least some black slaves had been freed and were purchasing their own land.

Indeed, quite a few of the ingredients of slavery are found in Virginia: the feverish boom that sparked the demand for human labor; the mortality rate that encouraged survivors to become callous about human life; the servants bought and sold, treated almost as if they were property. If we were looking in the abstract to construct a society in which social and economic pressures combined to encourage the development of human slavery, Virginia would seem to fit the model neatly. Yet the actual records do not quite confirm the hypothesis.

The earliest-known record of Africans in Virginia is a muster roll of March 1619 (discovered only in the 1990s), which shows thirty-two Africans (fifteen men and seventeen women) "in the service of sev[er]all planters." But are these Africans working as servants or as slaves? The muster roll doesn't say. Historians have gone through court records, inventories, letters, wills, church documents—anything that might shed light on the way blacks were treated. What little information that has surfaced indicates that very few Africans came to Virginia in the colony's first half century. People of African descent made up no more than 5 percent of the population at any time during those years.

Were the first Africans in Virginia servants or slaves?

Furthermore, the status of those Africans who did come varied widely. Before 1660 some were held as slaves for life, but others worked as servants. Still others either were given their freedom or were able to purchase it. Even the names in the record supply a clue to the mixed status of these early African newcomers. In the eighteenth century, once slavery was well established, planters tried to control the naming process, giving their slaves diminutive names such as Jack or Sukey, or perhaps a classical Caesar or Hercules, bestowed in jest. But during Virginia's early years, Africans tended to keep their full names—names that often reflected the complex cultural landscape of the African coast, where Europeans and Africans of many backgrounds mixed: Bashaw Farnando, John Graweere, Emanuel Driggus. Other Africans tried to assimilate into English life. The man who first appeared in the colony's records as only "Antonio a Negro" changed his name to Anthony Johnson. "Francisco a Negroe" eventually became the freeman Frank Payne.

Only during the 1660s did the Virginia assembly begin to pass legislation that separated blacks from whites, defining slavery, legally, as an institution. Black Virginians, in other words, lived with white Virginians for more than forty years before their status became fully and legally debased. The facts in the records force us to turn the initial question around. If the 1620s, with its boom economy, was such an appropriate time for slavery to have developed, why didn't it?

Here, the talents of historians are stretched to their limits. They can expect no obvious explanations from contemporaries such as John Rolfe, Captain Smith, or William Capps. The development of slavery was something that came gradually to Virginia. Most settlers were not thinking or writing about a change that developed over many decades. Even the records left by the clerks are scant help. The best we can do is intelligent conjecture, based on the kind of society that has been reconstructed.

Was it a matter of the simple availability of slaves? Perhaps. While Virginia was experiencing its boom of the 1620s, West Indian islands like Barbados and St. Kitts were also being settled. There, where the cultivation of sugar demanded even more intensive labor than tobacco did, the demand for slaves was extremely high, and slavery developed more rapidly. If traders sailing from Africa could carry only so many slaves, and if the market for them was better in Barbados than in Virginia, why sail all the way up to Chesapeake Bay? Slave traders may not have found the effort worth it. That is the conjecture of one historian, Richard Dunn. Other historians and economists have argued that Chesapeake planters preferred white servants but that during the 1670s the supply of servants from England began to decrease, sending prices higher. At the same time, an economic depression in the West Indies sent the price of slaves falling and sent slave dealers looking to sell more slaves along the Chesapeake.

Edmund Morgan has suggested another possibility, based on the continuing mortality rate in Virginia. Put yourself in the place of the planter searching for labor. You can buy either servants or slaves. Servants come cheaper than slaves, of course, but you get to work them for only seven years before they receive their freedom. Slaves are more expensive, but you get their labor for the rest of their lives, as well as the labor of any offspring. In the long run, the more expensive slave would have been the better buy. But in Virginia in the 1620s? Everyone is dying anyway. What are the chances that either servants or slaves are going to live for more than seven, five, even three years? Wouldn't it make more sense to pay less and buy servants on the assumption that whoever is bought may die shortly anyway?

It is an ingenious conjecture, but it must remain that. No plantation records have been found indicating that planters actually thought that way. Available evidence does suggest that the high death rate in Virginia began to drop only in the 1650s. It makes sense that only then, when slaves became a profitable commodity, would laws come to be passed formally establishing their legal status. Whatever the reasons may have been, Virginia remained until the 1680s and 1690s what historian Ira Berlin has termed a "society with slaves" rather than a full-fledged "slave society" whose economy and culture revolved around the institution of slavery based on race. During the boom of the 1620s, slavery did not flourish markedly.

Sometime between 1629 and 1630 the economic bubble popped. The price of tobacco plummeted from 3 shillings to a penny a pound. Virginians tried desperately to prop it up again, either by limiting production or by simple edict, but they did not succeed. Planters still could make money, but the chance for a quick fortune had vanished—"into smoke," as Sandys or one of his disillusioned investors would no doubt have remarked. It is much to the credit of historians that the feverish world of the Chesapeake has not, like its cash crop, entirely vanished in similar fashion.

Additional Reading

The vigorous prose of Captain John Smith struts, bounces, jars, and jounces from one page to the next. A sampling of his writings are gathered in Karen Ordahl Kupperman, ed., *Captain John Smith: A Select Edition of His Writings* (Chapel Hill, 1988). Frederick Fausz perceptively discusses white–Native American relations in early Virginia in William W. Fitzhugh, ed., *Cultures in Contact: The Impact of European Contacts on Native American Cultural Institutions, A.D. 1000–1800* (Washington, DC, 1985), pp. 225–268. Edmund S. Morgan brilliantly reconstructs boom-country Virginia in *American Slavery, American Freedom* (New York, 1975). Much of the new scholarship on the development of slavery in Virginia (and elsewhere in North America) can be found in the judicious synthesis of Ira Berlin, *Many Thousands Gone: The First Two Centuries of Slavery in North America* (Cambridge, MA, 1998), and Allan Kulikoff, *Tobacco and Slaves: The Development of Southern Cultures in the Chesapeake, 1680–1800* (Chapel Hill, NC, 1986). Anthony Parent Jr. argues that the planter class knew exactly what it was doing in establishing the institution of slavery in late-seventeenth-century Virginia in *Foul Means: The Formation of a Slave Society in Virginia, 1660–1740* (Chapel Hill, NC, 2003).

Is Slavery Dead?

The slave named Enung was desperate and starving. Outside, she saw a stranger near the bushes. Neither of her masters was anywhere in sight. So she ran out, wearing only the ragged clothes that had been given her. Having been brought from a continent halfway across the world, she knew only a few words of English. As she ran up, the man caught sight of her, astonished at how emaciated she seemed. Then she said the word that had been on her mind:

"Doughnut." And repeated it: "Doughnut."

The man, a landscape gardener, went to his truck and gave her the half-dozen doughnuts he happened to have in the cab.

This is not an account like the fictional baseball game narrated by Captain John Smith. The event actually occurred in a pleasant suburb on Long Island, New York. Enung was Indonesian, brought to the United States by two naturalized Indian citizens, who were tried in 2007 for hiring her and another woman under conditions of virtual slavery. The two "servants" were forced to sleep in closets, beaten with rolling pins and brooms, given little to eat, and for five years never allowed out of the house except to take out the garbage.

Slavery was officially outlawed by the Slavery Convention of 1926, sponsored by the League of Nations. Yet human rights organizations estimate that today some 27 million people are enslaved, which is to say, forced to labor without pay under the threat of violence. The CIA estimates that anywhere from 14,500 to 16,000 people are brought to the United States annually under such conditions. The most common type of slavery, accounting for well over half of all slaves, is debt bondage. Sex slavery constitutes another widespread abuse; a third category is forced labor, in which the promise of good jobs and wages lures people into isolated areas, such as mining compounds, where they cannot escape the harsh work set before them. But pleasant suburbs can be isolated, too, as Enung discovered when she was brought to the United States.

What factors allow slavery to persist to such a great degree, even when it has been outlawed internationally? How do those factors compare with the forces encouraging the growth of slavery in the seventeenth century?

CHAPTER 3
The Visible and Invisible Worlds of Salem

What sparked the witchcraft hysteria of 1692? Historians studying the psychological and social contexts of this tragic incident have turned up unexpected answers.

If historians are in the business of reconstruction, it follows that they must make some of the same kinds of decisions as architects or builders. Before they begin their work, they must decide on the scale of their projects. How much ground should be covered? A year? Fifty years? Several centuries? How will the subject matter be defined or limited? The story of slavery's arrival in Virginia might be ranked as a moderately large topic. It spans some sixty years and involves thousands of immigrants and an entire colony. Furthermore, the topic is large because of its content and themes. The rise of slavery surely ranks as a central strand of the American experience. To grasp it well requires more breadth of vision than, for instance, understanding the history of American hats during the same period. The lure of topics both broad and significant is undeniable, and there have always been historians willing to pull on their seven-league boots.

The great equalizer of such grand plans is the twenty-four-hour day. Historians have only a limited amount of time, and the more years covered, the less time available to research the events in each year. Conversely, the narrower the area of research, the more the historian can become immersed in a period's details. A keen mind working on an apparently small topic may uncover relationships and connections whose significance goes beyond the subject matter's original boundaries.

Salem Village in 1692 is such a microcosm—one familiar to most students of American history. That was the place and the time witchcraft came to New England with a vengeance, dominating the life of the village for ten months. Because the witchcraft episode exhibited well-defined boundaries in both time and space, it shows well how an oft-told story may be transformed by the intensive research of small-scale history. Traditionally, the outbreak at Salem has been viewed as an incident separate from the events of everyday village life. Even to label the witchcraft episode as an "outbreak" suggests that it is best viewed as an epidemic, alien to the community's normal functions. The "germs" of bewitchment break out suddenly and inexplicably—agents, presumably, of some invading disease.

Over the past decades, however, historians have studied the traumatic experiences of 1692 in great detail. In so doing they have created a more sophisticated model of the mental world behind the Salem outbreak. They have also suggested ways in which the witchcraft episode was tied to the everyday events of village life. The techniques of small-scale history, in other words, have provided a compelling psychological and social context for the events of 1692.

BEWITCHMENT AT SALEM VILLAGE

The baffling troubles experienced in Salem Village began during the winter of 1691–1692 in the home of the village's minister, Samuel Parris. There, Parris's nine-year-old daughter Betty and his niece Abigail Williams had taken strangely ill, claiming that they had been "bitten and pinched by invisible agents; their arms, necks, and backs turned this way and that way, and returned back again . . . beyond the power of any Epileptick Fits, or natural Disease to effect." Later traditions—not necessarily reliable—suggested that the afflictions came after a group of girls met to divine what sort of men their future husbands might be, a subject of natural enough interest. Lacking a crystal ball, they used the next available substitute, the white of a raw egg suspended in a glass of water. At some point during these conjurings, things went sour. One of the girls thought she detected "a specter in the likeness of a coffin" in the glass—a threatening omen. Betty, the youngest of the girls, began complaining of pinching, prickling sensations, knifelike pains, and the feeling that she was being choked. In the weeks that followed, three more girls exhibited similar symptoms.

Whatever the cause of the young girls' symptoms, the Reverend Parris was baffled by them, as were several doctors and ministers he brought in to observe the strange behaviors. When one doctor hinted at the possibility of witchcraft, a neighbor, Mary Sibley, suggested putting to use a bit of New England folklore to reveal whether there had been any sorcery. Sibley persuaded two slaves living in the Parris household, John Indian and his wife, Tituba, to bake a "witch cake" made of rye meal and urine given them by the girls. The cake was fed to a dog—the theory of bewitchment confirmed, presumably, if the dog suffered torments similar to those of the afflicted girls.

This experiment seems to have frightened the girls even more, for their symptoms worsened. Thoroughly alarmed, adults pressed the girls for the identity of the specters they believed were tormenting them. When the girls named three women, a formal complaint was issued, and on February 29 the suspects were arrested. That was the obvious action to take, for seventeenth-century New Englanders conceived of witchcraft as a crime. If the girls were being tormented, it was necessary to punish those responsible.

Two of the women arrested, Sarah Good and Sarah Osbourne, were already unpopular in the village. The third accused was Parris's Indian slave, Tituba. Tituba may have been purchased by Parris during a visit to the Caribbean and was perhaps originally from South America, Florida, or the Georgia Sea Islands. When questioned by village magistrates, Sarah Good angrily denied the accusations, suggesting instead that Sarah Osbourne was guilty. Osbourne denied the charges, but the dynamics of the hearings changed abruptly when Tituba confessed to being a witch. One account of the trials, published eight years later, reported that her admission came after an angry Reverend Parris had beaten Tituba. For whatever reason, she testified that four women and a man were causing the afflictions of the young women. Good and Osbourne were among them. "They hurt the children," Tituba reported. "And they lay all upon me and they tell me if I will not hurt the children, they will hurt me." The tale continued, complete with apparitions of black and red rats, a yellow dog with a head like a woman, "a thing all over hairy, all the face hairy," and midnight rides to witches' meetings where plans were being laid to attack Salem.

During New England's first seventy years, few witchcraft cases had come before the courts. Those that had were dispatched quickly, and calm soon returned. Salem proved different. In the first place, Tituba had described several other witches and a wizard, though she said she was unable to identify them. The villagers felt they could not rest

During New England's first seventy years, the few witchcraft cases that surfaced were dispatched quickly. Salem proved different.

so long as these agents remained at large. Furthermore, the young women continued to name names—and now not just community outcasts, but a wide variety of villagers, some respectable church members. The new suspects joined Tituba, Sarah Good, and Sarah Osbourne in jail. By the end of April, the hunt even led to a former minister, George Burroughs, then living in Maine.

If the accused refused to admit guilt, the magistrates looked for corroborating proof. Physical evidence, such as voodoo dolls and pins found among the suspect's possessions, were considered incriminating. Furthermore, if the devil made a pact with someone, he supposedly required a physical mark of allegiance and thus created a "witch's tit" where either he or his familiar, a likeness in animal form, might suck. Prisoners in the Salem trials were often examined for any abnormal marks on their bodies.

Aside from physical signs, the magistrates considered evidence that a witch's ill will might have caused a victim to suffer. This kind of black magic—harm by occult means—was known as *maleficium*. Villager Sarah Gadge, for example, testified that she had once refused Sarah Good lodging for the night. According to Gadge, Good "fell to muttering and scolding extreamly and so told said Gadge if she would not let her in she should give her something . . . and the next morning after . . . one of the said Gadges Cowes Died in a Sudden terrible and Strange unusuall maner."

The magistrates also considered what they called "spectral evidence"—ghostly likenesses of the witches that victims reported seeing during their torments. In an attempt to confirm that these specters were really links to the accused witches, the magistrates kept the afflicted women in the court-room and observed them while the accused were being examined. "Why doe you hurt these children?" one of the magistrates asked Sarah Osbourne, in a typical examination. "I doe not hurt them," replied Osbourne. The record continues: "The children abovenamed being all personally present accused her face to face which being don, they ware all hurt, afflicted and tortured very much: which being over and thay out of theire fitts thay sayd that said Sarah Osburne did then Come to them and hurt them."

The problem with spectral evidence was that it could not be corroborated by others. Only the victim saw the shape of the tormentor. Such testimony was normally controversial, for theologians in Europe as well as in New England believed that spectral evidence should be treated with caution. After all, what better way for the devil to spread confusion than by assuming the shape of an innocent person? In Salem, however, the magistrates considered spectral testimony as paramount. When they handed down indictments, almost all the charges referred only to the spectral torments exhibited by accusers during the pretrial hearings.

On June 2 a court especially established to deal with the witchcraft out-break heard its first case, that of a woman named Bridget Bishop. Even before the Salem controversy, Bishop had been suspected of witchcraft by a number of villagers. She was quickly convicted and, eight days later, hanged from a scaffold on a nearby rise. The site came to be known as Witch's Hill—with good reason, since on June 29 the court again met and convicted five more women. One of them, Rebecca Nurse, had been found innocent, but the court's chief justice disapproved the verdict and con-vinced the jurors to change their minds. On July 19 Nurse joined the other four women on the scaffold, staunch churchwoman that she was, praying for the judges' souls as well as her own. Sarah Good remained defiant to the end. "I am no more a witch than you are a wizard," she told the attend-ing minister, "and if you take away my life, God will give you blood to drink."

Still the accusations continued; still the court sat. As the net was cast wider, more and more accused were forced to work out their response to the crisis. A few, most of them wealthy, went into hiding until the furor subsided. Giles Cory, a farmer whose wife, Martha, was executed as a witch, refused to submit to a trial by jury. The traditional penalty for such a refusal was the *peine fort et dure*, in which the victim was placed between two boards and had heavy stones placed on him until he agreed to plead innocent or guilty. Although that punishment had been outlawed in Massachusetts, the court nonetheless carried it out. Cory was slowly crushed to death, stubborn to the end. His last words were said to be, "More weight."

Some of the accused admitted guilt, the most satisfactory solution for the magistrates. Puritans could be a remarkably forgiving people. They were not interested in punishment for its own sake. If a lawbreaker gave evidence of sincere regret for his or her misdeeds, Puritan courts would often reduce or suspend the sentence. So it was in the witchcraft trials at Salem (unlike most trials in Europe, where confessing witches were executed). But the policy of forgiveness had unforeseen consequences. Those who were wrongly accused quickly realized that if they did not confess, they were likely to be hanged. If they did admit guilt, they could escape death but would have to demonstrate their sincerity by providing details of their misdeeds and names of other participants. The temptation must have been great to confess and, in so doing, to implicate other innocent people.

Given such pressures, the web of accusations continued to spread. August produced six more trials and five hangings. Elizabeth Proctor, the wife of a tavern keeper, received a reprieve because she was pregnant, the court being unwilling to sacrifice the life of an innocent child. Her husband, John, was not spared. September saw another eight victims hanged. More than a hundred suspected witches remained in jail.

Pressure to stop the trials had been building, however. One member of the court, Nathaniel Saltonstall, resigned in protest after the first execution. More important, the ministers of the province were becoming uneasy. In public they had supported the trials, but privately they wrote letters cautioning the magistrates. Finally, in early October, Increase Mather, one of the most respected preachers in the colony, published a sermon signed by fourteen other pastors that strongly condemned the use of spectral evidence. Mather argued that to convict on the basis of a specter, which everyone agreed was the devil's creation, in effect took Satan at his own word. That, in Mather's view, risked disaster. "It were better that ten suspected witches should escape, than that one innocent person should be condemned," he concluded.

Mather's sermon convinced the colony's governor, William Phips, that the trials had gone too far. He forbade any more arrests and dismissed the court. The following January a new court met to dispose of the remaining cases, but this time almost all the defendants were acquitted. Phips immediately granted a reprieve to the three women who were convicted and in April released the remaining prisoners. Satan's controversy with Salem was finished.

That, in outline, is the witchcraft story as it has come down to us for so many years. Rightly or wrongly, the story has become an indelible part of American history. The startling fits of possession, the drama of the court examinations, the eloquent pleas of the innocent condemned—all make for a superb drama that casts into shadow the rest of Salem's more pedestrian history.

Indeed, the episode is unrepresentative. Witchcraft epidemics were not a serious problem in New England and were even less of a problem in other American colonies. Such persecutions were much more common in Europe, where they reached frightening proportions. The death of 20 people at Salem is sobering, but the magnitude of the event diminishes considerably alongside the estimate of 40,000 to 60,000 people executed for witchcraft in early modern Europe.

Now, a curious thing has resulted from this illumination of a single, isolated episode. Again and again the story of Salem Village has been told, quite naturally, as a drama complete unto itself. The everyday history that preceded and followed the trials—the petty town bickerings, arguments over land and ministers—was for many years largely passed over. Yet the disturbances at Salem did not occur in a vacuum. They may indeed have constituted an epidemic, but not the sort caused by some germ pool brought into the village over the rutted roads from Boston. So the historian's first task is to take the major strands of the witchcraft affair and see how they are woven into the larger fabric of New England society. Salem Village was small enough that virtually every one of its residents can be identified. We can find out who owned what land, the amount of taxes each resident paid, what sermons people listened to on Sundays. In so doing, a richer, far more intriguing picture of New England life begins to emerge.

THE INVISIBLE SALEM

Paradoxically, the most obvious facet of Salem life that the historian must recreate is also the most insubstantial: what ministers of the period would have called the "invisible world." Demons, familiars, witchcraft, and magic all shaped seventeenth-century New England. For most Salem Villagers, Satan was a living, supernatural being who might appear to people, bargain with them, even enter into agreements. The men and women who submitted to such devilish compacts were said to exchange their souls in return for special powers or favors: money and good fortune, perhaps, or the ability to revenge themselves on others.

Most often, ordinary folk viewed witchcraft as a simple matter of *maleficium*: Sarah Gadge, for example, believing that Sarah Good caused one of her cows to die after a hostile encounter. The process by which such suspicions grew was described well in 1587 by George Gifford, an English minister who was himself quite skeptical of witchcraft:

> Some woman doth fall out bitterly with her neighbour: there followeth some great hurt . . . There is a suspicion conceived. Within few years after, [the same woman] is in some jar [argument] with another. He is also plagued. This is noted of all. Great fame is spread of the matter. Mother W is a witch. She had bewitched Goodman B. Two hogs died strangely: or else he is taken lame.
>
> Well, Mother W doth begin to be very odious and terrible unto many. Her neighbours dare say nothing but yet in their hearts they wish she were hanged. Shortly after, another [person] falleth sick and doth pine; he can have no stomach unto his meat, nor he cannot sleep. The neighbours come to visit

him. "Well neighbour," sayeth one, "do ye not suspect some naughty dealing: did ye never anger Mother W?" "Truly neighbour (sayeth he) I have not liked the woman a long time."

Such suspicions of witchcraft were widespread in the early modern world. Indeed, the belief in *maleficium* was only one part of a worldview filled with magic and wonders—magic that could be manipulated by some-one with the proper knowledge. Fortune-tellers provided a win-dow into the future; objects like horseshoes brought good luck; earthquakes and comets warned of God's judgments. People who possessed more than the usual store of supernatural knowledge were known as "cunning folk" who might be called upon in times of trouble to heal the illness of a sick villager, cast horoscopes for a merchant worried about a ship's upcoming voyage, or discover what sort of children a woman might bear.

> *The belief in witchcraft was only one part of a worldview filled with magic and wonders—magic that could be manipulated by someone with the proper knowledge.*

The outlines of such beliefs are easily enough sketched, but it can be dif-ficult to imagine how a Salem Villager who believed in such wonders might have behaved. People who hold beliefs foreign to our own do not always act the way that we think they should. Over the years, historians of the witchcraft controversy have faced the challenge of re-creating Salem's mental world.

One of the first people to review Salem's troubles was Thomas Hutchin-son, who in 1750 published a history of New England's early days. Hutchin-son did not believe in witchcraft; fewer and fewer educated people did as the eighteenth century progressed. Therefore he faced an obvious question, which centered on the motivations of the accusers. If the devil never actually covenanted with anyone, how were the accusers' actions to be explained? Some of Hutchinson's contemporaries argued that the bewitched were suf-fering from "bodily disorders which affected their imaginations." He dis-agreed: "A little attention must force conviction that the whole was a scene of fraud and imposture, begun by young girls, who at first perhaps thought of nothing more than being pitied and indulged, and continued by adult per-sons who were afraid of being accused themselves." Charles Upham, a min-ister who published a two-volume study of the episode in 1867, was equally hard on the young women. "There has seldom been better acting in a the-atre than displayed in the presence of the astonished and horror-stricken rulers," he concluded tartly.

Indeed, the historical record does supply some evidence that the possessed may have been shamming. When Elizabeth Proctor was accused of being a witch, a friend of hers testified that he had seen one of the afflicted women cry out, "There's Goody Procter!"* But when people in the room challenged

---

* *Goody* was short for *Goodwife*, a term used for most married women. Husbands were addressed as *Goodman*. The terms *Mr.* and *Mrs.* were reserved for those of higher social standing.

the woman's claim as evidently false, she backed off, saying only that "she did it for sport; they must have some sport."

Another of the tormented young women, Mary Warren, stopped having fits and began to claim "that the afflicted persons did but dissemble"—that is, that they were only pretending. But then the other accusers began to declare that Mary's specter was afflicting them. Placed on the witness stand, Mary again fell into a fit "that she did neither see nor hear nor speak." The examination record continued:

> Afterwards she started up, and said I will speak and cryed out, Oh! I am sorry for it, I am sorry for it, and wringed her hands, and fell a little while into a fit again and then came to speak, but immediately her teeth were set, and then she fell into a violent fit and cryed out, oh Lord help me! Oh Good Lord Save me!
>
> And then afterward cryed again, I will tell I will tell and then fell into a dead fit againe.
>
> And afterwards cryed I will tell, they did, they did they did and then fell into a violent fit again.
>
> After a little recovery she cryed I will tell they brought me to it and then fell into a fit again which fits continueing she was ordered to be had out.

The scene is tantalizing. It appears as if Mary Warren is about to confess when pressure from the other girls forces her back to her former role as one of the afflicted. In the following weeks, the magistrates questioned Mary repeatedly, with the result that her fits returned and she again joined in the accusations. Such evidence suggests that the girls may well have been acting.

Yet such a theory leaves certain points unexplained. If the girls were only acting, what are we to make of the many other witnesses who testified to deviltry? One villager, Richard Comans, reported seeing Bridget Bishop's specter in his bedroom. Bishop lay upon his breast, he reported, and "so oppressed" him that "he could not speak nor stur, noe not so much as to awake his wife" sleeping next to him. Comans and others who testified were not close friends of the girls; there appears no reason why they might be conspiring with each other. How does the historian explain their actions?

Were some of the "afflicted" girls merely willful adolescents having fun at the expense of their elders?

Even some of the afflicted women's behavior is difficult to explain as conscious fraud. It is easy enough to imagine faking certain fits: whirling through the room crying "whish, whish"; being struck dumb. Yet other behavior was truly sobering: being pinched, pummeled, nearly choked to death; contortions so violent several grown men were required to restrain the victims. Even innocent victims of the accusations were astounded by such behavior. Rebecca Nurse on the witness stand could only look in astonishment at the "lamentable fits" she was accused of causing. "Do you think these [afflicted] suffer voluntary or involuntary?" asked one examiner. "I cannot tell what to think of it," replied Nurse hesitantly. The prosecutor pressed others with similar results. What ails the girls, if not your torments? "I do not know." Do you think they are bewitched? "I cannot tell." What do you think does ail them? "There is more than ordinary."

"More than ordinary"—historians may accept that possibility without necessarily supposing the presence of the supernatural. Psychiatric research has long established what we now take almost for granted: that people may act for reasons they themselves do not fully understand; even more, that emotional problems may be the unconscious cause of apparently physical disorders. The rationalistic psychologies of Thomas

Conversion hysteria suggests that emotional problems may be the unconscious cause of apparently physical disorders.

Hutchinson and Charles Upham led them to reject any middle ground. Either the Salem women had been tormented by witches, or they were faking their fits. But given a fervent belief in devils and witches, the Salem episode can be understood not as a game of fraud gone out of control, but as a study in abnormal psychology on a community-wide scale.

Scholars of the twentieth century have been more inclined to adopt this medical model. Indeed, one of the first to make the suggestion was a pediatrician, Ernest Caulfield. The accused "were not impostors or pests or frauds," he wrote in 1943; "they were not cold-blooded malignant brats. They were sick children in the worst sort of mental distress—living in fear for their very lives and the welfare of their immortal souls." Certainly, the fear that gripped susceptible subjects must have been extraordinary. They imagined themselves pursued by agents of the devil, intent on torment or even murder, and locked doors provided no protection. Anthropologists who have examined witchcraft in other cultures note that bewitchment can be traumatic enough to lead to death. An Australian aborigine who discovers himself bewitched will

> stand aghast. . . . His cheeks blanch and his eyes become glassy. . . . He attempts to shriek but usually the sound chokes in his throat, and all that one might see is froth at his mouth. His body begins to tremble and the muscles twist involuntarily. He sways backwards and falls to the ground, and after a short time appears to be in a swoon; but soon after he writhes as if in mortal agony.

Afterward such victims often refuse to eat, lose all interest in life, and die. Although there is no record of bewitchment death in Salem, the anthropological studies indicate the remarkable depth of reaction possible in a community that believes in its own magic.*

Historian Chadwick Hansen compared the behavior of the bewitched with the neurotic syndrome that psychiatrists refer to as "conversion hysteria."

---

* A least one bewitchment death may have occurred, however. Daniel Wilkins believed that John Willard was a witch and meant him no good. Wilkins sickened, and some of the afflicted girls were summoned to his bedside, where they claimed that they saw Willard's specter afflicting him. The doctor would not touch the case, claiming it "preternatural." Shortly after, Wilkins died.

A neurosis is a disorder of behavior that functions to avoid or deflect intolerable anxiety. Normally, an anxious person deals with an emotion through conscious action or thought. If the ordinary means of coping fail, however, the unconscious takes over. Hysterical patients convert their mental worries into physical symptoms such as blindness, paralysis of various parts of the body, choking, fainting, or attacks of pain. These symptoms, it should be stressed, cannot be traced to organic causes. There is nothing wrong with the nervous system during an attack of paralysis, or with the optic nerve in a case of blindness. Physical disabilities are mentally induced. Such hysterical attacks often occur in patterns that bear striking resemblance to some of the Salem afflictions.

Pierre Janet, the French physician who wrote the classic *Major Symptoms of Hysteria* (1907), reported that a characteristic hysterical fit begins with a pain or strange sensation in some part of the body, often the lower abdomen. From there, it

> seems to ascend and to spread to other organs. For instance, it often spreads to the epigastrium [the region lying over the stomach], to the breasts, then to the throat. There it assumes rather an interesting form, which was for a very long time considered as quite characteristic of hysteria. The patient has the sensation of too big an object as it were, a ball rising in her throat and choking her.

Most of us have probably experienced a mild form of the last symptom— a proverbial "lump in the throat" that comes in times of stress. The hysteric's lump, or *globus hystericus,* is more extreme, as are the accompanying convulsions: "the head is agitated in one direction or another, the eyes closed, or open with an expression of terror, the mouth distorted."

Compare those symptoms with the fits of another tormented accuser, Elizabeth Brown:

> When [the witch's specter] did come it was as birds pecking her legs or pricking her with the motion of thayr wings and then it would rize up into her stamak with pricking pain as nayls and pins of which she did bitterly complayn and cry out like a women in travail and after that it would rise to her throat in a bunch like a pullets egg and then she would tern back her head and say witch you shant choak me.

The diagnosis of hysteria has gained ground over the past decades. Yet the issue of fraud cannot be put so easily to rest. Bernard Rosenthal, a scholar who has reexamined the Salem records, argues that fraud and hysteria were intermingled. What are we to make, for example, of testimony about the "torments" of one Susannah Sheldon?

> Susannah Sheldon being at the house of William Shaw she was tied her hands a cross in such a manner we were forced to cut the string before we could git her hand loose and when shee was out of her fit she told us it [was] Goody Dustin that did tye her hands after that manner, and 4 times shee hath been tyed in this manner in [two] weeks time[.] The 2 first times shee sayth it was Goody Dustin and the 2 last times it was Sarah Goode that did tye her.

A hysterical convulsive attack of one of the patients in Salpêtrière Hospital during the nineteenth century. J. M. Charcot, the physician in charge of the clinic, spent much of his time studying the disorder. Note the crossed legs, similar to some of the Salem girls' fits.

It is one matter to have "fits" through terror but another to have wrists tied four times by a specter. Unless we believe in invisible spirits, the only reasonable explanation would seem to be that Susannah Sheldon had a confederate who tied her hands. Similarly Deodat Lawson, a minister who devoutly believed in witchcraft, reported in March 1692 that

> some of the afflicted, as they were striving in their fits in open court, have (by invisible means) had their wrists bound fast together with a real cord, so as it could hardly be taken off without cutting. Some afflicted have been found with their arms tied, and hanged upon an hook, from whence others have been forced to take them down, that they might not expire in that posture.

The conclusion, argued Rosenthal, must be similar: "Whether the 'afflicted' worked these shows out among themselves or had help from others cannot be determined; but there is little doubt that such calculated action was deliberately conceived to perpetuate the fraud in which the afflicted were involved, and that theories of hysteria or hallucination cannot account for people being bound, whether on the courtroom floor or on hooks." Such evidence suggests a complex set of behaviors in which both hysteria and fraud played a part.

As for those who were accused of witchcraft, they were put under severe pressure by the court's decision to view confession as worthy of pardon while viewing denials of witchcraft as a sign of guilt. Indeed, the court magistrates appeared not to want to take no for an answer. John Proctor complained that when his son was examined, "because he would not confess that he was Guilty, when he was Innocent, they tyed him Neck and Heels till the Blood gushed out at his Nose, and would have kept him so 24 Hours, if one more Merciful than the rest, had not taken pity on him."

Sarah Churchill, a young woman of about seventeen, experienced similar pressures. She apparently succumbed to her fears and testified that she was a witch. Soon, however, she had second thoughts, for she came crying and wringing her hands to an older friend, Sarah Ingersoll. "I asked her what she ailed?" reported Ingersoll.

> She answered she had undone herself. I asked her in what. She said in belying herself and others in saying she had set her hand to the devil's Book whereas she said she never did. I told her I believed she had set her hand to the book. She answered crying and said no no no, I naver, I naver did. I asked then what had made her say she did. She answered because they threatened her and told her they would put her into the dungeon and put her along with Mr. Burroughs, and thus several times she followed [me] on up and down telling me that she had undone herself in belying herself and others. I asked her why she didn't tell the truth now. She told me because she had stood out so long in it that now she darst not. She said also that if she told Mr. Noyes [an investigating minister] but once that she had set her hand to the Book he would believe her, but if she told the truth and said she had not set her hand to the book a hundred times he would not believe her.

Thus psychological terrors sprang from more than one source. The frights of the invisible world, to be sure, led many villagers to fear for their lives and souls. But when the magistrates refused to accept the protests of innocence, they created equally terrifying pressures to lie in order to escape execution. As the witchcraft episodes spread to include hundreds of people in the community, it is not surprising that different individuals behaved in a wide variety of ways.

THE VISIBLE SALEM

It would be tempting, having explored the psychological dynamics of Salem, to suppose that the causes of the outbreak have been fairly well explained. There is the satisfaction of placing the symptoms of the modern hysteric side by side with those of the seventeenth-century bewitched and seeing them match, or of carefully reading the trial records to distinguish likely cases of fraud from those of hysteria. Yet by narrowing our inquiry to the motivations of the possessed, we have left other important facets of the Salem episode unexplored.

In the first place, the investigation thus far has dealt with the controversy on an individual rather than a social level. But step back for a moment. For whatever reasons, approximately 150 people in Salem and other towns found themselves accused. Why were those particular people singled out? Does any common *What if we view the witchcraft outbreak from within a social context rather than an individual one?* bond explain why they, and not others, were accused? Only after we have examined their social identities can we answer that question.

Another indication that the social context of Salem Village needs to be examined is the nature of hysteria itself. Hysterics are notably suggestible—that is, sensitive to the influence of their environment. Scattered testimony in the records suggests that sometimes when the young women saw specters whom they could not identify, adults suggested names. "Was it Goody Cloyse? Was it Rebecca Nurse?" If true, such conditions confirm the need to move beyond strictly personal motivations to the social setting of the community.

In doing so, a logical first step would be to look for correlations, or characteristics common to groups that might explain their behavior. Are the accusers all church members and the accused nonchurch members? Are the accusers wealthy and respectable and the accused poor and disreputable? The historian assembles the data, shuffles them around, and looks for matchups.

Take the two social characteristics just mentioned, church membership and wealth. Historians can compile lists from the trial records of both the accusers and the accused. With those lists in hand, they can begin checking the church records to discover which people on each list were church members. Or they can search tax records to see whose tax rates were highest and thus which villagers were wealthiest. Land transactions were recorded, indicating which villagers owned the most land. Inventories of personal property were made when a member of the community died, so at least historians have some record of an individual's assets at death, if not in 1692. Other records may mention a trade or occupation, which will give a clue to relative wealth or social status.

If you made such calculations for the Salem region, you would quickly find yourself at a dead end, a spot all too familiar to practicing historians. True, the first few accused witches were not church members, but soon enough the faithful found themselves in jail along with nonchurch members. A similar situation holds for wealth. Although Tituba, Sarah Good, and Sarah Osbourne were relatively poor, merchants and wealthy farmers were accused as the epidemic spread. The correlations fail to check.

This dead end was roughly the point that had been reached when two historians, Paul Boyer and Stephen Nissenbaum, were inspired to take literally the advice about going back to the drawing board. More than a hundred years earlier, Charles Upham had made a detailed map of Salem for his own study of the witchcraft episode. Upham examined the old town records, paced the actual sites of old houses, and established to the best of his knowledge the residences of a large majority of Salem Villagers. Boyer and Nissenbaum took their list of accusers and accused and noted the location of each village resident. The results were striking, as can be seen from the map on page 66.

Of the fourteen accused witches in the village, twelve lived in the eastern section. Of the thirty-two adult villagers who testified against the accused, thirty lived in the western section. "In other words," concluded Boyer and Nissenbaum, "the alleged witches and those who accused them resided on opposite sides of the Village." Furthermore, of twenty-nine residents who publicly defended the accused in some way, twenty-four lived in the eastern half of the village. Often they were close neighbors of the accused. It is moments like these that make the historian want to behave, were it not for the staid air of research libraries, like Archimedes leaping from his fabled bathtub and shouting "Eureka!"

The discovery is only the beginning of the task. The geographic chart suggests a division, but it does not indicate what that division is, other than a general east-west split. So Boyer and Nissenbaum began to explore the history of the village itself, expanding their microcosm of 1692 backward in time. They investigated a social situation that historians had long recognized but never associated with the Salem witch trials: Salem Village's uneasy relation to its social parent, Salem Town.

Salem Town's settlement followed the pattern of most coastal New England towns. Original settlers set up houses around a central location and carved their farmlands out of the surrounding countryside. As a settlement prospered, the land in its immediate vicinity came to be completely taken up. As houses were erected farther and farther away from the central meeting house, outlying residents found it inconvenient to come to church or attend to other civic duties. In such cases, they sought recognition as a separate village, with their own church, their own taxes, and their own elected officials.

Here the trouble started. The settlers who lived toward the center of town were reluctant to let their outlying neighbors break away. Everyone paid taxes to support a minister for the town church, to maintain the roads, and to care for the poor. If a chunk of the village split off, revenue would be lost. Furthermore, outlying settlers would no longer share the common burdens, such as guarding the town at night. So the centrally located settlers usually resisted any movement by their more distant neighbors to split off. Such disputes were a regular feature of New England life.

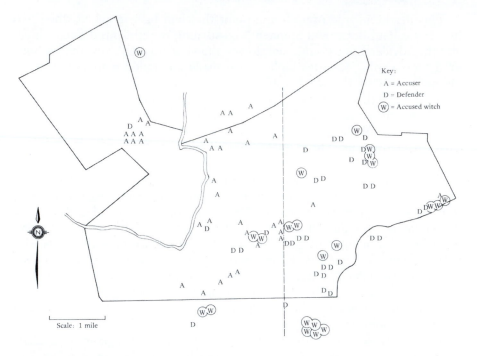

"The Geography of Witchcraft" (after Boyer and Nissenbaum, *Salem Possessed*, Harvard University Press, 1974)

Salem Town had followed this pattern. Its first settlers located on a pen-insula extending into Massachusetts Bay, where they pursued a prosperous colonial trade. By 1668 four outlying areas had already become separate towns. Now the "Salem Farmers," living directly to the west, were petition-ing for a similar settlement, and the "Townsmen" were resisting. In 1672 Massachusetts's legislature allowed Salem Village to build its own meeting house, but in other matters, the village remained dependent. Salem Town still collected village taxes, chose village constables, and arranged for village roads. The colony's records include petition after petition from villagers complaining about tax rates, patrol duties, boundary rulings.

Here, then, is one east-west split—between the village and the town. But the line drawn on Boyer and Nissenbaum's map is within the village. What cause would the village have for division?

Many causes, the records indicate—chief among them the choice of a minister. When the village built its own meeting house, it chose James Bayley to be its pastor in 1673. Soon enough, however, some churchgo-ers began complaining. Bayley didn't attend regularly to his private prayers. Church members had not been fully consulted before his selection. After a flurry of petitions and counterpetitions, Bayley left in 1680, and George Burroughs was hired. Three years later, Burroughs left in another dispute. He was succeeded by Deodat Lawson, who lasted through four more years

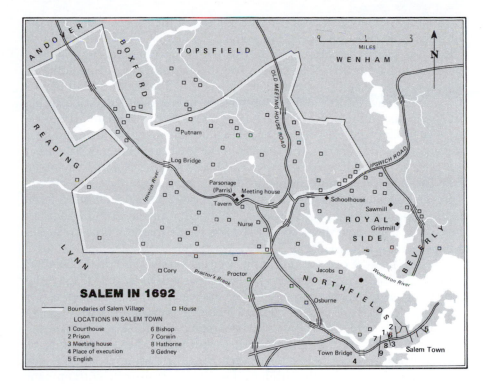

"Salem in 1692" (From *The Pursuit of Liberty: A History of the American People*, vol. 1, by R. Jackson Wilson, et al. Copyright 1966 by HarperCollins College Publishers. Reprinted by permission of Addison-Wesley Educational Publishers Inc.)

of quarrels. Finally, Samuel Parris occupied the pulpit after 1688. His term was equally stormy, and in 1696 his opponents finally succeeded in starving him out of the job by refusing to collect taxes to pay his salary.

The maneuverings that went on during the years of bickering seem bewilderingly complex. But Boyer and Nissenbaum recognized that the church records, as well as the petitions and counterpetitions, provided a key to local divisions. When the lists from the different quarrels were compared, Boyer and Nissenbaum found that the same names were being grouped together. The people who supported James Bayley usually supported George Burroughs and then opposed the second two ministers. Conversely, the supporters of Deodat Lawson and Samuel Parris had been the people who complained about Bayley and Burroughs. And—here is the link—the two lists from those disputes coincide closely with the divisions in 1692 between accusers and accused.

Suddenly the Salem witch trials take on an entirely new appearance. Instead of being a dramatic disruption that appears out of nowhere in a village kitchen and then disappears equally suddenly at the end of ten months, it becomes an elaboration of a quarrel that has gone on for nearly twenty years!

What lay behind the divisions? One reading of the evidence suggests that the larger split between Salem Town and Salem Village was reflected in the village itself, with the villagers on the east retaining enough in common with the town to continue their affiliation and the westerners favoring complete separation. Boyer and Nissenbaum argue that the division also went beyond the simple geographical one to a difference in lifestyle. Salem Town was becoming one of the major commercial centers of New England. It boasted a growing merchant class whose wealth would soon support the building of fine mansions. By contrast, the farmers in the western portion of Salem Village were more traditional: they practiced subsistence farming, led spartan daily lives, and were more suspicious of the commercial habits of offering credit and making speculative investments. Worse, the Salem farmers found themselves increasingly hard-pressed. The land available in the village was dwindling. What land there was proved less fertile than the broad plains on the eastern side of the village.

Look, too, at the occupations of the accused witches and their defenders. Many lived along the Ipswich Road, a route that passed by the village rather than through it, a main thoroughfare for travelers and for commerce. The tradespeople who had set up shop there included a carpenter, sawmill operator, shoemaker, and miller. And of course there were the taverns, mainstays of travelers, yet always slightly suspect to Puritans. The people along the Ipswich Road were not rich, most of them, but their commercial links were with Salem Town and with outsiders. They were small-scale entrepreneurs rather than farmers. Out of twenty-one villagers who lived along or near the road, only two signed petitions linking them with the western faction; thirteen signed petitions linking them with the eastern faction. Tavern keeper John Proctor was hanged as a witch; his wife Elizabeth barely escaped with her life.

Boyer and Nissenbaum's reconstruction of village factions thus suggests an alternate way of looking at the Salem trials. Traditional accounts place Samuel Parris and his supporters as leaders of the village, terrorizing innocent villagers and controlling the trials. Certainly Parris's supporters had their day in 1692, but from the longer perspective they appear to have been fighting a losing battle. If Boyer and Nissenbaum are correct, the Salem trials were an indirect yet anguished protest of a group of villagers whose agrarian way of life was being threatened by the rising commercialism of Salem Town.

The brilliance of Boyer and Nissenbaum's research lay in placing the individual dramas of Salem into a larger social context. But their maps are not the only maps that can be drawn, nor their connections the only connections to be made. Boyer and Nissenbaum focused their attention on Salem Village. But as the witchcraft trials gained momentum, the fever spread to a few neighboring villages. In the summer of 1692, several of the possessed women of Salem were invited to Andover by concerned residents. The resulting round of accusations led to the arrest of nearly forty Andover villagers. A month later, a smaller outbreak centered in the fishing port of

Gloucester, where six people were arrested. Several more of the accused from Salem had Gloucester ties. All these people were tried by the same court that dealt with the Salem cases.

Taking these additional episodes into account makes it more difficult to generalize about embattled farmers arrayed against a rising commercialism. Gloucester was a fishing port, while Andover, though it was just as agrarian as Salem Village, had no commercial "parent" the likes of Salem Town. But if rising commercialism was not the only, or primary, social factor influencing the Salem outbreak, what then?

Several historians, most recently Mary Beth Norton, have explored the connections between the trials and New England's Indian wars. Memories of King Philip's War of 1676 lingered in the region for many years, leaving inhabitants anxious and uneasy, especially along the frontier. Then came a new outbreak of violence in 1689, which the settlers referred to as "the second Indian war." In January 1692, just as the witchcraft controversy was getting started, word came from York, Maine,

A new outbreak of Indian-white violence on the Maine frontier left its mark on many of the women afflicted by witch torments.

that Indians had massacred residents there. Indeed, a number of the accusers at the Salem trials experienced firsthand the horrors of the conflict. Mercy Lewis—one of the principal accusers—only two years earlier had seen her mother, father, sister, and brother murdered in an Indian attack.

Analyzing the chronology of the trials, Norton pointed out that the number of witchcraft accusations rose sharply only in April 1692. It was at this point that Abigail Hobbs was brought before the magistrates because of her reputation for being flippant about the spreading crisis. (She was "not afraid of anything," she is said to have boasted, because she had "Sold her selfe boddy & Soull to the old boy"—that is, to Satan.) During the late 1680s, Hobbs had lived for some time along the Maine frontier. Under hostile questioning from the magistrates, she admitted that she had covenanted there with the devil—while "at Casko-bay." Having thus confessed, she quickly turned into an enthusiastic prosecution witness. Before her confession on April 17, only ten people had been charged with witchcraft. In the seven weeks that followed, the total jumped to sixty-eight. The spectral visions of Abigail Hobbs and Mercy Lewis led to the indictment of a number of folk from Maine, chief among them the Reverend George Burroughs, who seemed the ringleader of the devilish conspiracy, in the eyes of many. The anxieties spawned by the frontier attacks, argued Norton, were what pushed the Salem hysteria beyond the bounds of the usual witchcraft trials of seventeenth-century New England.

In addition to the fear of Indian "devils," did the accusers perhaps fear religious demons? For years the colony's ruling Congregationalists had worried about the heresies spread by Quakers, members of the Society of Friends. In the 1650s and 1660s, Massachusetts Bay hanged four Quaker missionaries on the Boston Common. Other members of this Protestant sect had been whipped, thrown into prison, or driven from the colony. The Quaker belief that every person possessed his or her own divine inner light seemed to Congregationalists to suggest the heretical notion that God could speak directly to individuals. Even more disquieting, Friends caught up in their enthusiasm would "quake" when the holy spirit possessed them, behavior that seemed all too much like the fits of the Salem afflicted. "Diabolical Possession was the thing which did dispose and encline men unto Quakerism," warned Boston minister Cotton Mather, the son of Increase, in 1689.

By 1692, Congregationalists no longer had the power to persecute Quakers, for Massachusetts' new charter guaranteed toleration to all Protestants. Yet many ordinary folk remained suspicious, and within Essex County, the largest concentration of Quakers lived in Salem and Gloucester. In Andover too, Quaker connections seemed to figure in the arrests. Rebecca Nurse, who was pious and well respected in other ways, had taken an orphaned Quaker boy into her family. John and Elizabeth Proctor, the tavern keepers, counted a large number of Quakers among Elizabeth's family.

"WOMEN ALONE"

While Boyer, Nissenbaum, and other historians pursued correlations based on the social geography of witchcraft, another striking connection can be made. That connection is the link between witchcraft and gender.

Out of the 178 accused Salem witches who can be identified by name, more than 3 out of 4 were female. And nearly half of the accused men were husbands, sons, or other relatives of accused women. The gender gap widens further when witchcraft outside Salem is examined. Of 147 additional accused witches in seventeenth-century New England, 82 percent were women. In the cases that actually came to trial, 34 involved women and only 7 involved men. Of the women tried, 53 percent were convicted. Of the men, only 2 were convicted, or 29 percent. And of those people who were not only convicted but executed, women outnumbered men 15 to 2.

When historian Carol Karlsen examined the trial records, she found that the authorities tended to treat accused women differently from men. Magistrates and ministers often put pressure on women to confess their guilt. In New England cases (excluding Salem), when that pressure led a woman to confess a "familiarity with Satan," she was invariably executed, in accordance with the biblical command, "Thou shalt not suffer a witch to live." But when men were accused, pressure was seldom applied to make them confess. In fact, confessions from men were not always accepted. In 1652 one John Broadstreet of Rowley admitted having familiarity with Satan. The court ordered him whipped and fined twenty shillings "for telling a lie." In 1674 Christopher Brown confessed to "discoursing with . . . the devil," but the court rejected his statement as being "inconsistent with truth."

Such evidence suggests that, by and large, most seventeenth-century New Englanders expected women to be witches, whereas men who confessed were seldom believed. But why should women be singled out for such attention?

Why was it that more women than men were accused of witchcraft?

Part of the answer, Karlsen argues, lay in the cultural position of women. Like Martin Luther and other Reformation theologians, the Puritans exalted the role of motherhood over the chaste life of the convent; they saw women as partners and helpmates in marriage. Even so, Puritans retained a distinctly hierarchical conception of marriage. They viewed families as miniature commonwealths, with the husband as the ruler and his family as willing subjects. "A true wife accounts her subjection [as] her honor and freedom," noted Governor John Winthrop of Massachusetts.

A wife's unequal status was reflected legally as well: she was known in law as a *feme covert*—one whose identity was "covered" by that of her husband. As such, she had no right to buy or sell property, to sue or be sued, or to make contracts. Similarly, the patterns of inheritance in New England were male dominated. A husband might leave his widow property—indeed, the law required him to leave her at least a third of his estate. But she was to "have and enjoy" that property only "during [the] term of her natural life." She could not waste or squander it, for it was passed on to the family's heirs at her death. Similarly, daughters might inherit property, but if they were already married, it belonged to the husband. If a young woman had not yet married, property usually seems to have been held for her, "for improvement," until she married.

Thus the only sort of woman who held any substantial economic power was a widow who had not remarried. Such a woman was known as a *feme sole*, or "woman alone." She did have the right to sue, to make contracts, and to buy or sell property. Even when remarrying, a widow could sometimes protect her holdings by having her new husband sign a prenuptial contract, guaranteeing before marriage that the wife would keep certain property as her own. In male-dominated New England, these protections made the *feme sole* stand out as someone who did not fit comfortably into the ordinary scheme of things.

So, women in Puritan society were generally placed in subordinate roles. At the same time, a significant number of accused witches were women who were *not* subordinate in some way. In refusing to conform to accepted stereotypes, they threatened the traditional order of society and were more likely to be accused of subverting it as witches.

A woman might stand out, for example, through a contentious, argumentative nature. If a woman's duty was to submit quietly to the rule of men and to glory in "subjection," then quite a few witches refused to conform to the accepted role. We have already seen how Sarah Good's "muttering and scolding extreamly" were perceived by Salem Villagers to have caused the death of cattle. Trial records are filled with similar accusations.

Older women—especially those who were reputed to have medical knowledge of herbs and potions—often came under suspicion of witchcraft both in England and in America. This English drawing of 1622 portrays the stereotypical willful older woman, a supposed witch by the name of Jenner Dibble. She was said to have been attended for forty years by a spirit in the shape of a great black cat called Gibb.

Often, more than short tempers were at stake. A remarkably high percentage of accused women were *femes sole* in an economic sense. Of the 124 witches whose inheritance patterns can be reconstructed from surviving records, as many as 71 (57 percent) lived or had lived in families with no male heirs. Another 14 accused witches were the daughters or granddaughters of witches who did not have brothers or sons to inherit their property. This figure is at least twice the number that would be expected, given the usual percentage of *femes sole* in the New England population. Furthermore, of the women executed at Salem, more than half had inherited or stood to inherit their own property. Such statistics suggest why witchcraft controversies so often centered on women.

TANGLED WEBS

The early modern world, including that of colonial New England, was uncertain, unpredictable, full of chance. Amidst so many unpredictable tragedies, witchcraft offered an explanation for misfortunes that otherwise might have seemed inexplicable.

Unlike diviners or witch doctors, historians have followed the example of the natural sciences in seeking testable, rational links between cause and effect. Yet the longing for a simple, coherent story remains strong. We all wish to see the confusing welter of events lock together with a clarity that leads us, like Archimedes, to cry Eureka—conversion hysteria! Or Eureka—the pressures of the new commercial economy! Or Eureka—*femes sole*!

Instead, the discipline of small-scale, local history forces humility. As historians sift the web of relationships surrounding the Salem outbreak, most have come to believe that its causes are multiple rather than singular. "Irreducible to any single source of social strain," concludes Christine Heyrman, the scholar who traced out the Quaker connections to witchcraft. No single "governing explanation," argues Bernard Rosenthal. The very fact that the witchcraft outbreak did not recur elsewhere in New England suggests that the magnitude of Salem's calamity depended on an unusual combination of psychological and social factors.

Certainly, an agrarian faction in the village did not consciously devise the trials to punish their commercial rivals or Quaker-loving neighbors. Nor was the male Puritan patriarchy launching a deliberate war against women. But the invisible world of witchcraft did provide a framework that amplified village anxieties and focused them. As the accusations of a small circle of young women widened and as controversy engulfed the town, it was only natural that long-standing quarrels and prejudices were drawn into the debate. The interconnections between a people's religious beliefs, their habits of commerce, even their dream and fantasy lives, are intricate and fine, entwined with one another like the delicate root system of a growing plant. Historians who limit their examination to a small area of time and space are able, through persistent probing, to untangle the strands of emotions, motivations, and social structures that provided the context for those slow processions to the gallows on Witch's Hill.

Additional Reading

David Hall's *Worlds of Wonder, Days of Judgment* (New York, 1988) provides an excellent introduction to the way witchcraft fits into the larger belief systems of popular religion and magic. Chadwick Hansen's *Witchcraft at Salem* (New York, 1969) presents the most detailed case for conversion hysteria among the accusers. But Bernard Rosenthal, in *Salem Story: Reading the Witch Trials of 1692* (New York, 1993), argues convincingly that conscious deception played some role, especially among the core accusers. Paul Boyer and Stephen Nissenbaum apply the techniques of social history with lucidity and grace in *Salem Possessed: The Social Origins of Witchcraft* (Cambridge, MA, 1974). Other historians, however, have been skeptical about leaning too hard on rising commercialism as the outbreak's chief catalyst. For the contribution of anxiety over war and Indian raids, see the authoritative study by Mary Beth Norton, *In the Devil's Snare: The Salem Witchcraft Crisis of 1692* (New York, 2002). Because of all the attention given the Salem trials, it is important to remember that most colonists' attitudes toward witchcraft were more ambiguous. For an instructive comparison, see Richard Godbeer's study of a contemporaneous trial (this one in Fairfield, Connecticut), *Escaping Salem: The Other Witch Hunt of 1692* (New York, 2004).

CHAPTER 4
Declaring Independence

Do actions speak louder than words? When analyzing a document like the Declaration of Independence, historians sometimes heed the old proverb, "Watch what I do, not what I say."

Good historians share with magicians a talent for elegant sleight of hand. In both professions, the manner of execution conceals much of the work that makes the performance possible. Like the magician's trapdoors, mirrors, and other hidden props, historians' primary sources are essential to their task. But the better that historians are at their craft, the more likely they will focus their readers' attention on the historical scene itself and not on the supporting documents.

Contrary to prevailing etiquette, we have gone out of our way to call attention to the problems of evidence to be solved before a historical narrative is presented in its polished form. As yet, however, we have not examined in detail the many operations to be performed on a single document. What at first seems a relatively simple job of collecting, examining, and cataloging can become remarkably complex.

So let us narrow our focus even more than in the previous two chapters by concentrating not on a region (Virginia) or a village (Salem), but on one document. The document in question is more important than most, yet brief enough to be read in several minutes: the Declaration of Independence.

The Declaration, of course, is one of the most celebrated documents in the nation's history. Drafted by Thomas Jefferson, adopted by the Second Continental Congress, published for the benefit of the world, hailed in countless patriotic speeches, it is today displayed within the rotunda of the National Archives, encased in a glass container filled with helium to prevent any long-term deterioration from oxygen. Every schoolchild knows that Congress declared the colonies' independence by issuing the document on July 4, 1776. Nearly everyone has seen the painting by John Trumbull that depicts members of Congress receiving the parchment for signing on that day.

So the starting place is familiar enough. Yet there is a good deal to establish even when unpacking the basic facts. Under what circumstances did Jefferson write the Declaration? What people, events, or other documents

The Committee of Five—Adams, Sherman, Livingston, Jefferson, and Franklin—
present their work to John Hancock, president of the Continental Congress, in
a detail from *The Declaration of Independence* by John Trumbull. When Hancock
finally put his elaborate signature to the engrossed copy, he is reported to have said,
"There! John Bull can read my name without spectacles, and may now double his
reward of £500 for my head."

influenced him? Only when such questions are answered in more detail does
it become clear that quite a few of the "facts" enumerated in the previous
paragraph are either misleading or incorrect. And the confusion begins in
trying to answer the most elementary questions about the Declaration.

THE CREATION OF A TEXT

In May 1776 Thomas Jefferson traveled to Philadelphia, as befit a proper
gentleman, in a coach-and-four with two attending slaves. He promptly took
his place on the Virginia delegation to the Second Continental Congress.
Even a year after fighting had broken out at Lexington and Concord, Congress was still debating whether the quarrel with England could be patched
up. Sentiment for independence ran high in many areas but by no means
everywhere. The greatest reluctance lay in the middle colonies, particularly in Pennsylvania, where moderates like John Dickinson still hoped for
reconciliation.

Such cautious sentiments infuriated the more radical delegates, especially John and Samuel Adams of Massachusetts. The two Adamses had worked for independence from the opening days of Congress but found the going slow. America, complained John, was "a great, unwieldy body. It is like a large fleet sailing under convoy. The fleetest sailers must wait for the dullest and the slowest." Jefferson also favored independence, but he lacked the Adamses' taste for political infighting. While the men from Massachusetts pulled their strings in Congress, Jefferson only listened attentively and took notes. Thirty-three years old, he was the youngest delegate, and no doubt his age contributed to his diffidence. Privately, he conversed more easily with friends, sprawling casually in a chair with one shoulder cocked high, the other low, and his long legs extended. He got along well with the other delegates.

The debate over independence sputtered on fitfully until late May, when Jefferson's colleague Richard Henry Lee arrived from Williamsburg, determined to force Congress to act. On Friday, June 7, based on orders from Virginia, he rose in Congress and offered the following resolutions:

> That these United Colonies are, and of right ought to be, free and independent States, that they are absolved from all allegiance to the British crown, and that all political connection between them and the state of Great Britain is, and ought to be, totally dissolved.
>
> That it is expedient forthwith to take the most effectual measures for forming foreign alliances.
>
> That a plan of confederation be prepared and transmitted to the respective colonies for their consideration and approbation.

On Saturday and again on Monday, moderates and radicals debated the propositions. The secretary of the Congress, Charles Thomson, cautiously recorded in his minutes only that "certain resolutions" were "moved and discussed"—the certain resolutions, of course, being treasonous in the extreme.

Still, sentiment was running with the radicals. When delegate James Wilson of Pennsylvania announced that he felt ready to vote for independence, Congress set the wheels in motion by appointing a five-member committee "to prepare a Declaration to the effect of the said first resolution." The events that followed can be traced, in bare outline at least, in a modern edition of Secretary Thomson's minutes (*Journals of the Continental Congress: 1774–1789*). From it we learn that on June 11, 1776, Congress constituted Jefferson, John Adams, Benjamin Franklin, Roger Sherman, and Robert Livingston as a "Committee of Five" responsible for drafting the declaration. Then for more than two weeks, Thomson's journal remains silent on the subject. Only on Friday, June 28, does it note that the committee "brought in a draught" of an independence declaration.

On Monday, July 1, Congress resolved itself into a "Committee of the Whole," in which it could freely debate the sensitive question without leaving any official record of debate or disagreement. (Thomson's minutes did not record the activities of committees.) On July 2 the Committee of the Whole went through the motions of "reporting back" to Congress (that is, to itself). The minutes note only that Richard Lee's resolution, then "being read" in formal session, "was agreed to."

Thus the official journal makes it clear that Congress voted for independence on July 2, not July 4, adopting Richard Henry Lee's original proposal of June 7. When John Adams wrote home on July 3 to his wife, Abigail, he enthusiastically predicted that July 2 would be remembered as "the most memorable Epoca in the History of America. I am apt to believe that it will be celebrated, by succeeding Generations, as the great anniversary Festival. . . . It ought to be solemnized with Pomp and Parade, with Shews, Games, Sports, Guns, Bells, Bonfires and Illuminations from one End of this Continent to the other from this Time forward forever more."

As it turned out, John Adams picked the wrong date for celebrating American independence.

As it turned out, Adams picked the wrong date for the fireworks. Although Congress had officially broken the tie with England, the declaration explaining the action had not yet been approved. On July 3 and 4 Congress again met as a Committee of the Whole. Only then was the formal declaration reported back, accepted, and sent to the printer. Thomson's journal notes, "The foregoing declaration was, by order of Congress, engrossed, and signed by the following members. . . ." Here is the enactment familiar to everyone: the "engrossed" parchment (one written in large, neat letters) beginning with its bold "In Congress, July 4, 1776," and concluding with the president of the Continental Congress's signature, so flourishing that we still speak of putting our John Hancock to paper. Below that, the signatures of fifty-five other delegates appear more modestly inscribed.

If mention of the Declaration in Thomson's minutes concluded with the entry on July 4, schoolchildren might emerge with their memories reasonably intact. But later entries of the journal suggest that in all likelihood, the Declaration was not signed on July 4 after all, but on August 2. To muddy the waters further, not all the signers were in Philadelphia even on August 2. Some could not have signed the document until October or November.

So the upshot of the historian's preliminary investigation is that (1) Congress declared independence on the second of July, not the fourth; (2) most members officially signed the engrossed parchment only on the second of August; and (3) all the signers of the Declaration never met together in the same room at once, despite the appearances in John Trumbull's painting. In the matter of establishing the basic facts surrounding a document, historians are all too ready to agree with John Adams's bewildered search of his recollections in old age: "What are we to think of history? When in less than 40 years, such diversities appear in the memories of living men who were witnesses."

Yet even with the basic facts in place, many important points remain to be answered about the Declaration's creation. Although Jefferson drafted it, what did the Committee of Five contribute? If the delegates made changes during the congressional debate on July 3 and 4, for what purpose? A historian will want to know which parts of the completed document were most controversial; surviving copies of earlier drafts could shed valuable light on these questions.

The search for accurate information about the Declaration's drafting began even while the protagonists were still living. Some forty years after the signing, both Jefferson and John Adams tried to set down the sequence of events. Adams recalled the affable and diplomatic Jefferson suggesting that Adams write the first draft. "I will not," replied Adams.

"You shall do it," persisted Jefferson.

"Oh no!"

"Why will you not do it? You ought to do it."

"I will not."

"Reasons enough." Adams ticked them off. "Reason 1st. You are a Virginian and a Virginian ought to be at the head of this business. Reason 2nd. I am obnoxious, suspected and unpopular; you are very much otherwise. Reason 3rd. You can write ten times better than I can."

"Well," said Jefferson, "if you are decided, I will do as well as I can."

Jefferson, for his part, did not remember this bit of diplomatic shuttlecock. In a letter to James Madison in 1823 he asserted that the Committee of 5 met . . . [and] they unanimously pressed on myself alone to undertake the draught. I consented; I drew it; but before I reported it to the committee I communicated it separately to Dr. Franklin and Mr. Adams requesting their corrections; . . . and you have seen the original paper now in my hands, with the corrections of Dr. Franklin and Mr. Adams interlined in their own handwriting. Their alterations were two or three only, and merely verbal [that is, changes of phrasing, not substance].

So far, so good. Jefferson's "original paper"—which he endorsed on the document itself as the "original Rough draught"—is preserved in the Library of Congress. Indeed, the draft is even rougher than Jefferson suggested. As historian Carl Becker pointed out,

> the inquiring student, coming to it for the first time, would be astonished, perhaps disappointed, if he expected to find in it nothing more than the "original paper . . . with the corrections of Dr. Franklin and Mr. Adams interlined in their own handwriting." He would find, for example, on the first page alone nineteen corrections, additions or erasures besides those in the handwriting of Adams and Franklin. It would probably seem to him at first sight a bewildering document, with many phrases crossed out, numerous interlineations, and whole paragraphs enclosed in brackets.

These corrections make the rough draft more difficult to read, but in the end also more rewarding. For the fact is, Jefferson continued to record on this copy successive changes of the Declaration, not only by Adams and Franklin, but by Congress in its debates of July 3 and 4.

Jefferson wrote out a rough draft of the Declaration, which this illustration from 1897 envisions him reading to Franklin at his lodgings. In 1883 those lodgings were still standing, dwarfed by a four-story building next door that housed a tavern.

Thus by careful comparison and reconstruction, we can accurately establish the sequence of changes made in one crucial document, from the time it was first drafted, through corrections in committee, to debate and further amendment in Congress, and finally on to the engrossed parchment familiar to history. The changes were not slight. In the end, Congress removed about a quarter of Jefferson's original language. Eighty-six alterations were made by one person or another, including Jefferson, over those fateful three weeks of 1776.

THE TACTICS OF INTERPRETATION

Having sketched the circumstances of the Declaration's composition, the historian must attempt the more complicated task of interpretation. And here, historians' paths are most likely to diverge. To determine a document's historical significance requires placing it within the larger context of events. There is no single method for doing this, of course. If there were, historians would all agree on their reconstructions of the past, and history would be a good deal duller. On the other hand, historians do at least share certain tactics of analysis that have consistently yielded profitable results.

What follows, then, is one set of tactical approaches to the Declaration. These approaches are by no means the only ways of making sense of the document. But they do suggest some range of the options historians normally call upon.

The document is read, first, to understand its surface content. This step may appear too obvious to bear mentioning, but not so. The fact is, most historians examine a document from a particular and potentially limiting viewpoint. A diplomatic historian, for instance, may approach the Declaration with an eye to the role it played in cementing a formal alliance with France. A historian of political theory might prefer to focus on the theoretical justifications of independence. Both perspectives are legitimate, but by beginning with such specific interests, historians risk prejudging the document. They are likely to notice only the kinds of evidence they are seeking.

So it makes sense to begin by putting aside any specific questions and approaching the Declaration as a willing, even uncritical reader. Ask only the most basic questions. How is the document organized? What are its major points, briefly summarized?

The Unanimous Declaration of the Thirteen United States of America.

When in the Course of human events, it becomes necessary for one people to dissolve the political bands, which have connected them with another, and to assume among the powers of the earth, the separate and equal station to which the Laws of Nature and of Nature's God entitle them, a decent respect to the opinions of mankind requires that they should declare the causes which impel them to the separation.—We hold these truths to be self-evident, that all men are created equal, that they are endowed by their Creator with certain unalienable Rights, that among these are Life, Liberty and the pursuit of Happiness.—That to secure these rights, Governments are instituted among Men, deriving their just powers from the consent of the governed,—That whenever any Form of Government becomes destructive of these ends, it is the Right of the People to alter or to abolish it, and to institute new Government, laying its foundation on such principles and organizing its powers in such form, as to them shall seem most likely to effect their Safety and Happiness. Prudence, indeed, will dictate that Governments long established should not be changed for light and transient causes; and accordingly all experience hath shewn, that mankind are more disposed to suffer, while evils are sufferable, than to right themselves by abolishing the forms to which they are accustomed. But when a long train of abuses and usurpations, pursuing invariably the same Object evinces a design to reduce them under absolute Despotism, it is their right, it is their duty, to throw off such Government, and to provide new Guards for their future security. Such has been the patient sufferance of these Colonies; and such is now the necessity which constrains them to alter their former Systems of Government. The history of the present King of Great Britain is a history of repeated injuries and usurpations, all having in direct object the establishment of an absolute Tyranny over these States. To prove this, let Facts be submitted to a candid world.—He has refused his Assent to Laws, the most wholesome and necessary for the public good.—He has forbidden his Governors to pass Laws of immediate and pressing importance, unless suspended in their operation till his Assent should be obtained; and when so suspended, he has utterly neglected to attend to them.—He has refused to pass other Laws for the accommodation of large districts of people, unless those people would relinquish the right of Representation in the Legislature, a right inestimable to them and formidable to tyrants only.—He has called together legislative bodies at places unusual, uncomfortable, and distant from the depository of their public Records, for the sole purpose of fatiguing them into compliance with his measures.—He has dissolved Representative Houses repeatedly, for opposing with manly firmness his invasions on the rights of the people.—He has refused for a long time, after such dissolutions, to cause others to be elected; whereby the Legislative powers, incapable of Annihilation, have returned to the People at large for their exercise; the State remaining in the meantime exposed to all the dangers of invasion from without, and convulsions within.—He has endeavoured to prevent the population of these States; for that purpose obstructing the Laws for Naturalization of Foreigners; refusing to pass others to encourage their migrations hither, and raising the conditions of new Appropriations of Lands.—He has obstructed the Administration of Justice, by refusing his Assent to Laws for establishing judiciary powers.—He has made judges dependent on his Will alone, for the tenure of their offices, and the amount and payment of their salaries.—He has erected a multitude of New Offices, and sent hither swarms of Officers to harass our people, and eat out their substance.—He has kept among us, in times of peace, Standing Armies without the Consent of our legislatures.—He has affected to render the Military independent of and superior to the Civil power.—He has combined with others to subject us to a jurisdiction foreign to our constitution, and unacknowledged by our laws; giving his Assent to their Acts of pretended Legislation.—For quartering large bodies of armed troops among us:—For protecting them, by a mock Trial, from punishment for any Murders which they should commit on the inhabitants of these States:—For cutting off our Trade with all parts of the world:—For imposing Taxes on us without our Consent:—For depriving us in many cases, of the benefits of Trial by Jury:—For transporting us beyond Seas to be tried for pretended offenses:— For abolishing the free System of English Laws in a neighboring Province, establishing therein an Arbitrary government, and enlarging its Boundaries so as to render it at once an example and fit instrument for introducing the same absolute rule into these Colonies:—For taking away our Charters, abolishing our most valuable Laws, and altering fundamentally the Forms of our Governments:—For suspending our own Legislatures, and declaring themselves invested with power to legislate for us in all cases whatsoever.—He has abdicated Government here, by declaring us out of his Protection and waging War against us.—He has plundered our seas, ravaged our Coasts, burnt our towns, and destroyed the lives of our people.—He is at this time transporting large Armies of foreign Mercenaries to compleat the works of death, desolation and tyranny, already begun with circumstances of Cruelty & perfidy scarcely paralleled in the most barbarous ages, and totally unworthy the Head of a civilized nation.—He has constrained our fellow Citizens taken Captive on the high Seas to bear Arms against their Country, to become the executioners of their friends and Brethren, or to fall themselves by their Hands.—He has excited domestic insurrections amongst us, and has endeavoured to bring on the inhabitants of our frontiers, the merciless Indian Savages, whose known rule of warfare, is an undistinguished destruction of all ages, sexes and conditions. In every state of these Oppressions We have Petitioned for Redress in the most humble terms: our repeated Petitions have been answered only by repeated injury. A Prince whose character is thus marked by every act which may define a Tyrant, is unfit to be the ruler of a free people. Nor have We been wanting in attentions to our Brittish brethren. We have warned them from time to time of attempts by their legislature to extend an unwarrantable jurisdiction over us. We have reminded them of the circumstances of our emigration and settlement here. We have appealed to their native justice and magnanimity, and we have conjured them by the ties of our common kindred to disavow these usurpations, which would inevitably interrupt our connections and correspondence. They too have been deaf to the voice of justice and of consanguinity. We must, therefore, acquiesce in the necessity, which denounces our Separation, and hold them, as we hold the rest of mankind, Enemies in War, in Peace Friends.

We, therefore, the Representatives of the United States of America, in General Congress, Assembled, appealing to the Supreme Judge of the world for the rectitude of our intentions do, in the Name, and by Authority of the good People of these Colonies, solemnly publish and declare, That these United Colonies are, and of Right ought to be Free and independent States; that they are Absolved from all Allegiance to the British Crown, and that all political connection between them and the State of Great Britain, is and ought to be totally dissolved: and that as Free and independent States, they have full Power to levy War, conclude Peace, contract Alliances, establish Commerce, and to do all other Acts and Things which independent States may of right do.—And for the support of this Declaration, with a firm reliance on the protection of divine Providence, we mutually pledge to each other our Lives, our Fortunes and our sacred Honor.

As befits a reasoned public document, the Declaration can be separated fairly easily into its key parts. The first sentence begins by informing the reader of the document's purpose. The colonies, having declared their independence from England, intend to announce "the causes which impel them to the separation."

The causes that follow, however, are not all of a piece. They break naturally into two sections: the first, a theoretical justification of revolution, and the second, a list of the specific grievances that justify this revolution.

Because the first section deals in general, "self-evident" truths, it is the one most often remembered and quoted. "All men are created equal," "unalienable Rights," "Life, Liberty and the pursuit of Happiness," "consent of the governed"—these principles have meaning far beyond the circumstances of the colonies in the summer of 1776.

But the Declaration devotes far greater space to a list of British actions that Congress labeled "a long train of abuses and usurpations" designed to "reduce [Americans] under absolute Despotism." Because the Declaration admits that revolution should never be undertaken lightly, it proceeds to demonstrate that English rule has been not merely inconvenient, but so full of "repeated injuries" that "absolute Tyranny" is the result. What threatens Americans most, the Declaration proclaims, is not the individual measures, but the existence of a deliberate plot by the king to deprive a "free people" of their liberties.

The final section of the Declaration turns to the colonial response. Here the Declaration incorporates Richard Lee's resolution passed on July 2 and ends with the signers solemnly pledging their lives, fortunes, and sacred honor to support the new government.

Having begun with this straightforward reading, the historian is less likely to wrench out of context a particular passage, magnifying it at the expense of the rest of the document. Yet taken by itself, the reading of "surface content" may distort a document's import. Significance, after all, depends on the circumstances under which a document was created. Thus historians must always seek to place their evidence in context.

The context of a document may be established, in part, by asking what the document might have said but did not. When Jefferson retired to his second-floor lodgings on the outskirts of Philadelphia, placed a portable writing desk on his lap, and put pen to paper, he had many options open to him. Yet the modern reader, seeing only the final product, is tempted to view the document as the logical, even inevitable result of Jefferson's deliberations. Perhaps it was, but the historian needs to ask how it might have been otherwise. What might Jefferson and the Congress have declared but did not?

We can get a better sense of what Congress and Jefferson rejected by looking at a declaration made some ten years earlier by another intercolonial gathering, the Stamp Act Congress. Like Jefferson's, this declaration, protesting the Stamp Act as unjust, began by outlining general principles. In reading the first three resolves, note the difference between their premises and those of the Declaration.

A decade earlier, the Stamp Act Congress was unwilling to go as far as the Continental Congress in separating from Great Britain.

I. That his Majesty's Subjects in these Colonies, owe the same Allegiance to the Crown of Great-Britain, that is owing from his Subjects born within the Realm, and all due Subordination to that August Body the Parliament of Great-Britain.

II. That his Majesty's Liege Subjects in these Colonies, are entitled to all the inherent Rights and Liberties of his Natural born Subjects, within the Kingdom of Great-Britain.

III. That it is inseparably essential to the Freedom of a People, and the undoubted Right of Englishmen, that no Taxes be imposed on them, but with their own Consent, given personally, or by their Representatives.

The rights emphasized by the Stamp Act Congress in 1765 differ significantly from those emphasized in 1776. The Stamp Act resolutions claim that colonials are entitled to "all the inherent Rights and Liberties" of "Subjects, within the Kingdom of Great-Britain." They possess "the undoubted Right of Englishmen." Nowhere in Jefferson's Declaration are the rights of Englishmen mentioned as justification for protesting the king's conduct. Instead, the Declaration magnifies what the Stamp Act only mentions in passing—natural rights inherent in the "Freedom of a People," whether they be English subjects or not.

The shift from English rights to natural rights resulted from the changed political situation. In 1765 Americans were seeking relief within the British imperial system. Logically, they cited rights they felt due them as British subjects. But in 1776 the Declaration was renouncing all ties with its parent nation. If the colonies were no longer a part of Great Britain, what good would it do to cite the rights of Englishmen? Thus the natural rights "endowed" all persons "by their Creator" took on paramount importance.

The Declaration makes another striking omission. Nowhere in the long list of grievances does it use another word that appears in the first resolve of the Stamp Act Congress—"Parliament." The omission is all the more surprising because the Revolutionary quarrel had its roots in the dispute over Parliament's right to tax and regulate the colonies. The Sugar Act, the Stamp Act, the Townshend duties, the Tea Act, the Coercive Acts, the Quebec Act—all place Parliament at the center of the dispute. The Declaration alludes to those legislative measures but always in the context of the king's actions, not Parliament's. Doing so admittedly required a bit of evasion: in laying out parliamentary abuses, Jefferson complained, rather indirectly, that the king had combined with "others"—namely Parliament—"to subject us to a jurisdiction foreign to our constitution, and unacknowledged by our laws; giving his Assent to their Acts of pretended Legislation."

Obviously, the omission came about for much the same reason that Jefferson excluded all mention of the "rights of Englishmen." At the Stamp Act Congress of 1765, virtually all Americans were willing to grant Parliament some jurisdiction over the colonies—not the right to lay taxes without American representation, certainly, but at least the right to regulate colonial trade. Thus Congress noted (in Resolve I) that Parliament deserved "all due Subordination."

By 1775 more radical colonials would not grant Parliament any authority over the colonies. They had come to recognize what an early pamphleteer had noted, that Americans could be just as easily "ruined by the powers of legislation as by those of taxation." The Boston Port Bill, which closed Boston harbor, was not a tax. Nor did it violate any traditional right. Yet Parliament used it to take away Americans' freedoms.

Although many colonials had totally rejected all parliamentary authority by 1775, most had not yet advocated independence. How, then, were the colonies related to England if not through Parliament? The only link was through the king. The colonies possessed their own sovereign legislatures, but they shared with all British subjects one monarch. Thus when the final break with England came, the Declaration carefully laid all blame at the king's feet. That was the connection that needed to be severed.

What the Declaration does not say, then, proves to be as important as what it did say. Historians can recognize the importance of such unstated premises by remembering that the actors in any drama possess more alternatives than the ones they finally choose.

A document may be understood by seeking to reconstruct the intellectual worlds behind its words. We have already seen, in the cases of the De Soto expedition, slavery in Virginia, and witchcraft in Salem, the extent to which history involves the task of reconstructing whole societies from fragmentary records. The same process applies to the intellectual worlds that lie behind a document.

The need to perform this reconstruction is often hidden, however, because the context of the English language has changed over the past two hundred years—and not simply in obvious ways. For example, what would Jefferson have made of the following excerpt out of a computer magazine?

> Macworld's Holiday Gift Guide. It's holiday shopping season again. Macworld advises you on the best ways to part with your paycheck. . . . It could be an audio CD, but it could also be a CD-ROM containing anything from an encyclopedia to a virtual planetarium to an art studio for the kids.

To begin with, terms like "audio CD" and "CD-ROM" would mystify Jefferson simply because they come from a totally unfamiliar world. Beyond the obvious, however, the excerpt contains words that might seem familiar but would be deceptively so, because their meaning has changed over time. Jefferson probably would recognize "planetarium," though he might prefer the more common eighteenth-century term *orrery*. He would recognize "virtual" as well. But a "virtual planetarium"? Today's notion of virtual reality would be lost to him unless he read a good deal more about the computer revolution.

Even more to the point, look at the innocuous phrase "It's holiday shopping season again." The words would be completely familiar to Jefferson, but the world that surrounds them certainly would not. To understand the phrase, he would have to appreciate how much the Christmas holiday has evolved into a major commercial event, bearing scant resemblance to any eighteenth-century observance. (In John Adams's Puritan New England, of course, even to celebrate Christmas would have been frowned upon as a popish superstition.) Or to make an even subtler linguistic point: unlike a magazine article from the 1950s, this one from the 1990s never uses the word Christmas. The social reasons for this deliberate omission would undoubtedly interest Jefferson, for it reflects a multicultural nation sensitive to the questions of equality and the separation of church and state. But unless he were aware of the ways in which American society had evolved, Jefferson would miss the implications hidden within language that to us seems reasonably straightforward.

By the same token, eighteenth-century documents may appear deceptively lucid to twentieth-century readers. When Jefferson wrote that all men were "endowed by their Creator with certain unalienable Rights," including "Life, Liberty and the pursuit of Happiness," the meaning seems clear.

Sometimes the same word means different things in different centuries.

But as essayist and historian Garry Wills has insisted, "To understand any text remote from us in time, we must reassemble a world around that text. The preconceptions of the original audience, its tastes, its range of reference, must be recovered, so far as that is possible."

In terms of reassembling Jefferson's world, historians have most often followed Carl Becker in arguing that its center lay in the political philosophy of John Locke. Locke's *Second Treatise on Government* (1690) asserted that all governments were essentially a compact between individuals based on the principles of human nature. Locke speculated that if all the laws and customs that had grown up in human society over the years were stripped away, human beings would find themselves in "a state of perfect freedom to order their possessions and persons, as they think fit, within the bounds of the law of nature." But because some individuals inevitably violate the laws of nature—robbing or murdering or committing other crimes—people have always banded together to make a compact, Locke suggested, agreeing to create governments that will order human society. And just as people come together to allow themselves to be governed, likewise they can overturn those governments wherein the ruler has become a tyrant who "may do to all his subjects whatever he pleases."

Jefferson's colleague Richard Henry Lee in later years commented that Jefferson, in writing the Declaration, had merely "copied from Locke's treatise on government." Yet as important as Locke was, his writings were only one aspect of the Enlightenment tradition flourishing in the eighteenth century. Jefferson shared with many European philosophes the belief that human affairs should be studied as precisely as the natural world. Just as Sir Isaac Newton in the 1680s had used mathematical equations to derive the laws of gravity, optics, and planetary motion, so the philosophes of Jefferson's day looked to quantify the study of the human psyche.

The results of such efforts seem quaint today, but the philosophes took their work seriously. Garry Wills has argued that even more important to Jefferson than Locke were the writings of Scottish Enlightenment thinkers,

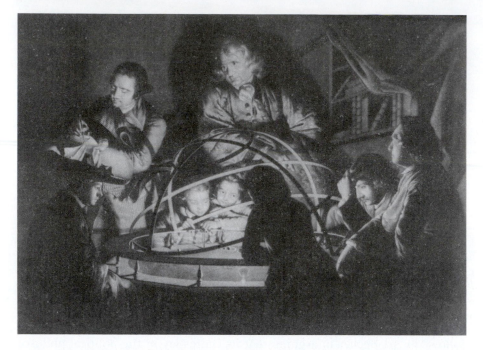

An orrery, shown in this engraving from 1768, traced the orbits of the planets around the sun. If it was possible to discover the relationships within the natural order, Jefferson and other Enlightenment thinkers reasoned, why not map the relationships of the human psyche?

chief among them Francis Hutcheson. In 1725 Hutcheson attempted to quantify such elusive concepts as morality. The result was a string of equations in which qualities were abbreviated by letters (B = benevolence, A = ability, S = self-love, I = interest) and placed in their proper relations:

$$M = (B + S) \times A = BA + SA; \text{ and therefore}$$
$$BA = M - SA = M - I, \text{ and } B = \frac{M-I}{A}$$

Jefferson possessed a similar passion for quantification. He repeatedly praised the American astronomer David Rittenhouse and his orrery, a mechanical model of the solar system whose gears replicated the relative motions of the earth, moon, and planets. Jefferson also applied classification and observation as a gentleman planter. If it were possible to discover the many relationships within the natural order, he reasoned, farmers might better plant and harvest to those rhythms. Even in the White House, Jefferson kept his eye on the Washington markets and recorded the seasons' first arrivals of thirty-seven different vegetables.

Wills argues that Jefferson conceived the "pursuit of Happiness" in equally precise terms. Francis Hutcheson had suggested that a person's actions be judged by how much happiness that person brought to other people. "That action is best," he argued, "which accomplishes the greatest happiness for the greatest number." According to Enlightenment science, because happiness could be quantified, a government's actions could be weighed in the balance scales to discover whether they hindered a citizen's right to pursue happiness as he or she saw fit. Thus, for Jefferson, the pursuit of happiness was not a phrase expressing the vague hope that all Americans should have the chance to live happily ever after. His language reflected the conviction that the science of government, like the science of agriculture or celestial mechanics, would gradually take its place in the advancing progress of humankind.

Jefferson, mind you, never said explicitly that he was relying on Scottish moral philosophy when he wrote the Declaration. This is Garry Wills's reconstruction, based on circumstantial evidence, such as the presence of Francis Hutcheson's works in Jefferson's library and the topics Jefferson's professors lectured on during his college years—and even, more generally, what ideas and opinions were "in the air." Whether or not Wills's specific case is convincing, his method of research is one that historians commonly employ. By understanding the intellectual world from which a document arose, we come to understand the document itself.

ACTIONS SPEAK LOUDER?

More than a few historians, however, become uneasy about depending too heavily on a genealogy of ideas. Certainly, a historian can speak of theories as being "in the air" and of Jefferson, as it were, inhaling. But that approach may neglect the noisy world outside his Philadelphia lodgings. By June 1776 Congress was waging a war, and a hundred and one events demanded its daily attention. The morning that Richard Henry Lee submitted his motion for independence, delegates had to deal with troops being raised in South Carolina and complaints about the gunpowder manufactured by a certain Mr. Oswald of Eve's Mill. Over the following days they learned that the British fleet had sailed from Halifax, on its way to attack New York City. Events large and small kept Jefferson and the rest of Congress from sitting down quietly to ponder over a single document.

Thus to understand the Declaration we must also set it within the context of contemporary events. "What was Jefferson thinking about on the eve of his authorship of the Declaration of Independence?" asked a recent biographer, Joseph Ellis. "The answer is indisputable. He was not thinking . . . about John Locke's theory of natural rights or Scottish commonsense philosophy. He was thinking about Virginia's new constitution." Throughout May and June, couriers brought news to Jefferson of doings in Williamsburg, the capital of his own "country," as he called it. There, on June 12, the Virginia convention adopted a preamble to its state constitution, written by

George Mason. "All men are created equally free and independent and have certain inherent and natural rights," wrote Mason, ". . . among which are the enjoyment of life and liberty, with the means of acquiring and possessing property, and pursuing and obtaining happiness and safety."

These words reached Philadelphia little more than a week before Jefferson penned his immortal credo "that all men are created equal, that they are endowed by their Creator with certain unalienable Rights, that among these are Life, Liberty and the pursuit of Happiness." The point is not to expose Jefferson as a plagiarist, for he substantially improved Mason's version. Nor is it to deny that John Locke or Francis Hutcheson may have played a role in shaping Jefferson's (and Mason's) thinking. But comparing Jefferson's language with Mason's makes it clear how much Jefferson was affected by actions around him rather than the books and words in his library.

Often enough, actions do speak louder than words. Yet a problem remains. Despite the proverb about actions, we are still talking about words, whether Jefferson's or George Mason's. The point of the maxim is that we cannot always take words at face value—that often, actions are what reveal true feelings. We need not reject the Declaration's heartfelt sentiments in order to recognize that the Congress (or, for that matter, colonials themselves) may have had reasons for declaring independence that they did not proclaim loudly.

Consider the vexed topic of slavery, especially relevant to a document proclaiming that "all men are created equal." It has become commonplace to point out the contradiction between the Declaration's noble embrace of human liberties and the reality that many delegates to Congress, including Jefferson, were slave owners; or similarly, the inconsistency between a declaration of equality and the refusal to let women participate in the equal rights of citizenship.

Although such contradictions seem now to be almost truisms, they deserve to be pointed out again and again. Indeed, much of American history can be seen as an effort to work out the full meaning of "all men are created equal"—whether in the Civil War, which ended slavery only after a vast and bloody carnage, or at the Seneca Falls Convention of 1848, mounted by women to proclaim an equality of the sexes in their own Declaration of Sentiments. The theme could be applied to the populist and progressive movements of the late nineteenth century, which challenged the monopoly powers of big business, or to the twentieth-century debates over civil rights and affirmative action. The implications of the Declaration have engaged the republic for more than two centuries and will continue to do so.

So let's return to the notion of actions and examine the intriguing way in which slavery appears in the Declaration. At first glance, it doesn't seem to appear at all. The only allusion comes in the document's long list of grievances, where Congress notes that the king has "excited domestic insurrections amongst us"—a rather indirect way of saying that the king had encouraged slaves to rise up against their patriot masters. The five words slip by so quickly that we hardly notice them.

Slavery did not slip by so quickly in Jefferson's rough draft. His discussion of the institution appeared not as a grace note, but as the climax of his long list of grievances against the king:

> He has waged cruel war against human nature itself, violating its most sacred rights of life and liberty in the persons of a distant people who never offended him, captivating & carrying them into slavery in another hemisphere or to incur miserable death in their transportation thither. This piratical warfare, the opprobrium of infidel powers, is the warfare of the Christian king of Great Britain. Determined to keep open a market where Men should be bought & sold, he has prostituted his negative [that is, used his veto power] for suppressing every legislative attempt to prohibit or to restrain this execrable commerce. And that this assemblage of horrors might want no fact of distinguishing die, he is now exciting those very people to rise in arms among us, and to purchase that liberty of which he has deprived them, by murdering the people on whom he also obtruded them: thus paying off former crimes committed against the Liberties of one people, with crimes which he urges them to commit against the lives of another.

Jefferson's rough draft of the Declaration said a lot more about slavery than what appeared in the final draft.

The passage is both revealing and astonishing. It reveals, first, that Jefferson was very much aware of the contradiction between slavery and the Declaration's high sentiments. Not once but twice he speaks out. The enslavement of black Africans violates the "most sacred rights of life and liberty," he admits. And again: enslavement amounts to "crimes committed against the Liberties of one people." Yet in admitting the wrong, he blames the king for it! Jefferson based his charge on the fact that several times during the eighteenth century, Virginia's legislature passed a tariff designed to put a brake on the importation of slaves. The lawmakers did so not so much from humanitarian motives (although these were occasionally mentioned) but because the colony's slave population was expanding rapidly. Importing too many Africans would lower the price of domestic slaves whom Virginia planters wanted to sell. The British administration, however, consistently vetoed such laws—and thus the king had "prostituted his negative" to prevent the slave trade from being restrained. For their part, white Georgians and South Carolinians were generally happy to see the trade continue, as were many New England merchants whose income depended on it.

To accuse the king of enslaving black colonials was far-fetched enough, but Jefferson then turned around and hotly accused the king of *freeing* black colonials. In November 1775 the loyal Governor Dunmore of Virginia proclaimed that any slave who deserted his master to fight for the king would be freed. Dunmore's Proclamation, as it was called, outraged many white patriots. Hence Jefferson called King George to account for the vile "crime" of freeing slaves who remained loyal to the crown.

What the delegates in Congress thought of the passage does not survive. But their actions spoke loudly. In the final draft, Jefferson's long passage vanished. All that remained was the accusation that the king had "excited domestic insurrections." Most likely Congress rejected Jefferson's logic as being so strained that it could hardly withstand public scrutiny. The less said, the better.

DECLARING FOR FREEDOM

Saying less, however, is not the same as saying nothing. By not deleting the accusation regarding "domestic insurrections," Congress revealed that this particular issue remained a sensitive one. Indeed, many other declarations of independence, issued by various states and towns on their own, complained loudly about Dunmore's Proclamation. Marylanders protested that slaves "were proclaimed free, enticed away, trained and armed against their lawful masters." Pennsylvanians objected that the British had incited "the negroes to imbrue their hands in the blood of their masters." North Carolina echoed that sentiment nearly word for word. The frequency of this complaint raises a question. Leave aside for a moment the issue of white attitudes toward slavery and liberty. How did the actions of *African Americans* affect the drafters of the Declaration?

On the face of it, the chance of answering that question seems far-fetched. The approximately 400,000 black slaves living in the colonies in 1776 could not leave a trail of resolutions or declarations behind them, for most were not allowed to. Yet the Declaration's complaint that Britain was stirring up American slaves brings to mind the similar laments of proslavery advocates in the 1850s and of segregationists during the 1950s and 1960s. Both repeatedly blamed "outside agitators" for encouraging southern blacks to assert their civil rights. In the eighteenth century, the phrase most commonly used was "instigated insurrection." "The newspapers were full of Publications calculated to excite the fears of the People," wrote one indignant South Carolinian in 1775, "Massacres and Instigated Insurrections, were words in the mouth of every Child." And not only children: South Carolina's First Provincial Congress voiced its own "dread of instigated insurrections." North Carolinians, too, warned that "there is much reason to fear, in these Times of general Tumult and Confusion, that the Slaves may be instigated, encouraged by our inveterate Enemies to an Insurrection."

Were the British "instigating" rebellion? Or were they taking advantage of African Americans' own determination to strike for freedom? As historian Sylvia Frey has pointed out, the incidence of flight, rebellion, or protest among slaves increased significantly in the decade following the Stamp Act, despite the long odds against success. In 1765 the Sons of Liberty paraded around Charleston shouting "Liberty! Liberty and stamp'd paper!" Soon after, slaves organized a demonstration of their own, chanting "Liberty!"

Planter Henry Laurens believed the ruckus was merely a "thoughtless imitation" of white colonials, but it frightened many South Carolinians.

With good reason. Look more closely at events in Virginia leading up to Governor Dunmore's proclamation. Six months before Dunmore offered freedom to all able-bodied slaves who would serve the king, he had confiscated some of the colony's gunpowder to prevent the rebels from getting it. At that point, "some Negroes . . . offered to join him and take up arms." What was Dunmore's reaction? He ordered the slaves "to go about their business" and "threatened them with his severest resentment, should they presume to renew their application." Patriot forces, on the other hand, accused Dunmore of seizing the gunpowder with the intention of "disarming the people, to weaken the means of opposing an insurrection of the slaves." Hearing this charge, Dunmore became "exceedingly exasperated" and threatened to "declare freedom to the slaves and reduce the City of Williamsburg to ashes."

In other words, the slaves, not Dunmore, made the first move in this game of chess! And far from greeting the slaves' offer with delight, Dunmore shunned it—until patriot fears about black insurrections made him consider the advantages that black military support might provide. Similarly, in 1773 and again in 1774 the loyal governor of Massachusetts, General Thomas Gage, received five separate petitions from "a grate Number of [enslaved] Blacks" offering to fight for him if he would set them free. "At present it is kept pretty quiet," Abigail Adams reassured her husband, John, who was off at the First Continental Congress.

Who was "instigating" rebellion—the British or African American slaves?

By 1775 slave unrest was common in many areas of the Carolinas and Georgia. Charleston had taken on "rather the appearance of a garrison town," reported one observer, because the militia were patrolling the streets at night as well as during the day, "to guard against any hostile attempts that may be made by our domesticks." White fears were confirmed when a black harbor pilot, Thomas Jeremiah, was arrested, tried, hanged, and burned to death for plotting an insurrection that would enlist the help of the British navy. Jeremiah told other blacks that "there was a great War coming soon" that "was come to help the poor Negroes." According to James Madison, a different group of slaves in Virginia "met together and chose a leader who was to conduct them when the English troops should arrive." The conspiracy was discovered and suppressed. Islands along the coasts of South Carolina and Georgia, as well as English navy ships, attracted slaves striking for freedom. The slaves were not "inticed," reported one captain; they "came as freemen, and demanding protection." He could "have had near 500 who had offered."

The actions of these and other enslaved African Americans clearly affected the conduct of both British officials and colonial rebels. The British, who (like Dunmore) remained reluctant to encourage a full-scale rebellion, nevertheless saw that the mere possibility of insurrection might be used as an effective psychological threat. If South Carolinians did not stop opposing British policy, warned General Gage ominously, "it may happen that your Rice and Indigo will be brought to market by negroes instead of white People." For their part, southern white colonials worked energetically to suppress both the rebellions and all news of them. As two Georgia delegates to the Continental Congress informed John Adams, slave networks could carry news "several hundreds of miles in a week or fortnight." Madison saw clearly the dangers of talking about the slave conspiracy in his state: "It is prudent such things should be concealed as well as suppressed," he warned a friend. Maryland's provisional government felt similarly about Governor Dunmore's proclamation in neighboring Virginia. It immediately outlawed all correspondence with the state, either by land or water. But word spread anyway. "The insolence of the Negroes in this county is come to such a height," reported one Eastern Shore Marylander, "that we are under a necessity of disarming them which we affected [sic] on Saturday last. We took about eighty guns, some bayonets, swords, etc."

Thus the actions of African Americans helped push the delegates in Congress toward their final decision for independence, even though the Declaration remained largely silent on the subject. By striking for liberty, slaves encouraged the British to use them as an element in their war against the Americans. Lord North expected that British troops sent to Georgia and the Carolinas in 1775 would meet with success, especially because "we all know the perilous situation ... [arising] from the great number of their negro slaves, and the small proportion of white inhabitants."

The Americans were pushed toward independence by this knowledge. Georgia delegates told John Adams that their slaves were eager to arise, and if "one thousand regular [British] troops should land in Georgia, and their commander ... proclaim freedom to all the negroes who would join his campaign, twenty thousand would join it from [Georgia and South Carolina] in a fortnight." James Madison, worrying about Lord Dunmore, warned that a slave insurrection "is the only part in which this Colony is vulnerable; & if we should be subdued, we shall fall like Achilles by the hand of one that knows the secret." Washington, too, perceived the threat. Dunmore must be crushed instantly, he warned in December 1775, "otherwise, like a snowball, in rolling, his army will get size." Although southern delegates wanted to forbid black Americans from serving in the Continental Army, Washington changed his mind and supported the idea, having come to believe that the outcome of the war might depend on "which side can arm the Negroes the faster." Until recently, few historians have appreciated the role African Americans played in shaping the context of independence.

Actions do speak louder than words—often enough. Still, the Declaration's words and ideals have outlasted the sometimes contradictory actions of its creators. Jefferson's entire life embodied those contradictions. More than any president except Lincoln, Jefferson contributed to the downfall of

---

RUN away from *Hampton*, on *Sunday* laſt, a luſty Mulatto Fellow named A R G Y L E, well known about the Country, has a Scar on one of his Wriſts, and has loſt one or more of his fore Teeth; he is a very handy Fellow by Water, or about the Houſe, *&c.* loves Drink, and is very bold in his Cups, but daſtardly when ſober. Whether he will go for a Man of War's Man, or not, I cannot ſay; but I will give 40 s. to have him brought to me. He can read and write.
    N O V E M B E R 2, 1 7 7 5.   J A C O B W R A Y.

RUN away from the Subſcriber, in *New Kent*, in the Year 1772, a ſmall new New Negro Man named G E O R G E, about 40 Years of Age, mith a Nick in one Ear, and ſome Marks with the Whip. He was about *Williamſburg* till laſt Winter, but either went or was ſent to Lord *Dunmore's* Quarter in *Frederick* County, and there paſſes for his Property. Whoever conveys him to me ſhall have 5 l. Reward.
    1 ‖   J A M E S M O S S.

Masters whose slaves ran away commonly posted notices in newspapers offering rewards for their return. The advertisements often assumed that slaves had gone to join kin. But these advertisements from an issue of the *Virginia Gazette* in November 1775 indicate that slaveowners were frequently convinced that their male slaves might have gone to offer service to Lord Dunmore or to the British navy ("a Man of War's Man").

slavery. In addition to penning the Declaration's bold rhetoric, he pushed for the antislavery provision in the Northwest Ordinance of 1787, which served as a model for later efforts to stop slavery's expansion. Yet for all that, he depended on the labor of enslaved African Americans throughout his life. Although he apparently maintained a sexual relationship with one of his slaves, Sally Hemings, upon his death he freed none, except five members of the Hemings family. Sally was not among them.

It lay with Abraham Lincoln to express most eloquently the notion that a document might transcend the contradictions of its creation. In 1857 Lincoln insisted that in proclaiming "all men are created equal," the founders of the nation

> did not mean to assert the obvious untruth that all were then actually enjoying that equality. They meant to set up a standard maxim for free society, which should be familiar to all, and revered by all, constantly looked to, constantly labored for, and even though never perfectly attained, constantly

approximated, and thereby constantly spreading and deepening its influence, and augmenting the happiness and value of life to all people of all colors everywhere.

"For the support of this Declaration," Jefferson concluded, "we mutually pledge to each other our Lives, our Fortunes and our sacred Honor." This sentiment was no idle rhetoric. Many delegates took the final step toward independence only with great reluctance. If the war was lost, they faced a hangman's noose. Even in victory, more than a few signers discovered that their fortunes had been devastated by the war. Yet it does no dishonor to the principles of the Revolution to recognize the flawed nature of Jefferson's attempt to reconcile slavery with liberty. Even less does it dishonor the Revolution to appreciate the role enslaved African Americans played in forcing the debates about independence. They, too, risked all in the actions—declarations made without words—that so many of them took to avail themselves of life, liberty, and the pursuit of happiness.

Additional Reading

Carl Becker's venerable work, *The Declaration of Independence: A Study in the History of Political Ideas* (New York, 1942) is still an engaging introduction. Garry Wills provides wide-ranging contextual analysis of the document in *Inventing America: Jefferson's Declaration of Independence* (New York, 1978). Many states and local governments issued their own declarations, which have been discussed in Pauline Maier, *American Scripture: Making the Declaration of Independence* (New York, 1997). Maier also examines how the Declaration outgrew its position of relative obscurity during the half century following the Revolution to become one of the "scriptural" texts of American history. Sylvia Frey's fine *Water from the Rock: Black Resistance in a Revolutionary Age* (Princeton, 1991) outlines the actions taken by African Americans during the Revolutionary years. For the relation of African American rebellion and the Declaration itself, see Sidney Kaplan, "The Domestic Insurrections of the Declaration of Independence," *Journal of Negro History* 61 (1976): 243–255.

CHAPTER 5
Material Witness

Do possessions define us? The study of everyday objects reveals much about the early republic—from small habits to the fundamental ways in which society was being transformed.

Here's a mute witness, like many to be encountered in this chapter. It survives now in the collections of Memorial Hall Museum in Deerfield, Massachusetts. The Museum's best estimate is that the object was hammered together around 1820, somewhere in New England. It measures about 21 inches tall and 18 inches square. It would be seen around some, though not all, American houses during this era. Any guesses as to its use?

A crate, perhaps, for storage? If so, the material being stored would have to be bulky or it would fall out the rather large spaces between the slatting. A contraption for holding wood by the fireplace? Not particularly practical, for the crate's shape would make it difficult to stack wood horizontally, and almost as awkward to do so vertically. Furthermore, the amount of firewood burned on a winter's day in New England would be far greater than what this crate could hold.

Also, look closely at the object. About halfway down on the back side is a horizontal piece of wood within the container that appears to be a small ledge. What could that be for?

In fact, the goods being "stored" in this container (for a container of sorts it is) were much more valuable to the occupants of the house than any firewood. Americans of the early nineteenth century would have recognized this contraption as a "baby tender," or "standing stool," used by parents to help toddlers stand but keep them from straying into mischief. The small ledge allowed the child to sit and rest. Tenders with wheels were also available, but the fancier versions actually possessed a certain disadvantage, because babies using them could propel themselves across the floor. This feature posed a significant danger in a house in which open fires for cooking or heating were regularly kept going. The records of Henniker, New Hampshire, make that clear. Between 1790 and 1830, seven children in that small town alone were scalded to death in accidents involving hot water, soups and stews, or hazards from similar housekeeping chores, such as boiling soap. Two other Henniker youngsters died falling into the fireplace during the same time period. And that total does not include lesser injuries, in which the children survived.

The baby tender was only one among hundreds of objects that played an intimate part in the everyday routines of Americans during the early republic, the period between the 1780s and the 1820s. A great many of those items are foreign to us today, despite the fact that versions of some have survived to the present. (Toddlers still careen around in wheeled "walkers," occasionally launching themselves into harm's way when parents forget to close gates at the tops of stairs.) Like the changing context of the words examined in

the previous chapter ("pursuit of happiness," for example), the context surrounding material objects has shifted as well. If historians are to understand
the lives of past Americans both great and small, they need to breathe life
not only into the abstract sentiments of the Declaration, but also the contours of the material environment—the stuff of everyday life.

Heat, one variable shaping those contours, is something we tend to take
for granted in a fully industrialized society. But keeping warm, particularly
during the harsh New England winters, shaped the material environment
in dozens of ways. Sarah Emery of Newburyport, Massachusetts, recalled
that in the cold winter of 1820–1821, "china cups cracked on the tea table
from the frost, before a rousing fire, the instant the hot tea touched them;
and plates set to drain in the process of dishwashing froze together in front
of the huge logs, ablaze in the wide
kitchen fireplace." Most homes
in the early republic had only one
central fireplace, and the older the
house, the larger and draftier it was
likely to be. Seventeenth-century fireplaces were 2 to 3 yards wide—large
enough to walk into—and their broad chimneys swept most of the heat
straight up out of the house. In such breezy conditions, seating benches like
the "kitchen settle" pictured here were designed to face the fire and shelter
those sitting in them from the drafts. (Notice that the high back extends all
the way to the floor to help keep the sitters' legs warm.)

*Extremes of heat and cold defined
many of the hazards of household
life in the early republic.*

If the main room was drafty despite the presence of a fire, other
rooms in the house were downright frigid. More than wind could whistle

through the chinks of exterior walls and the cracks around windows. Abner Sanger's diary for December 19, 1793, noted laconically that he used his time "to clean out chambers [i.e., his rooms] of snow." Youngsters, who often slept in garrets, were not surprised to find light drifts along the floor and rime from their breath frosting the tops of their blankets. Some folk moved their beds to the warmest room possible, in front of the main fireplace—but then they had to worry about stray sparks setting fire to their covers. Rooms abutting the chimney on the second floor or in the attic gained some secondary warmth and could be used for storing foods such as apples, squashes, onions, potatoes, carrots, and beets, all of which needed to be protected from freezing. When the thermometer really plummeted, however, "people's roots were frozen in the garret," as another diarist noted in 1788. Digging into the ground provided more reliable food storage; a "root cellar" penetrating deep enough beyond the frost line kept temperatures above freezing.

For those who could afford them, curtains draped on four-poster beds created a tent to conserve the warmer air generated by the bed's occupants. And siblings as well as husbands and wives doubled up to benefit from the shared body heat. Indeed, the practice was so common that sleeping alone seemed a bit odd. One young apprentice recorded several times in his diary the search for one or another nighttime companion: "I got Albert Field to sleep with me last night, & I must go and get somebody to sleep with me tonight for it is rather lonesome to lie alone." Many New Englanders also "banked" their houses, protecting the root cellar and first story by piling up insulation around the outside walls every autumn. They used leaves, tanbark, cornstalks, sand, or even "chip-dung."

Baby tenders, root cellars, and bed curtains are all items of everyday life that historians define as material culture. Those historians who make that field their specialty realize how much the lives of Americans of this era were constrained, day in, day out, by circumstances far different from today's world. If it was a woman's task to spin wool, should she ask her husband or son to move the "great wheel" into a heated room? (Julia Smith of Glastonbury, Connecticut, did because she knew her fingers would not be nimble enough otherwise.) What sorts of trees supplied the most useful firewood, and when was the best time to lay in the year's supply? (For baking, coals from hickory or birch served well; and the winter snow cover facilitated hauling logs from the woodlot in a sleigh.)

Reconstructing the material culture of a people requires both hard work and imagination. Some information can be gleaned by examining objects discovered in attics or passed down by the descendants of those who first used them. The baby tender pictured at the opening of this chapter arrived at Memorial Hall Museum in 1960 with a tag identifying it as an "18th century primitive baby tender used in Mrs. Sheldon Howe's family for many years." But in examining the tender's 113 nails, the museum discovered that 100 of them were a type known as "cut nails," not commonly in use until after 1820.

Thus the tender was more likely constructed in the early nineteenth century, which is only to say that the traditions handed down along with the objects are not always accurate. Scholars of material culture use a wide variety of written records and physical analysis to identify surviving objects and place them in their broader context.

We have already encountered some sources of evidence. Reconstructing the social world of Salem Village, historians drew upon household inventories taken upon the death of the house's owner. Such inventories provide room-by-room lists of the house's contents—not only major pieces of furniture, but often minor objects as well, whose value might be only a few pennies. Such inventories are not unfailingly reliable. When death was preceded by a long illness, some possessions might have already been passed on to other relatives. What else are we to make of a list including a fancy mirror and silver plates but no beds? However, by sampling enough estates, patterns emerge.

The bed curtains just mentioned, for example, were expensive. Did that limit their ownership solely to the rich? Historians have surveyed enough inventories to suggest that by the 1770s at least half the households in some towns used them. Although the cost may have been high, the warmth gained on cold nights apparently justified the expense. Other documentary records include family account books, which note daily expenses, extraordinary purchases, and even the number of cords of wood burned over time. More arcane records, such as fire insurance documents filed by prosperous homeowners, yield details about how many fireplaces were used at different times of the year. (Some rooms were shut up for the coldest months, it seems, because they were too much trouble and expense to heat.) And of course, diaries supply wonderfully concrete descriptions of everyday lives.

Yet some details elude us, as in the case of the fired clay object shown here, dated around 1820. Any guesses as to its function? We should note immediately that its dimensions are too large to make it a cup for drinking. It was delicately referred to as a "chamber pot," used in an era when "privies" (outhouses) were often constructed at some distance from the house and inconvenient to reach, especially in the middle of the night or in winter. Historian Jane Nylander, whose study of material culture has illuminated

many of the previously noted strategies for keeping warm, confessed herself at a loss for information when it came to chamber pots:

> Chamber pots are listed in a few inventories, but they are conspicuously absent from many others. Considering the frequency with which they are excavated by historical archaeologists and the heavy reliance [by Americans of that day] on cathartics as medical remedies, it seems likely that the care of these useful vessels was an important daily chore. However, it is difficult to know the conventions associated with their use. . . . Abner Sanger's diary gives us two clues in this obscure area: on July 7, 1794, he purchased a "urine mug," and on November 19, 1778, he made a "shit house." Perhaps that was really the difference.

ROOM FOR IMPROVEMENT

It would be understandable, of course, if Sanger's descendants were not eager to hand down his chamber pot as an heirloom. Indeed, the wonder is that so many chamber pots—and other objects—survived the winnowing process that death inevitably brings. If you were to die suddenly, how many of your possessions would be saved and passed along? Valued photographs or letters, perhaps—but that old computer, whose processor is nearly worthless, with its dial-up modem? The kitchen dish towels or the plastic Pocahontas tumbler from McDonald's, which somehow survived a purging? A lot of your own material culture would likely disappear into the landfill, simply because the remnants are old and worn or their personal significance is lost on others.

Yet material objects that have disappeared in real life often survive in paintings or photographs, which become visual archives for historians. A variety of material culture from the early republic can be seen in the paintings of John Lewis Krimmel, for example. Krimmel, a German immigrant who came to Philadelphia, was one of America's earliest painters of "genre scenes"—paintings of ordinary life rather than formal portraits of the well-to-do or grand paintings of historic events. Krimmel recorded bustling parades and election-day crowds; indoors he painted weddings and tavern scenes. *Quilting Frolic,* shown on the following page, depicts the end of a day on which a number of women have been working on the quilt at left. A woman is cutting it free from its frame just as several other folk arrive to celebrate the project's completion. There will likely be some dancing, since a black fiddler is there to provide the music.

The room is filled with a veritable treasure trove of material culture. In examining the painting, we intend to follow the method of many preachers of the era, which was to present a text out of scripture and then "improve" (or elaborate on) its verses one by one. But before beginning, it may be useful for readers to try "improving" the painting themselves. Take a pencil and paper and jot down half a dozen items of material culture displayed in

Quilting Frolic. Then consider how each might be used to illuminate the lives of the people pictured.

The likeliest place to begin is with the quilt itself, for quilting conjures up picturesque images of the young republic's simpler days. Sewing was women's work that young girls learned almost as soon as they could hold a needle. Harriet Kidder of Newark, New Jersey, recorded proudly in her diary that daughter Katy "has nearly completed her quilt. . . . She has pieced every block—put them all together in long strips & assisted in sewing together these strips." A month later the Kidders celebrated that completion with a party, for it was Katy's fifth birthday. The age of five was a common marker of when a child might complete a quilt—at least when this particular diary was written, in 1847.

But the date is important, for by 1847 we are already well into the mid-nineteenth century, and it is a nostalgic misconception to envision quilting as an integral part of life during the colonial period, or even in 1820. Today, recycling is a virtue; we imagine stitching together a patchwork blanket as a thrifty way to reuse old scraps of cloth. Yet before the 1820s, such quilting would have struck most Americans as a sign of abundance, for it required patterned cloth, and such cloth was an imported luxury throughout nearly all of the eighteenth century. Most clothing was made of

> *A patchwork quilt was not so much a sign of old-fashioned habits as it was the coming of the Industrial Revolution.*

simple homespun. Paradoxically, the "rustic" practice of quilting was a by-product of the Industrial Revolution, which made low-cost patterned textiles readily available.

During the early years of the republic, quilts were simpler affairs, not made up of multiple pieces of cloth or decorative materials appliquéd to the cloth. A diary that mentioned a quilt in 1780 was more likely referring to a woman's petticoat, which was finished with the characteristic crisscross stitch. The example shown here, from the later eighteenth century, was bright red and finished off with an elegant leaf-and-flower design that could have peeked through the fashionable open-front skirts of gowns of the period.

As for quilting a blanket, that was done by joining two large pieces of cloth that enclosed an insulating padding of carded wool or tow (fibers made from flax); the three layers were kept together by the crisscross stitch. The display side of the blanket was usually made of calamanco, a lustrous worsted wool, while the hidden side was a simpler homespun. In Krimmel's scene, painted around 1813, the quilt appears to be of a single color and not made of piecework.

The social nature of the quilting frolic, however, was characteristic of both the colonial period and the nineteenth century. When work was arduous or lonely, especially in sparsely populated rural areas, Americans looked for ways to enjoy each other's company. New Englanders called the practice "changing works"—that is, one person helped another who would later return the favor in an exchange of work. We "spun and sang songs," recorded Ruth Henshaw in her diary in 1789, when her friend Sally came by for two days. When such get-togethers involved more people and ended with a celebration, they were called "frolics," and completing a quilt was only one of many excuses for sociability. Esther Cooper, living on Long Island in the 1760s and 1770s, recorded going to "spinning frolics" on several occasions; her husband Simon proposed a wood-chopping frolic, for which the women "were very busie cooking for the work men."

Quilting was by no means the only occupation that went on in rooms like this one. Historian Laurel Thatcher Ulrich tallied the references to work in the diary of Betty Foot, a Connecticut girl, from January through May 1775:

> Spinning appeared on twenty-three days, knitting on twenty-three, sewing fifteen, carding [wool] thirteen, and a cluster of other activities—quilting, hatcheling [separating flax fibers], spooling and quilling—on five. Betty mentioned her own weaving only once, on March 7, 1775, when "I stay'd at home & finish'd Molly's Worsted Stockings and fix'd two Gowns for Welch's Girls which came to 1s 6d [1 shilling, sixpence] and I wove while Nabby went to Milking." Her fifteen sewing entries included nine occasions on which she "fix'd" gowns for other people.

Krimmel's painting itself suggests the variety of activities. The woman kneeling on the ground has her left arm resting on a sewing basket, and in the lower foreground at least two other similar workbaskets can be seen.

Turning to another set of objects, look at the cups and saucers on the tray carried by the young black servant (see the detail from the painting above), and the plates and napkins on the tablecloth to the left. To modern eyes such objects seem unexceptional, yet they reveal much, particularly when we consider change over time. During the eighteenth century, dining habits in the colonies were often primitive, especially in rural areas and among poorer folk. One physician traveling in 1744 wrote about being offered a meal by a ferryman along the Susquehanna River

The ferryman's family ate fish out of a single dirty, deep, wooden dish, "cramming down skins, scales, and all" with their bare hands.

> whom I found att vittles with his wife and family upon a homely dish of fish without any kind of sauce. They desired me to eat but I told them I had no stomach. They had no cloth upon the table, and their mess [i.e., food] was in a dirty, deep, wooden dish which they evacuated with their hands, cramming

down skins, scales, and all. They used neither knife, fork, spoon, plate, or napkin because, I suppose, they had none to use.

Even in the late eighteenth century, dining could be primitive. At breakfast "my father and mother would eat out of one bason, myself and two sisters, out of the other," recalled Seth Sprague of Duxbury, Massachusetts. John Weeks of Salisbury, Vermont, remembered "the custom of setting the large six-quart dish in the centre of the table, while half a dozen or more children stood around it, each with a spoon, partaking of this homely but healthful repast of samp and milk." Samp, a Narragansett Indian term for cornmeal mush, was only one of many stews, soups, puddings, and porridges common at the time. Such fare was eaten easily enough out of an all-purpose dish known as a "porringer," a bowl that could be used to drink out of or to hold a semiliquid meal eaten with a spoon. Early porringers were often earthenware, like the one pictured here, imported from England around 1690. After 1750, however, pewter and silver models became more common. In his autobiography, Benjamin Franklin recalled that his wife presented him with new dining ware, because she thought "her husband deserv'd a silver spoon and China bowl as well as any of his neighbors. This was the first appearance of [silver] plate and China in our house."

Given the dining habits prevailing at the beginning of the nineteenth century, Krimmel's portrayal of proper china cups and plates and napkins suggests that his Philadelphia frolickers prided themselves on their civilized fare. The tablecloth, too, is a mark of refinement. If you look closely you can see the fashionable fringe at its edges; by this date many American weavers were adding fringe to their homemade linen cloths. The painting is not detailed enough to show whether silverware is present. Although it almost certainly would have been used, we have no way of knowing whether the guests considered themselves polite enough to convey food to their mouths by using a fork rather than a knife, in the manner of the French and English. One manual of etiquette from the 1830s advised, "if you think as I do that Americans have as good a right to their own fashions . . . you may choose the convenience of feeding yourself with your right hand armed with a [knife's] steel blade; and provided you do it neatly and do not put in large mouthfuls, or close your lips tight over the blade, you ought not to be considered as eating ungenteely."

Another mark of refined dining, significant in its own right, is the cupboard at the left of Krimmel's painting. It displays china through its windows, so guests can admire the household's prosperity and good taste. The doors were unusual for 1813 in that they slid sideways rather than swinging out on hinges, an advantage in crowded quarters. Cupboards played a crucial role as a repository for family valuables—particularly valuables belonging to women. Like other possessions, cupboards themselves could be passed along in the family and treasured for their own sake.

One such heirloom, astonishing in its beauty, is the cupboard shown here belonging originally to Hannah Barnard of Hadley, Massachusetts. Made sometime in the decade after 1710, its design reflected a local tradition among cabinetmakers in the Connecticut River region around Springfield. Cabinetmakers there both carved and painted designs on the wood, including the bright blue turned columns on the upper half of the Barnard cupboard. About 250 examples of these "Hadley chests" or similar items, created between 1680 and 1740, have survived. To have the owner's name painted in large letters was unusual, but out of 126 similar chests, at least 115 incorporated the owner's initials into the design. Other characteristic motifs include the two-petaled tulips joined to a single large leaf (seen to the inside of the letters of Hannah Barnard's name), the inverted hearts and diamonds below the tulips, the semicircles, and the twining vines flanking each side of the drawers.

In addition, the Hadley chests exhibit a revealing naming pattern. Barnard was Hannah's maiden name, though the chest was very probably made in anticipation of her marriage. Similarly, the great majority of initials displayed on other Hadley chests corresponded with maiden names, and only 6 bore the initials of both the wife and husband. In other words, the cabinets were associated with the woman of the household far more than with the man. As Laurel Ulrich has noted, the reason seems to be that such cabinets held goods that women traditionally owned—linens, damask napkins, embroidered samplers—passed down through the female line of a family, mother to daughter. We have already seen, in discussing the status of women during the colonial period, that the law treated men and women differently. That was the case in terms of inheritance. Traditionally "real" property—woodlands, fields, houses, barns, and other real estate—passed from one male to another. Because such property was not moveable, it could not travel from place to place.

By contrast, when a woman married, she moved from her own family to the home of her husband and took his name. Her possessions tended to be what the law referred to as "moveables"—property that could travel with her, including domestic animals and personal possessions such as a cupboard and its contents. As Ulrich observed,

A woman's possessions tended to be "moveables," property that could travel with her when she married.

this division of property was not neutral. "In such a system, women themselves became 'movables,' changing their names and presumably their identities as they moved from one male-headed household to another." In 1813, when Krimmel painted *Quilting Frolic,* Hannah Barnard's cupboard was still being used by her descendants, a century after its manufacture. It left the family only when Hannah's great-granddaughter, Hannah Barnard Hastings Kellogg, was forced to part with it upon making the long trek to California. In an age of increasing mobility, even "moveables" had their limits.

Notice the broom lying on the floor at the lower right of *Quilting Frolic.* This broom is an advance over the coarser versions used in most homes in the 1780s. Older twig brooms could only banish leaves or clots of mud and dirt, leaving finer dust behind. Given those limitations, a careful housewife camouflaged the remaining dust by scattering a bit of clean white sand on the floor and brushing it into a pleasing herringbone pattern. "A white floor sprinkled with clean white sand . . . decorated a parlour genteely enough for any body," recalled one woman who grew up in Philadelphia near the turn of the century. Around 1800, however, some farmers began using the thinner stalks of sorghum grass (which came to be called "broomcorn") to manufacture a broom that swept up finer dust as well. This seems to be the variety used by Krimmel's quilters. By the 1830s millions had been sold.

In the right-hand corner of Krimmel's room stands a tall case clock, about 6 feet high—another reflection of the owner's good taste. In the first years of the republic, such a clock could be afforded only by the reasonably well-to-do. American clockmakers worked by hand, producing no more than about

ten "movements" per year. The purchaser was expected to find a cabinet-maker to build a case for the movement. By 1813 Eli Terry and other manu-facturers had devised ways to turn out over a thousand movements a year, also significantly smaller and capable of fitting in cases only 20 inches high. The new clocks were cheaper, too. Over the next decades they would be hawked far and wide by Yankee peddlers to Americans eager to add a bit of refinement to houses and even rude cabins.

As material culture, such clocks provided an ambiguous message about the world their owners occupied. The clock in Krimmel's painting was a mark of gentility as much or more than it was a precise timepiece. To be sure, urban Americans had some use for dividing the day into hours and minutes. Yet natural rhythms of light and dark often provided equally practical divisions of the day. Farmers knew quite well how far along the day had come merely by look-ing out a window, and often they made fine distinctions. One Illinois farmer in the 1830s divided the hours before sunrise into no less than eight stages: long before day, just before day, just coming day, just about daylight, good light, before sunup, about sunup, and (finally) sunup. The faces of many clockworks reflected this affinity to the natural world; the one shown here gives not only the time but, above the clock face, a calculation of the moon's current phase. It was useful to know when a full moon was available, to provide better light for traveling or working at night. At the same time, the penetration of clocks into ordinary homes reflected an increased need to appear punctually either at work or at social events. A Massachusetts diarist in 1830 recorded having a fine time at a sleighing party: "They sing, going and returning, which sounds very prettily. Have some hot coffee, and return at half past nine." Krimmel's clock, then, was a part of the material environment that looked both backward to the genteel culture of the late eighteenth century and forward to an industrial era in which the hours of the day were more strictly regimented.

THE REFINING OF AMERICA

Thus far we have been dealing with material culture on a piecemeal basis— object by object, looking to tease out how each item shaped everyday life. But the case clock reminds us that with the passage of time, material culture is constantly changing. Quilting, we saw, meant something different in 1840 than it did in 1780. If material culture is constantly evolving, then a study of it may help chart the broader evolution of American society as well.

What longer-term trends are revealed by the objects in *Quilting Frolic?* Return to the painting's plates and napkins, and recall the physician's account of dinner with the ferryman's family, written some seventy-five years earlier. Contrasting the two ways of dining suggests that over time, more refined habits were coming into play. Yet that evolution is not a simple progression from the "barbarities" of 1744 to the "civilized" behavior of 1813. Some people in 1744 (including that disgusted physician) felt it uncouth to eat without silverware or napkins—and those folk, obviously, came from the higher ranks of society.

The spread of refinement, therefore, involved the diffusion of habits first practiced by social elites downward to Americans in the middle of the social spectrum—to a middle class that was itself becoming a distinctive part of American society during those years. Historian Richard Bushman has traced this process over several hundred years. The changes were gradual and usually appeared first in urban areas, where new cultural influences spread more easily. They appeared also where industrialization took hold earlier, in New England and the Mid-Atlantic states, rather than in the South and the West—though those regions showed signs of change as well.

Genteel behavior was modeled after the manners of kings, queens, and the nobility. Over the centuries, guides were published, known as "courtesy books," that instructed in the intricacies of proper conduct. *Rules of Civility*, a French publication of 1671 (also used in Britain), explained that those men and women with the highest social rank assumed the greatest places of honor, whether in a room (the space farthest from the door) or in a carriage (the back right seat) or in a bedroom (the bed itself). Behaviors of the smallest sort came under regulation: a servant of inferior rank was never to knock at the door of a nobleman—only to scratch! Such rules were extreme for

eighteenth-century America, but George Washington as a young man copied maxims out of a similar courtesy book: "In Company of those of Higher
Quality than yourself Speak not ti[ll] you are ask'd a Question then Stand
upright put of[f] your Hat and Answer in few words."

As these formulas made clear, genteel manners specified the proper relation to material objects such as doors, carriage seats, and beds. Hats were
doffed to show respect—not only in
Washington's day but in Krimmel's;
note the guest in *Quilting Frolic* who
is tipping his hat courteously. We
have also seen how china, tablecloths,
and clocks all served as markers of civility. One item missing in this array is
a carpet—not surprising, for in 1813 such adornments were still relatively
rare. In 1770 most Americans would have found it odd indeed to cover a
room's wide plank flooring. *Rug* usually referred to a bed blanket, also called
a "coverlid."

"Refined" manners specified even the proper relation to objects such as doors, carriage seats, and beds.

To modern eyes, a carpet would seem hardly to merit mention as an
object toward which proper behavior must be paid. But in 1813 (and earlier)
there were good reasons for not using carpets. Walking any distance out of
doors coated shoes with mud or dirt that could easily deface fine rugs. Over
time, dirt became less an issue in cities with paved or cobblestone streets and
sidewalks. In 1824 novelist Lydia Sigourney wrote a story based in part on
a real experience, about a farmer mystified to see a rug on the parlor floor.
Trying his level best to avoid getting it dirty, he worked his way around the
edge of the room until blocked by a table. "I must tread on the kiverlid,"
he apologized; and when told that the carpet was meant to be walked on,
replied, "I ha'nt been used to seeing kiverlids spread on the floor to walk on.
We are glad to get 'em to kiver us up a' nights."

The trend toward refinement included more than the spread of genteel
objects, for such ornaments were displayed within a larger setting. Thus we
must examine not just the objects themselves but the space enclosing them, for
space, too, was undergoing a steady evolution within the American home.

The earliest houses in British America were quite basic. Perhaps a third
to a half or even more built during the seventeenth century featured a door
that opened directly into the main room, known since medieval days as the
"hall." Against one wall of this hall stood the large, drafty fireplace, which
doubled as a kitchen area. Later in the century, houses were more likely to
have two rooms on the first floor and another two on the second. On the
first floor the additional room was known as the "parlor," but in effect it
was the "best bedroom," where the mother and father slept and in which
the most valuable furniture was kept, such as beds and dressers. Additional
sleeping and storage space on the second floor was usually accessible by
either a ladder or a stairway, the latter walled off to keep the heat in the main
room from escaping upward. Windows were only about 2 feet square, also to
keep heat in, which guaranteed dark and gloomy surroundings. Glass panes

were preferred, but more than a few houses made do with oilcloth, which let through even less light.

Ordinary folk continued to use such houses during the eighteenth century, but those who could afford them increasingly built more spacious Georgian brick homes, which were coming into fashion in Britain. The main door no longer opened directly onto the central room, but onto an elegant hallway and staircase. No longer walled off and hidden, these stairs became part of the welcoming entryway. The main hall, which before had been a multi-functional space for eating, cooking, and sleeping, became more formal and finished, sometimes known as the "entertaining room." Walls were plastered and painted or wallpapered, instead of showing wood planking. The ceiling was finished, too, no longer revealing the rafters and flooring of the room above. Corner moldings added refinement, and chair rails—molding at waist height—protected walls from being scratched by the elegant seats placed along a room's perimeter. More light brightened the rooms: sash windows ("the newest fashion" in 1710) allowed in more daylight than the old-fashioned casements, and the eighteenth-century gentry took advantage of the new cleaner-burning (though more expensive) spermaceti candles to light their homes in the evening.

Improvements in heating also reshaped rooms toward the end of the eighteenth century. Benjamin Thomas, a Massachusetts man also known as Count Rumford, redesigned the traditional fireplace to make it smaller, less drafty, and more efficient. Benjamin Franklin's stove, inserted into a fireplace, also allowed more heat to radiate into the room. The smaller fireplaces were less convenient for cooking, but since the new houses had more space, the kitchen could be moved to a separate room at the back of the house, to the cellar, or, especially in the southern colonies, to an outbuilding behind the main house. (Krimmel's room features a smaller fireplace.)

Comfort was part of the rationale behind the changes. But they were not merely about practicality. The newer architecture reflected the leisure that colonial elites enjoyed. (The traditional definition of a gentleman was that he did not need to work to support himself or his family.) The more money spent on furnishing the parlor—the most expensive room in the house—the less the parlor was involved with practical, everyday economic activities such as eating, spinning, cooking, or sleeping. Estate inventories tell the tale. As the eighteenth century progressed, fewer and fewer large houses listed beds located in the parlor room. Instead we find tea tables, chairs, and cupboards displaying the best china. And entertainment in the finest houses was not confined to the parlor; second-floor rooms might be outfitted for tea or even fine dining. That was one reason the open staircase and central hallway were so important. "The staircase must present itself boldly and freely to the sight," advised one British architectural authority, "otherwise all has a confused and poor aspect. It looks as if the house had no good upper floor." Historian William Thomas O'Dea has pointed out that the increase of candles used in sconces and candelabra was not "the result of utilitarian pressures for better lighting, but of the evolution of a way of life whose chief objects were entertainment and display."

Display indeed. Both O'Dea and Bushman have emphasized the theatrical quality of the newer architecture. Colonial elites saw themselves as leaders of their communities, and they felt obliged to present their leadership in highly visible ways. George Washington was painfully aware of being watched at all times, as the maxims he copied from his courtesy book demonstrated: "In the Presence of Others Sing not to yourself with a humming Noise, nor Drum with your fingers and Feet." Washington's visibility was peculiarly high, but all gentlefolk recognized that "in the Presence of Others," they must behave to a standard. "Wherever you are, imagine that you are observed," insisted a popular eighteenth-century ladies' handbook, "and that your Behaviour is attentively scanned by the rest of the Company all the while; and this will oblige you to observe yourself, and to be constantly on your Guard."

Given such attitudes, the houses of the elite were designed to display the elite and their possessions advantageously. Visitors traveled a path, which was often landscaped, toward an imposing mansion whose exterior walls were painted or constructed of brick, in marked contrast to most weather-beaten, unpainted houses. Ushered through a formal garden or courtyard, guests entered an impressive hallway and were led into rooms aglow with as many as a dozen candles, whose light was multiplied and reflected back by the silver plate, candlesticks, and trays. Mirrors on the wall and polished chairs and tables further magnified space and light. The activities that went on within these rooms were not so different from those enjoyed by ordinary folk—card playing, tea drinking, and dancing. It was the refinement that made the difference. The objects, the spaces, and the vistas all ennobled those who took their place on these stages.

THE MATERIAL IDENTITIES
OF A MIDDLE CLASS

During the early republic, the tastes of gentlemen and gentlewomen were increasingly adopted by Americans with less income and status. The process of refinement helped create a distinctive middle class, defined in part by the increase in urban living and in part by the habits of life its members adopted and the sorts of objects with which they surrounded themselves. Yet as Richard Bushman pointed out, the process was not merely one of imitation. *Refinement* itself was evolving because of who these middling sorts were and how their lives required them to live.

Unlike gentlemen, members of the middle classes were obliged to work. Tableware, china, carpets, and clocks were eagerly purchased, but they did not come cheap. Where would the money be found to buy them? The census of 1810 provided one revealing answer, for it collected information on Americans' occupations and work habits. Both farm families and urban residents earned extra income through household manufacturing, producing textiles like the fringed tablecloth in Krimmel's painting or the new sorghum-grass brooms. Tench Coxe, who created a digest of the 1810 census, noted that cloth manufactured on home-based looms contributed "to the comfort and happiness" of the women who manufactured it and left men free "for the duties of the farm." With southern plantations producing ever more cotton since the invention in 1793 of Eli Whitney's cotton gin, Coxe hoped that home manufacturing might increase and in the process "render every industrious female an artizan, whenever her household duties do not require her time."

Thus the quilting frame so prominent in Krimmel's painting was actually a sign of the conflicting forces of leisure and work. On the one hand, the room exhibited many signs of refinement and a desire to rise above the older, simpler ways of life. Yet work, not leisure, provided the rationale for the frolic, no matter how much fun was to be had. Nearly 90 percent of the households in Topsham, Maine—to take one example—were making cloth of some sort. Over half of these households had looms, and the cloth making went on in families whose male heads were tanners, shipwrights, joiners, and blacksmiths, among others. Even a few men whom the census takers styled "gentlemen" found it profitable to manufacture clothing.

The spaces in a gentleman's house focused on a display of wealth and status; the new middle-class homes were refuges that valued privacy.

How the cloth was used varied from one house to the next. Some was created only for the family's shirts, dresses, and trousers. Other households were more ambitious. "My mother would change [i.e., exchange] work with Zerniah's mother and other women, knitting and sewing for them while they would weave cotton and flax into cloth which we would get dressed into fustian [a strong fabric] at the mill for the boys and also for Father's summer working dress," recalled Mary Palmer Tyler. From this entry alone, it becomes clear that cloth making involved a patchwork of relationships, with the exchange of work between families and friends going on as of old—but now also with the presence of a "mill." In the early 1800s more and more mills were dotting the New England countryside. The census of 1810 listed over 600 carding mills, where wire-brush machines combed out wool or flax in preparation for spinning. Over 110 cotton-spinning factories sold thread to women who could weave it into cloth in their own homes. The women would then sell the cloth back to the factories. Thus home industry at first complemented the new factories, and the parlors of the middle class remained places where work mixed with leisure, and where spinning wheels and even looms crowded other furniture.

But with the coming of larger-scale factories like the Lowell mills, established in 1820, cheaper cloth could be turned out in quantity, making it more difficult for home manufacturers to compete. The decades following 1830 saw the separation of the workplace and the home into increasingly distinct spheres. The daughters of farmers began to take jobs in factories, rather than

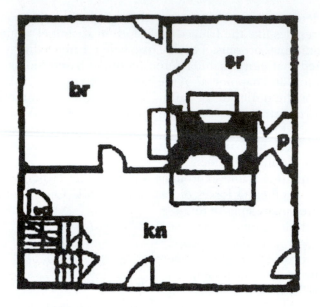

staying home to help mothers make cloth to be sold at market. As one New England minister noted, "The transition from mother-and-daughter power to water-and-steam power" produced "a complete revolution of domestic life." For middle-class families the home was becoming less a workplace and more a refuge from the workaday world beyond. Women were the moral guardians of this domestic domain, and working men retreated to it after the day's labor, expecting comfort and repose. By the mid-nineteenth century the "cult of domesticity," as historians have come to call it, was in full swing.

Historians can plot the material contours of these changes in the histories of individual houses, as they were remodeled and improved over the years. When Old Sturbridge Village moved the home of blacksmith Emerson Bixby from Barre, Massachusetts, to its museum grounds, it carefully studied Bixby's account books, the alterations of the house walls, and the layers of paint and wallpaper in order to document the process of refinement over time. In 1807 the dwelling was still primitive. Its somewhat uncharacteristic three-room configuration had a kitchen in the rear, with a parlor and sitting room in front. The parlor, also known as the "best room" (*br* on the plan) included a bed where the previous owners had slept. Although the front door opened directly onto that room, at least it could boast wallpaper on the upper half of the walls, as well as chair rails and wainscoting (a wood paneling) on the lower half, painted Prussian blue. Yet despite those refinements, the owners not only slept in the best room but ate there as well. The kitchen stairway was enclosed, following the old style, and a central chimney served the fireplace in each room. A small pantry was used for storage. In short, although a few eighteenth-century refinements had been introduced into the parlor, the house in 1807 functioned as had most simple seventeenth-century houses.

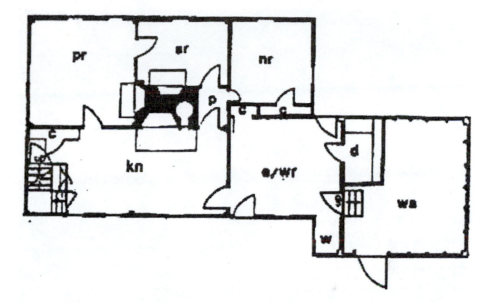

By the time Bixby finished a series of renovations around 1845, the size of the house and the functions of its rooms had changed (see the enlarged floor plan). A few features remained as they were. There was no easy way to add a central stairway and a front entry hall, so access to the second floor remained through the kitchen. But the best room had become a full-fledged parlor; the door to the outside had been removed and was replaced by a window. A room (*nr*) was added on the first floor for Mr. and Mrs. Bixby, which allowed their bed to be moved from the parlor. And the interior walls were plastered throughout, and all the rooms were either wallpapered or painted a fashionable gray.

The exterior received attention as well. Bixby had the unpainted siding removed and new clapboard installed and painted white, a color that had come into fashion by the mid-1800s. (Eighteenth-century owners preferred a yellow or sand, or even russet or green, if brick was not used.) Also, the notion of a front lawn as an aesthetic element of a refined home came into play.

When a refined home came to include a pleasing front lawn, residents stopped throwing their garbage out the windows.

We know this because archaeologists from Old Sturbridge excavated around the original site of the house. In the layers of the soil deposited before the 1840s, a good deal of refuse can be found: broken plates, ashes, and food scraps. Such garbage was simply thrown out through a convenient window, indicating no concern for the house's external appearance. After the 1840s, however, garbage was usually collected in designated spots at the rear.

We do not know for sure, but it would have made sense for the Bixbys to have added a fence around the yard, as many middle-class homes were doing. Contemporary architects were also recommending that shrubbery be

used to decorate the house and soften its appearance. The contrast with the more open display of eighteenth-century mansions is instructive: these new middle-class houses, envisioned as refuges, preferred to appear sheltered from the public bustle.

Given these changes in the home environment, look at one final engraving of a parlor, this one done about fifteen years after *Quilting Frolic*. Having analyzed the objects seen in Krimmel's painting, take a moment to catalog the material culture shown here. What differences do you notice, and how would you relate them to the social transformations under way?

In terms of objects, a number of items jump out. First, a pair related to size: the fireplace and the window. The former is much smaller and the latter much larger than would have been seen a century earlier. A close look at the fire in the grate reveals that the flames are no longer fueled by wood but instead coal, which was increasingly used by urban residents. There is a carpet on the floor, which is conspicuously absent from *Quilting Frolic*. Other objects worth commenting on—we leave you the opportunity for a little research and speculation—are the clock over the mantel, the globe, the draperies, the footstools, the lamp in the window, and the vase in the right foreground.

Perhaps an even more interesting question revolves around the objects we do not see in the engraving. An inspector from Scotland Yard once famously inquired of Sherlock Holmes whether there was any clue crucial to determining the whereabouts of a missing racehorse. Attention must be paid to "the curious incident of the dog in the nighttime," Holmes replied. "The dog did nothing in the nighttime," protested the inspector. "That was the curious incident!" replied Holmes. In *Quilting Frolic* we see a plethora of objects related to the work activities of the people in the parlor: sewing baskets, a broom, a quilting frame, a grinder of some sort on the stool. These are nowhere to be seen in the engraving from 1831. Work has been banished from the parlor. Furthermore, there is no cupboard full of dishes. Why not? What has replaced it?

Equally telling are the people in the engraving. Krimmel documents a boisterous social occasion, with thirteen people in the room. Here we see only three figures in an intimate family setting. The artist, whose engraving was titled *There Is No School Like the Family School,* clearly portrays a moral lesson about what should go on at home. We see now a nuclear family rather than extended one: only a father, mother, and daughter. In Krimmel's painting, by contrast, a grandfather sits by the fire and perhaps three siblings are evident, as well as their mother, seated to the left of the fireplace. As the young republic became more urban and less agricultural, the average family size began to drop. On a farm, a large family made good economic sense, since boys could help fathers in the field, and daughters could assist mothers in sewing, spinning, weaving, and doing household chores. The growing urban middle class, on the other hand, recognized that an education was paramount to securing a good job and a comfortable home; and education was more expensive to provide for large families.

Finally, compare the notion of refinement revealed in the engraving of a middle-class family with the sort of refinement reflected in eighteenth-century architecture. For the well-to-do of the late eighteenth century, rooms made it possible for one to see and be seen in a public way, as the leaders of society. This notion of leadership could not extend to members of the much larger middle class of the 1830s. So while more folk enjoyed many of the consumer goods that had been available only to the upper classes fifty years earlier, the focus of that enjoyment was turned inward. Calvert Vaux, a leading architect of the 1850s, spoke for changing tastes when he referred to the parlor as "the general living-room of the family" that functioned quite differently from the traditional genteel parlor. The genteel parlor was kept immaculate, its door tightly shut,

> always ready for—what? For daily use? Oh, no; it is in every way too good for that. For weekly use? No, not even for that—but for company use; and thus the choice room, with the pretty view, is sacrificed, to keep up a conventional show of finery that pleases no one. . . . All this is absurd. No room in any house, except, perhaps, in a very large mansion, ought to be set apart for company use only . . . certainly not the most agreeably situated apartment in the house, which should be enjoyed daily.

Over time, Vaux's notion of a house centered on family activities gained in one home after another. That was certainly the case with Emerson Bixby. Virtually every existing house in his neighborhood had been remodeled in one way or another by the time his renovations got under way. Bixby was, in fact, a classic example of a fellow "keeping up with the Joneses."

DEFINING OURSELVES

In the end, the study of material culture insinuates itself into the smallest crannies of everyday life, as historians and archaeologists examine faded porringers, chip the paint off moldings, and grub about in the dirt to reconstruct even the garbage of a household. Yet material culture can lead as well to larger questions about our collective identities. There is an old German adage with an aggressively materialist bent: *Mann ist was Mann ißt* (one is what one eats). If we broaden the saying, there is much to be said for the notion that people construct their identities—that they become what they are—by the way they make use of the things all around them. The "middling sorts" of people in the early republic incorporated eighteenth-century notions of what gentlefolk ought to own and how they ought to behave. Yet their own notions of refinement took on a different form, in which refuge from work became more important than the social display of the eighteenth-century gentry.

Material culture thus helps us trace the young republic's first steps away from an agrarian society toward an urban and industrial nation. This story has been often told, but usually by focusing on the rise of factories like the Lowell mills, as they turned out products on a large scale. The shorthand we use to name this transformation is, of course, the Industrial Revolution.

Yet by focusing on the material interactions of ordinary folk, the perspective shifts. Industrial America was only in its infancy during the early republic. The first factories had not yet displaced the work that was going on at home. While Emerson Bixby worked as a blacksmith in Barre, his wife Laura and her three daughters helped pay for their renovations by braiding straw for hats, as well as sewing shoe uppers that could be sold to shoe manufacturers. At the same time, they received income from the sale of the farm's cheese and butter.

In other words, even *before* factories came to dominate the American economy, ordinary folk were working harder in a host of different ways to earn additional income to buy goods that would refine their lives, give them more comfort, and allow them to enjoy some of the luxuries that the gentry possessed. Swap an old clay porringer for finer china,

Historians speak of an "industrious revolution," in which people began to work harder to earn money to buy consumer goods.

insisted Franklin's wife. Historians have begun to recognize the importance of this transformation, referring to a "consumer revolution" in eighteenth-century Britain and in America. To use the economists' metaphor of supply and demand, instead of talking about an industrial revolution that begins to *supply* a host of new goods to buyers, historians speak increasingly of an "industrious revolution" that began earlier in the eighteenth century, during which the *demand* for everything from silverware to printed textiles led more people of the middling sort to work harder, and vary the sort of work that went on in the home, in order to produce and to purchase such coveted consumer goods. Material culture has supplied a key to understanding how an emerging middle class evolved, as well as a market economy.

Yet the identities of material culture are not only collective and large scale, but also small and intensely personal. More than we realize, perhaps, the texture of our lives is built from the material world we incorporate in our lives: a familiar mug in our hand as we nurse hot coffee every morning, the comfort of a well-worn chair, the sheen of a pitcher passed down by a grandmother, the slim cell phone in our pocket. Material culture is in constant flux. New items become necessities; old items grow less relevant, though often still cherished. How long does one hold onto a treasured cupboard like Hannah Barnard's? We can all appreciate the material bond with the past expressed by Elizabeth Shackleton, an Englishwoman who in 1779 left the house she had lived in for many years because her son Thomas had taken possession of it upon marrying:

> On this day I emptied all and everything belonging unto me out of my mahogany bookcase, bureau and drawers given unto me by my own tender, good, most affectionate parent. They were made and finished by Henry Chatburne on Saturday December the eighth one thousand seven hundred and fifty. I value them much but relinquish the valuable loan with great satisfaction to my own dear child Thomas Parker.

We are more than we eat, assuredly; more, even, than we build and make and buy. But close attention to such matters reveals how intimately material culture has shaped our lives, and the lives of those who came before us.

Additional Reading

Jane C. Nylander, *Our Own Snug Fireside: Images of the New England Home, 1760–1860* (New York, 1993), is an engaging introduction to material culture. A good example of how historians use diaries and material culture to illuminate everyday life is Laurel Thatcher Ulrich, *A Midwife's Tale: The Life of Martha Ballard, Based on Her Diary, 1785–1812* (New York, 1990). For more on the artist who painted *Quilting Frolic,* see Anneliese Harding, *John Lewis Krimmel* (Winterthur, DE, 1994). Color reproductions of the painting on the Web may be found by searching for "Quilting Frolic" at the Images tab at www.google.com. Memorial Hall Museum of Old Deerfield has an online archive (http://www.old-deerfield.org/museum.htm) containing hundreds of everyday objects that can be easily accessed and examined.

Richard L. Bushman, *The Refinement of America: Persons, Houses, Cities* (New York, 1992), superbly places material culture within a broader context, as does Laurel Thatcher Ulrich, *The Age of Homespun: Objects and Stories in the Creation of an American Myth* (New York, 2001). For the consumer revolution of the late eighteenth century, see John Brewer and Roy Porter, eds., *Consumption and the World of Goods* (London, 1993). T. H. Breen, *The Marketplace of Revolution: How Consumer Politics Shaped Revolution* (New York, 2004), also contains useful material. For the creation of a market economy in the United States, see Winifred Barr Rothenberg, *From Market-Places to a Market Economy: The Transformation of Rural Massachusetts* (Chicago, 1992), and Stuart M. Blumin, *The Emergence of the Middle Class: Social Experience in the American City, 1760–1900* (New York, 1989).

Inside the Information Revolution

You had to be there is the cliché suggesting that an event is difficult to understand without having lived through it. For the historian, the opposite is often true: you have to *not* have been there to understand it.

This chapter's exploration of material culture has looked at change over decades, seeing how an industrial (or industrious) revolution transformed American lives. But unlike the wrenching events of the French Revolution, the changes of the Industrial Revolution took place gradually. They are harder to see as revolutionary when living in their midst, plodding along day by day.

For the past several decades, the world has been in the middle of an information revolution. Though its larger contours are difficult to analyze as it flows around us, we can employ the same process used in this chapter: examine the material culture of our own time as it has evolved. In 1990 landline telephones were the norm and big, blocky mobile phones were exotic high-tech devices flaunted by special agents in movies. Over the next two decades, the phone was transformed. The Masai in Africa and Filipinos in rural villages now have slim cell phones that function as cameras, map locators, text messengers, game players, as well as voice carriers.

Here is a list of objects whose alterations can be traced in similar fashion: the vinyl record, the book, the motion picture film, the letter or telegram, the typewriter. Each of these pieces of material culture has been used to convey information. Each has evolved over several decades. LPs become CDs become MP3 files. Letters become faxes become e-mails. The implications for society have been huge, in terms of commercial enterprise, labor practices, family ties and friendship networks, and even the way the ideas of the culture are disseminated.

Can you try *not* "being there" for a moment? Step back and ask how the experience of childhood has changed because of the shift in information technology. Which workers have gained more advantage and which less from the information revolution? Has the Web been a force promoting a democratic culture or an authoritarian one?

CHAPTER 6
Jackson's Frontier— and Turner's

The theories we use determine the questions we ask, whether we are looking at the closing of one frontier or the opening of many others.

Ceremony, merriment, and ballyhoo came to Chicago in the summer of 1893, and predictably, the crowds swelled the fairgrounds to get a taste of it. Buffalo Bill's Wild West Show went through its usual broncobusting, war-whooping routines. Visitors gawked at a giant map of the United States fashioned entirely from pickles. Also on display were a huge telescope, destined for Yerkes Observatory; a long-distance telephone, connected with New York City; and a four-story-high cross section of a new ocean liner. The amusement park—the Midway Plaisance—even boasted exotic exhibits in the living flesh: Irish peasants boiled potatoes over turf fires, Arabian veiled women and turbaned elders occupied their own village, while "Prince Pomiuk" of the Eskimos drove a dogsled through the warm summery dust.

The excuse for the fuss was Chicago's World's Columbian Exposition, held ostensibly to salute the 400th anniversary of Columbus's arrival in the Americas. More plausibly, the fair allowed proud Chicagoans to prove that they were more than hog butchers to the world and that they could out-exposition any metropolis on the globe. Given the total attendance of more than 12 million people over six months, the city made its case.

To further the exposition's reputation, several scholarly congresses were convened, including the World's Congress of Historians and Historical Students. And so on July 12, the curious tourist had the opportunity (or misfortune) of straying away from the booming cannibal drums of the Midway Plaisance and into the Art Institute, where five eager historians waited to present the fruits of their labors. On this hot evening, the papers were read back-to-back without relief, ranging from a discussion of "English Popular Uprisings in the Middle Ages" to "Early Lead Mining in Illinois and Wisconsin." The hardy souls who had not been driven off by the first four talks saw a young man in starched collar rise to present yet another thesis, this one titled "The Significance of the Frontier in American History."

124

The young man was Frederick Jackson Turner, a historian from the University of Wisconsin. Although none in the audience could have suspected it, his essay would spark four generations of scholarship and historical debate. The novelty of Turner's frontier thesis resulted not from his discovery of any previously unknown facts but from his proposal of a new theory, one that took old facts and placed them in an entirely different light.

THE SIGNIFICANCE OF THEORY

Turner's thesis is only one of many theoretical concepts that historians have used to bring order out of the chaotic past. Yet thus far, this book has avoided a direct discussion of the term *theory*. It is time to make amends, for theory is an essential part of the discipline of history, profoundly affecting the way historians go about their work. Indeed, if history is not merely "the past" itself but instead a reconstruction of it, theory could be said to supply the blueprints needed to raise the edifice.

At one level, *theory* can be defined simply as hypothesis. In this sense, it is the analysis that explains a relationship between two or more facts. During the Salem witch trials, certain "afflicted" townspeople acted in violent but consistent ways. Before historians could conclude that these acts might constitute symptoms of neurotic behavior, they had to accept the concept of conversion hysteria as a valid theoretical explanation. Note that the Salem records do not provide this interpretation; theory is what supplies it.

In a broader sense, *theory* can be defined as a body of theorems presenting a systematic view of an entire subject. We use the term this way when speaking of the "theory of wave mechanics" or a "germ theory of disease." Often, small-scale theoretical constructs are a part of a larger theoretical framework. Conversion hysteria is only one of many behavioral syndromes classified as neuroses. In turn, the concept of neurosis is only one part of the larger body of theory accepted by modern psychology. Physicists, chemists, and other natural scientists often use mathematical formulas to summarize their general theories, but among social scientists and humanists, theorems become less mathematic and more elastic. Even so, when historians discuss a "theory of democracy" or a "theory of economic growth," they are applying a set of coherent principles to explain specific events.

Because historians study an event or period in its entirety, historical narrative usually incorporates many theories rather than just one. The historian of early Virginia will draw on theories of economic behavior (the development of joint stock companies as a means of capital formation), sociology (the rise of slavery as an institution of color), psychology (the causes of friction between white and black laboring classes), and so on. In this broadest sense, historical theory encompasses the entire range of a historian's training, from competence in statistics to opinions on politics and philosophies of human nature. It is derived from formal education, from reading, even from informal discussions with academic colleagues and friends.

Turner in 1893, the year he presented his thesis at the World's Columbian Exposition; and the Johns Hopkins University seminar room for history students. At the head of the table is Professor Herbert Baxter Adams, who argued that American democratic institutions could be traced to British and European roots. Turner resented the lack of interest in the West at Hopkins. "Not a man I know here," he commented, "is either studying, or is hardly aware of the country behind the Alleghenies."

It follows that theory in this wider sense—"grand theory," as it might be called—plays a crucial role in historical reconstruction. While small-scale theory is called on to explain specific puzzles (why didn't slavery become entrenched in Virginia before 1660?), grand theory is usually part of a historian's mental baggage before he or she is immersed in a particular topic. Grand theory encourages historians to ask certain questions and not others. It tends to single out particular areas of investigation as worthy of testing and to dismiss other areas as either irrelevant or uninteresting.

While small-scale theory is used to explain specific puzzles, grand theory is usually a part of the mental baggage historians bring to a topic.

Thus anyone who ventures into the field of history—the lay reader as well as the professional researcher—needs to be aware of how grand theory exerts its influence. Nowhere in American history is this influence better illustrated than in Frederick Jackson Turner's venerable frontier thesis.

Turner began his Chicago lecture with a simple yet startling fact he had found in the recently released census of 1890. "Up to and including 1880, the country had a frontier of settlement," the census reported, "but at present the unsettled area has been so broken into by isolated bodies of settlement that there can hardly be said to be a frontier line." Turner seized upon this "event"—the passing of the frontier—as a "great historic moment." The reason for its importance to him seemed clear: "Up to our own day, American history has been in a large degree the history of the colonization of the Great West. The existence of an area of free land, its continuous recession, and the advance of American settlement westward, explain American development."

Turner's broad assertion—a manifesto, really—challenged on several counts the prevailing historical wisdom. Scholars of Turner's day had approached their subject with an Atlantic Coast bias. They viewed the East, and especially New England, as the true bearer of American culture. Developments beyond the Appalachian range were either ignored or treated sketchily. Turner, who had grown up in the rural setting of Portage, Wisconsin, and had taken his undergraduate degree at the University of Wisconsin, resented that attitude.

In addition, the reigning scholarship focused almost exclusively on political and constitutional developments. "History is past Politics and Politics present History" ran the slogan on the wall of the Johns Hopkins seminar room in which Turner had taken his PhD. In contrast, young Turner strongly believed that this narrow political perspective neglected the broader contours of social, cultural, and economic history. Historians who took the trouble to examine those areas, he felt, would discover that the unique physical and cultural conditions of the frontier, and not eastern cities, had shaped American character.

The frontier's effect on American character had been recognized in a casual way by earlier observers, but Turner attempted a more systematic analysis. In doing so, he drew on the scientific grand theory most prominent in his own day—Charles Darwin's theory of evolution. Whereas Darwin had proposed an explanation for evolution in the natural world, Turner suggested that America was an ideal laboratory for the study of cultural evolution. The American frontier, he argued, returned human beings to a primitive state of nature. With the trappings of civilization stripped away, the upward process of evolution was reenacted. Dramatically, Turner recreated the sequence for his audience:

The wilderness masters the colonist. It finds him a European in dress, industries, tools, modes of travel, and thought. It takes him from the railroad car and puts him in the birch canoe. It strips off the garments of civilization and arrays him in the hunting shirt and the moccasin. It puts him in the log cabin of the Cherokee and Iroquois and runs an Indian palisade around him. Before long he has gone to planting Indian corn and plowing with a sharp stick; he shouts the war cry and takes the scalp in orthodox Indian fashion. In short, at the frontier the environment is at first too strong for the man. He must accept the conditions which it furnishes, or perish, and so he fits himself into the Indian clearings and follows the Indian trails. Little by little he transforms the wilderness, but the outcome is not the old Europe. . . . The fact is that here is a new product that is American.

Turner suggested that the evolution from frontier primitive to civilized town dweller occurred not just once but time and time again, as the frontier moved west. Each time, settlers shed a bit more of their European ways; each time, a more distinctively American culture emerged. That was why the perspective of eastern historians was so warped: they stubbornly traced American roots to English political institutions or, worse, the medieval organization of the Germanic town. "The true point of view in the history of this nation is not the Atlantic coast," Turner insisted, "it is the Great West."

From this general formulation of the frontier's effects, Turner deduced several specific traits that the recurring evolutionary process produced. Chief among them were nationalism, independence, and democracy.

Nationalism, Turner argued, arose as the frontier broke down the geographic and cultural identities of the Atlantic Coast: New England with its Yankees and the tidewater South with its aristocratic planters. The "mixing and amalgamation" of sections was most clearly demonstrated in the middle states, where both Yankees and southerners migrated over the mountains, where Germans and other northern Europeans joined the English in seeking land. There a new culture developed, possessing "a solidarity of its own with national tendencies. . . . Interstate migration went steadily on—a process of cross-fertilization of ideas and institutions." (Once again, note the Darwinian metaphor of "cross-fertilization.")

"The true point of view in the history of this nation is not the Atlantic coast," Frederick Jackson Turner insisted, "it is the Great West."

The frontier also promoted independence, according to Turner. The first English settlements had depended on the home country for their material goods, but as settlers pressed farther west, England found it difficult to extend that supply. Frontier towns became self-sufficient, and eastern merchants increasingly provided westerners with American rather than English products. The economic system became more American, more independent.

Most important, suggested Turner, the individualism of the frontier promoted democracy and democratic institutions. "Complex society is precipitated by the wilderness into a kind of primitive organization based on the family," Turner argued. "The tendency is anti-social. It produces antipathy to control, and particularly to any direct control." Thus westerners resented being taxed without being represented, whether by England and Parliament or by Carolina coastal planters. The frontier also broke down social distinctions that were so much a part of the East and Europe. Given the fluid society of the frontier, poor farmers or traders could and did become rich almost overnight. Social distinctions disappeared when placed against the greater necessity of simple survival.

Turner even argued that the West, with its vast supply of "free land," encouraged democracy in the East. The frontier acted as a safety valve, he suggested, draining off potential sources of discontent before they disrupted society. "Whenever social conditions tended to crystallize in the East, whenever capital tended to press upon labor or political restraints to impede the freedom of the mass, there was this gate of escape to the free conditions of the frontier. . . . Men would not accept inferior wages and a permanent position of social subordination when this promised land of freedom and equality was theirs for the taking."

The upshot of this leveling process was nothing less than a new American character. Turner waxed eloquent in his description of frontier traits:

> That coarseness and strength combined with acuteness and inquisitiveness; that practical, inventive turn of mind, quick to find expedients; that masterful grasp of material things, lacking in the artistic but powerful to effect great ends; that restless, nervous energy; that dominant individualism, working for good and for evil, and withal that buoyancy and exuberance which comes with freedom—these are the traits of the frontier, or traits called out elsewhere because of the existence of the frontier.

What Turner offered his Chicago listeners was not only "the American, this new man," as Hector St. John de Crèvecoeur had called him in 1778, but also a systematic explanation of how the new American had come to be.

It would be proper etiquette here to scold Turner's Chicago audience for failing to recognize a masterpiece when they were read one. But in some ways it is easier to explain his listeners' inattention than to account for the phenomenal acceptance of the frontier thesis by later historians. Undeniably, Turner's synthesis was fresh and creative. But as he himself admitted, the essay was a hypothesis in need of research and testing. Of this, Turner proved constitutionally incapable. Although he loved to burrow in the archives for days on end, he found writing to be an unbearable chore.

Consequently, Turner published only magazine articles in the influential *Atlantic Monthly* and other journals. But these articles, along with numerous lectures and a gaggle of enthusiastic students, proved sufficient to make Turner's reputation. Publishers flocked to Wisconsin, seeking books by the celebrated historian. Turner, with hopelessly misplaced optimism, signed contracts with four publishers to produce eight separate manuscripts. None saw the light of day. The single book he completed (*The Rise of the West*, 1906) appeared only through the frantic efforts of editor Albert Bushnell Hart, who wheedled, cajoled, and threatened in order to obtain the desired results. "It ought to be carved on my tombstone," Hart later remarked, "that I was the only man in the world that secured what might be classed an adequate volume from Turner."

Why Turner's remarkable success? Certainly not because of his detailed research, which remained unpublished. Success was due to the attraction of his grand theory. Later critics have taken Turner to task for imprecision and vagueness, but these defects are compensated by an eloquence and magnificence of scale. "The United States lies like a huge page in the history of society," Turner would declaim, and then proceed to lay out history with a continental sweep. The lure of his hypothesis for historians was much like the lure of a unified field theory for natural scientists—a set of equations, as physicist Freeman Dyson has remarked, that would "account for everything that happens in nature . . . a unifying principle that would either explain everything or explain nothing." In similar (though less galactic) fashion, Turner's theory captured historians' imaginations. "The existence of an area of free land, its continuous recession, and the advance of American settlement westward, explain American development." That proposal is about as all-encompassing as a historian could desire!

The theory seemed encompassing, too, in its methods. The techniques of social science in historical research are so familiar today that we forget the novelty and brilliance of Turner's insistence on unifying the tools of research. Go beyond politics, he argued; relate geography, climate, economics, and social factors to the political story. Not only did he propose this unification; Turner also provided a key focus—the frontier—as the laboratory in which these variables could be studied. The fresh breeze of Turner's theory succeeded in overturning the traditional approaches of eastern historians.

Turner's critics complained that his definition of the "frontier" was vague. Was it a geographical place? The mechanism a safety valve? A type of personality produced by a process?

By the time Turner died in 1932, a tide of reaction had set in. Some critics pointed out that the frontier thesis severely minimized the democratic and cultural contributions of the English heritage. Others attacked Turner's vague definition of the "frontier." (Was it a geographical place? A type of population, such as trappers, herders, and pioneers? Or a process wherein European traits were stripped off and American ones formed?) Other critics disputed the notion of the frontier as a "safety valve" for the East. Few European immigrants actually settled on the frontier; if anything, population statistics showed more farmers moving to the cities.

For our own purposes, however, it would be misleading to focus on these battles. Whether or not Turner was right, his theory dramatically influenced the investigations of other historians. To understand how, we need to take Turner's general propositions and look at the way he and others applied them to a specific topic.

An ideal subject for this task is the man whose name Turner himself shared—Andrew Jackson.* Jackson is one of those figures in history who, like Captain John Smith, seems always to be strutting about the stage just a bit larger than life. Furthermore, Jackson's wanderings took him straight into the most central themes of American history. Old Hickory, as his troops nicknamed him, led land-hungry pioneers into the southeastern United States, displacing Native Americans from lands east of the Mississippi, expelling the Spanish from Florida, and repelling the British from New Orleans. As president, he launched the war against the "monster" Bank of the United States, placing himself at the center of the perennial American debate over the role of economic power in a democracy. Above all, he came to be seen as the

---

* The sharing of names is more than coincidence. Frederick Jackson Turner's father, Andrew Jackson Turner, was born in 1832 and named in honor of President Jackson, reelected that year.

political champion of the common people. Here is a man whose career makes it impossible to avoid the large questions that grand theory will suggest.

How, then, did Turner's frontier hypothesis shape historians' perception of Jackson? What features of his career did it encourage them to examine?

JACKSON: A FRONTIER DEMOCRAT (TARNISHED)

For Frederick Turner, Andrew Jackson was not merely "one of the favorites of the West," he was "the West itself." By that rhetorical proclamation Turner meant that Jackson's whole life followed precisely the pattern of frontier evolution wherein eastern culture was stripped bare and replaced by the "contentious, nationalistic democracy of the interior."

Jackson's Scotch-Irish parents had joined the stream of eighteenth-century immigrants who landed in Pennsylvania, pushed westward until they bumped up against the Appalachians, and then filtered southwest into the Carolina backcountry. This was the process of "mixing and amalgamation" that Turner outlined in his essay. Turner had also shown how the frontier stripped away higher social organizations, leaving only the family as a sustaining bond. Andrew Jackson was denied even that society. His father died before Jackson's birth; his only two brothers and his mother died during the Revolution. At the age of seventeen, Andrew left Waxhaw, his boyhood home, never to return again. In effect, he was a man without a family—but not, as Turner saw it, a man without a backcountry.

Jackson first moved to the town of Salisbury, North Carolina, reading law by day and, with the help of high-spirited young friends, raising hell by night. Brawling in barrooms, sporting with young ladies, moving outhouses in the wee hours past midnight—such activities gave Jackson a reputation as "the most roaring, game-cocking, horse-racing, card-playing, mischievous fellow that ever lived in Salisbury," according to one resident.

In 1788 the footloose Jackson grabbed the opportunity to become public prosecutor for the western district of North Carolina, a region that then stretched all the way to the Mississippi. There, in the frontier lands that now constitute Tennessee, Jackson hoped to make his reputation. Once settled in Nashville, he handled between a quarter and a half of all court cases in his home county during the first few years of his arrival. And he dispensed justice with the kind of "coarseness and strength" Turner associated with the frontier personality. When one enraged defendant stepped on prosecutor Jackson's toe to indicate his displeasure, Jackson calmly coldcocked the offender with a stick of wood. On another occasion, after Jackson had been appointed superior court judge in the newly created state of Tennessee, he stalked off the bench to summon a defendant before the court when no one else dared, including the sheriff and posse. The man in question, one Russell Bean, had threatened to shoot the "first skunk that came within ten feet," but when Jackson came roaring out of the courthouse, Bean pulled in his

Jackson the frontiersman: Russell Bean surrenders to Justice Jackson, as depicted in an 1817 biography. Wrote Turner, "If Henry Clay was one of the favorites of the West, Andrew Jackson was the West itself . . . the very personification of the contentious, nationalistic democracy of the interior."

horns. "I looked him in the eye, and I saw shoot," said Bean, "and there wasn't shoot in nary other eye in the crowd; and so I says to myself, says I, hoss, it's about time to sing small, and so I did."

All in all, Jackson seemed a perfect fit for frontier democrat. Turner described in characteristic terms Jackson's election to Congress in 1796:

> The appearance of this frontiersman on the floor of Congress was an omen full of significance. He reached Philadelphia at the close of Washington's administration, having ridden on horseback nearly eight hundred miles to his destination. Gallatin (himself a western Pennsylvanian) afterwards graphically described Jackson, as he entered the halls of Congress, as "a tall, lank, uncouth-looking personage, with long locks of hair hanging over his face, and a cue down his back tied in an eel-skin; his dress singular, his manners and deportment those of a rough backwoodsman." Jefferson afterwards testified to Webster: "His passions are terrible. When I was President of the Senate, he was a Senator, and he could never speak, on account of the rashness of his feelings. I have seen him attempt it repeatedly, and as often choke with rage." At length the frontier, in the person of its leader, had found a place in the government. This six-foot backwoodsman, angular, lantern-jawed, and thin, with blue eyes that blazed on occasion; this choleric, impetuous, Scotch-Irish leader of men; this expert duellist and ready fighter; this embodiment of the contentious, vehement, personal west, was in politics to stay.

This was Turner at his rhetorical best, marshaling all the striking personal details that supported his theory. But he was not writing a full-length biography and so confined his discussion of Jackson mostly to a few paragraphs of detail.

One of Turner's graduate students went further. Thomas Perkins Abernethy studied at Harvard during the period when the university had lured Turner east from his home ground at the University of Wisconsin. Abernethy believed that to test the frontier thesis, it ought to be examined on a local level, in more detail. In this respect, he felt, previous historians had not been scientific enough. "Science is studied by the examination of specimens, and general truths are discovered through the investigations of typical forms," he asserted. In contrast, "history has been studied mainly by national units, and the field is too broad to allow of minute examination." But Tennessee provided a perfect "specimen" of the western state. It broke away from its parent, North Carolina, during its frontier days; it was the first area of the nation to undergo territorial status; and from its backwoods settlements came Andrew Jackson himself. Why not trace the leavening effects of the frontier within this narrower compass? Abernethy set out to do just that in his book *From Frontier to Plantation in Tennessee.*

He had learned the techniques of his mentor well. Turner emphasized the role of free land as a crucial factor in the West. Abernethy agreed that land was "the chief form of wealth in the United States in its early years" and carefully studied the political controversies over Tennessee's vast tracts of land. Always he determined to look beyond the surface of the political arena to the underlying economic and geographic considerations.

Such techniques were Turner's, but the results produced anything but Turner's conclusions. *From Frontier to Plantation* is dedicated to Frederick Jackson Turner, but the book directly refutes Turner's optimistic version of western history.

As Abernethy began unraveling the tangled web of Carolina-Tennessee politics, he discovered that Americans interested in western land included more than pioneer squatters and yeoman farmers of the "interior democracy." Prosperous speculators who preferred the comforts of the civilized East saw equally well that forested, uncultivated land would skyrocket in value once settlers poured over the Appalachians in search of homesteads.

The scramble for land revealed itself in the strange and contradictory doings of the North Carolina legislature. During the Revolution, inflation had plagued the state, largely because the legislature had continuously issued its own paper money when short of funds. The value of this paper money plummeted to a fraction of its original face value. After the war, the legislature retrenched by proclaiming that all debtors would have to repay their debts in specie (that is, in gold or silver coins) or its equivalent in paper money. If, for example, the going rate set $1 in silver or gold as equal to $400 in paper notes and a person owed $10, the debtor would owe $4,000 in paper money. In effect, the legislature was repudiating its paper currency and saying that only gold or silver would be an acceptable medium of exchange.

This move made sense if the legislature was trying to put the state's finances on a stable footing. But Abernethy noticed that in the same session, the legislature turned around and issued a new run of paper money—printing up $100,000. Why issue more paper money when you've just done your best to get rid of the older stuff?

Abernethy also noticed that during the same legislative session, land offices were opened up to sell western lands—but only under certain conditions. The claimant had to go out into the woods and mark some preliminary boundaries, then come back and enter the claim at a designated land office. Finally, a government surveyor would survey the lot, submit a report to the secretary of state for the governor's authentication, and enter it in the county register.

The situation hardly confirmed Turner's democratic conception of the frontier, Abernethy concluded. First, who ended up being able to buy the new land? Not the squatter or yeoman farmer, certainly—few of them could fulfill the requirements of marking out land, returning East to register it, having it officially surveyed, and entering it. Instead, land speculators in the East, including state legislators, stepped in to make a killing. The career of William Blount, one of the most successful speculators, illustrated the process at work. As a state legislator, Blount helped write the new land laws. At the same time, he hired a woodsman to go west and mark out vast tracts. Blount, for his part, registered the claim and paid for the land.

The frontier seemed to be governed less by Turner's simple democrats than Abernethy's rich speculators.

Sometimes the money that paid for the land was the old paper currency, bought up for a fraction of its original price from poorer folk who had no means of claiming their own land. But the legislature also allowed purchasers to pay for the lands using the new paper money at face value. Was it coincidence only that Blount had been the legislator proposing the new issue of paper money? Abernethy thought not.

Instead of confirming Turner's version of a hardy democracy, then, Abernethy painted a picture of "free" Tennessee lands providing fortunes for already powerful men. Blount used "the entire Southwest [as] his hunting ground and he stuffed his pockets with the profits of his speculations in land. In the maw of his incredible ambition—or greed—there originated land grabs involving thousands of choice acres." And Blount was only one of many across the country. "In those days," Abernethy concluded, "America was run largely by speculators in real estate."

It was into this free-for-all country that Andrew Jackson marched in 1788, but Abernethy's new frame of reference placed his career in a different light. Compare Turner's description of Jackson's "pioneer" ride to Philadelphia with Abernethy's version of Jackson's horseback arrival in Tennessee. "Tradition has it," reported Abernethy, that Jackson arrived at Jonesboro . . . riding a fine horse and leading another mount, with saddlebags, gun, pistols, and fox-hounds. This was elaborate equipment for a struggling young lawyer, and within the year he increased it by the purchase of a slave girl. . . . Jackson still found time to engage in his favorite sport of horse-racing, and he fought a bloodless duel with Waightstill Avery, then the most famous lawyer in western North Carolina. All this makes it clear that the young man had set himself up in the world as a "gentleman." Frontiersmen normally fought with their fists rather than with pistols, and prided themselves more upon physical prowess, than upon manners. Though commonly looked upon as a typical Westerner, Jackson was ever an aristocrat at heart.

Jackson cemented his ties with the upper layers of society in more substantial ways. Turner had noted Jackson's practice as a "public prosecutor—an office that called for nerve and decision, rather than legal acumen." What frontier lawyering also called for, which Turner neglected to mention, was a knack for collecting debts, since Jackson most often represented creditors intent on recovering loans. During his first month of legal practice, he issued some seventy writs to delinquent debtors. This energetic career soon came to the notice of William Blount, who had by this time gotten himself appointed governor of the newly created Tennessee territory. He and Jackson became close political allies.

Jackson, too, had an eye for speculating, and it almost ruined him. Like Blount, he had cashed in on Tennessee's lands, buying 50,000 acres on the site of the future city of Memphis. In 1795 Jackson took his first ride to Philadelphia, a year before the one Turner eloquently described, in order to sell the Memphis land at a profit. Few Philadelphians wanted to buy, but Jackson finally closed a deal with David Allison, another of Blount's cronies. Allison couldn't pay in cash, so he gave Jackson promissory notes. Jackson, in turn, used the notes to pay for goods to stock a trading post he wanted to open in Tennessee.

Scant months after Jackson returned home, he learned that David Allison had gone bankrupt. Even worse, since Jackson had signed Allison's promissory notes, Allison's creditors were now after Jackson. "We take this early opportunity to make known to you that we have little or no expectations of getting paid from him," they wrote, "and that we shall have to get our money from you." This financial nightmare left Jackson "placed in the Dam'st situation ever a man was placed in," he admitted. To get himself out, he was forced to speculate even more. Buy a parcel of land here, sell it there. Cash in the trading post, make a small profit, invest it in more land, exchange the new land for another buyer's promissory note. And so on. Not until 1824 did he settle the final claims in the tangle. Clearly, Abernethy believed that Jackson's horseback rides on behalf of real estate deserved more emphasis than any romantic notions of a galloping frontier democrat.

Despite such a devastating attack on the frontier thesis, Abernethy's admiration for Turner was genuine, no doubt because he recognized how

Jackson the gentleman: Thomas Abernethy argued that the history of Jackson's Tennessee demonstrated how "the wealthy rose to the top of affairs even on the frontier, and combined through their influence and common interests to control economic legislation. From time to time they found it necessary to make some obvious concession to democracy, such as broadening the suffrage or lowering the qualifications for office. But, while throwing out such sops with one hand, they managed to keep well in the other the more obscure field of economic legislation." The aristocratic portrait of Jackson is by Thomas Sully.

much the thesis had guided his research. It is easy to conclude that the value of a theory rests solely on its truth. Yet even if Turner's hypothesis erred on many points, it provided a focus that prodded Abernethy to investigate important historical questions—the implications of western land policy, the effect of environment on character, the social and geographic foundations of democracy. All these topics had been slighted by historians.

Theory, in other words, is often as important for the questions it raises as for the answers it provides. In this sense it performs the same function in the natural sciences. Thomas Kuhn, a historian of science, has demonstrated how indispensable an older scientific theory is in pointing the way to the theory that replaces it. As the old theory is tested, attention naturally turns to problem areas—places where the results are not what the old theory predicts. The new theory emerges, Kuhn pointed out, "only for the man who, knowing with precision what he should expect, is able to recognize that something has gone wrong." Abernethy was able to discern that something had "gone wrong" in Tennessee politics, but only because Turner's hypothesis showed him what questions needed to be asked and where to look for answers.

JACKSON: LABORER'S FRIEND

Theory, then, can actually sharpen a historian's vision by limiting it—zeroing in on important issues and data. It stands to reason, however, that trade-offs are made in this game. If a theory focuses attention on certain questions, it necessarily also causes a historian to ignore other facts, trends, or themes. Theory can limit in a negative as well as a positive sense.

Abernethy's disagreement with Turner illustrates this problem. Although the two historians reached diametrically opposed conclusions about Jackson, they carried on the debate within the framework of Turner's thesis. Did Jackson embody the democratic, individualistic West? Yes, argued Turner. No, countered Abernethy. Yet both accepted the premise suggested by the thesis, that the influence of the West was crucial.

That conclusion might serve well enough for a study limited to Tennessee politics, but Jackson went on to achieve national fame by winning the Battle of New Orleans and was elected to the presidency in 1828. He triumphed in all the southern coastal states and in Pennsylvania, and he also received a majority of New York's electoral votes. In New York, too, he cemented an alliance with Martin Van Buren, the sophisticated eastern leader of the Albany Regency political faction.

Such facts call attention to something that Turner's frame of reference overlooked. As a national leader, Jackson made friends in the East as well as the West, in cities as well as in the country. Historian Arthur Schlesinger Jr., believing that both Abernethy and Turner overemphasized Jackson's western roots, determined to examine the eastern sources of Jackson's democratic coalition. The result was *The Age of Jackson* (1945), a sweeping study that highlighted the influence of eastern urban laboring classes on Jacksonian democracy.

In part, Schlesinger's theoretical approach was influenced by his upbringing. He spent his childhood within the civilized neighborhood of Cambridge, Massachusetts, where his father, Arthur Meier Schlesinger Sr., held a chair in history at Harvard. Unlike Frederick Jackson Turner, the senior Schlesinger emphasized the role of urban society and culture in American life. His article "The City in American History" sparked a generation of scholarship on peculiarly urban problems such as industrial labor and immigration. The article, Schlesinger later suggested generously, "did not seek to destroy the frontier theory but to substitute a balanced view: an appreciation of both country and city in the rise of American civilization." Nevertheless, Schlesinger Sr.'s interest clearly lay with the cities.

The younger Schlesinger admired his father and his work—so much so that at the age of fifteen he changed his name from Arthur Bancroft Schlesinger to Arthur Meier Schlesinger Jr. After schooling at the prestigious Phillips Exeter Academy, Arthur completed a brilliant undergraduate and graduate career at Harvard.* It was out of this intellectual training that Schlesinger wrote his book.

If the cities produced a democratic labor force solid for Andrew Jackson, why was "frontier democracy" so important?

The *Age of Jackson* also reflected a set of attitudes and emphases popular in the 1930s that distanced Schlesinger from the Progressive outlook Turner had shared at the turn of the century. The thirties saw the country plunged into a depression so severe that it shook many Americans' faith in the traditional economic system. Theories of class struggle, of conflict between capital and labor, became popular in scholarly circles. As an avid supporter of Franklin Roosevelt, Schlesinger by no means accepted the doctrines of the communist left, but he did believe that class conflict played a greater role in American history than the sectional disputes that Turner had emphasized.

Given Schlesinger's background, his research focused on substantially different aspects of Jackson's career. It portrayed Old Hickory as a natural leader who, though he came from the West, championed the cause of laborers in all walks of life—city "mechanicks" as well as yeoman farmers. Jackson's chief political task, argued Schlesinger, was "to control the power of the capitalist groups, mainly Eastern, for the benefit of the noncapitalist groups, farmers and laboring men, East, West, and South." Schlesinger made his opposition to Turner abundantly clear:

> The basic Jacksonian ideas came naturally enough from the East, which best understood the nature of business power and reacted most sharply against it. The legend that Jacksonian democracy was the explosion of the frontier, lifting into the government some violent men filled with rustic prejudices against big business does not explain the facts, which were somewhat more complex. Jacksonian democracy was rather a second American phase of that enduring struggle between the business community and the rest of society which is the guarantee of freedom in a liberal capitalist state.

Consequently, much of *The Age of Jackson* is devoted to people the Turner school neglected entirely: the leaders of workingmen's parties, the broader

---

*In fact, Schlesinger Sr. firmly believed in the virtues of public education. But he felt compelled to send Arthur Jr. to Exeter after discovering that his tenth-grade public school teacher taught that "the inhabitants of Albania were called Albinos because of their white hair and pink eyes."

Jackson, champion of the working people: "The legend that Jacksonian democracy was the explosion of the frontier, lifting into the government some violent men filled with rustic prejudices against big business does not explain the facts," wrote Arthur Schlesinger Jr. Here, the general public (dubbed "King Mob" by Jackson's genteel opponents) goes to work on a giant cheese at a White House celebration in 1837. The ordor of the cheese lingered for months.

labor movement, and the efforts of Democratic politicians to bring laborers within the orbit of Jackson's party. Abernethy's treatment of Jackson as land speculator is replaced by attention to Jackson's vigorous war on the Second Bank of the United States, where Democratic leaders are shown forging an alliance with labor. "During the Bank War," Schlesinger concluded, "laboring men began slowly to turn to Jackson as their leader, and his party as their party."

Like Turner, Schlesinger came under critical fire. Other historians have argued that much of Jackson's so-called labor support was actually middle- or even upper-class leaders who hoped to channel worker sentiments for their own purposes. At the same time, many in the real laboring classes refused to support Jackson. But again—what is important for our present purposes is to notice how Schlesinger's general concerns shaped his research. It is not coincidental that Jackson's celebrated kitchen cabinet, in Schlesinger's retelling, bears a marked resemblance to the "brain trusters" of Franklin Roosevelt's cabinet. It is not coincidental that Jackson attacks the "monster Bank" for wreaking economic havoc much the way that FDR inveighed against the "economic royalists" of the Depression era. Nor is it coincidental that *The Age of Jackson* was followed, in 1957, by *The Age of Roosevelt*. Schlesinger may have displayed his political and economic philosophy more conspicuously than most historians, but no scholar can escape bringing some theoretical framework to his or her research. One way or another, theory inevitably limits and focuses the historian's perspective.

JACKSON AND THE NEW WESTERN HISTORY

Perhaps precisely because Schlesinger does wear his political heart on his sleeve, we are forced to consider a notion that is potentially more troubling. The term *theory* implies that a historian, like some scientist in a lab, arrives at his or her propositions in a rigorous, logical way, setting aside the controversies of the present in order to study the past on its own terms. But in Schlesinger's case—like it or not—the events of his day clearly influenced his approach to Andrew Jackson. For that matter, Turner's original frontier thesis was a product of his times. It was the census of 1890, after all, that caught Turner's attention, with its declaration that the frontier was essentially closed. It was Turner's rural, midwestern upbringing that encouraged him to dissent from eastern-trained historians in his search for an explanation of democracy in America. Indeed, Turner would have been the first to recognize the pull of contemporary affairs. "Each age writes the history of the past anew with reference to the conditions uppermost in its own time," he commented in 1891.

The notion that historians' theories are tainted by a kind of presentism troubles many, including some historians. "The present-minded contend that in writing history no historian can free himself of his total experience," complained one scholar, who was clearly unhappy with the notion that others might think he could not help being swayed by contemporary "passions, prejudices, assumptions, prepossessions, events, crises and tensions." Surely he was right in believing that those who reconstruct the past should not do violence to it by making it over in the image of the present. Yet for better or for worse—perhaps we should say, for better and for worse—historical theories are shaped by the present in which they arise. There is no escaping current events—only, through careful self-discipline, the opportunity of using the perspectives of the present to broaden our understanding rather than lessen it. A case study of present-mindedness at work can be found among those historians who more recently have reexamined the field Turner championed. Their movement has come to be known as the "new western history."

The generation of historians spearheading the new western history came of age, by and large, during the social upheavals of the 1960s and 1970s, an era during which African Americans led a revolution for civil rights and equal treatment under the law. Other minorities, too, sought a greater voice in American society, whether they were Indians seeking tribal lands and tribal rights or Chicano migrant laborers organizing for fair working conditions. During these same years, feminists rallied to obtain equal treatment, and an environmental movement questioned the prevailing boom mentality in American life that equated all economic growth with progress. All these forces for change challenged traditional ways of thinking, and regardless of whether historians themselves became social activists, many were moved to reevaluate their perspectives on history. For historians of the West, the experiences of these decades were eye-opening in a host of different ways.

For historian Patricia Limerick, that seemingly innocuous phrase "free land" served as a big, flapping red flag.

Return for a moment to Turner's central proposition: "The existence of an area of free land, its continuous recession, and the advance of American settlement westward, explain American development." For historian Patricia Limerick, that seemingly innocuous phrase "free land" served as a big, flapping red flag. The ferment of the sixties and seventies made it much more evident that calling such land "free" loaded the dice. In framing a working hypothesis, historians glided over the inconvenient fact that the lands "were not vacant, but occupied," as Limerick pointed out, by Indians who used them either for hunting or for the cultivation of their own crops. "Redistributing those lands to the benefit of white farmers required the removal of Indian territorial claims and of the Indians themselves—a process that was never simple." The title of Limerick's book, *The Legacy of Conquest* (1987), framed the issue in blunt terms. Conquest was what made land "free," for the land had been taken either without permission or with only the most token of payments dispensed under dubious circumstances.

Consider another phrase plucked out of Turner's sentence: "the advance of American settlement westward." Turner tended to view the frontier as essentially one-dimensional. Americans—by which he meant Americans primarily of English heritage—moved westward across the "wilderness," evolving a new democratic society as they went. But the notion of wilderness was a theoretical construct that implicitly denied the existence of any significant borderland cultures other than Anglo-American. The new voices of the sixties and seventies—Indian, Latino, and African American—pushed historians to recognize that the frontiers of North America were both multicultural and multidirectional. Spanish settlers spread northward from Central America and the Caribbean into Florida, Texas, New Mexico, and California. Chinese and Japanese immigrants of the mid-nineteenth century moved from west to east as they crossed the Pacific to California. And for the various Indian tribes themselves, frontier lines were shifting in all directions during the unsettled centuries following European contact.

Turner showed little interest in the cultural mixing that went on in these regions, a defect the new western history sought to correct. "The invaded and subject peoples of the West must be given a voice in the region's history," argued Donald Worster in 1989. "Until very recently many western historians acted as though the West had either been empty of people prior to the coming of the white race or was quickly, if bloodily, cleared of them, once and for all, so that historians had only to deal with the white point of view." But Worster suggested that the "younger generation appearing in the 1970s and '80s" made the "new multicultural perspective their own." They replaced Turner's unidirectional frontier with a portrait of a West that "has been on the forward edge of one of modern history's most exciting endeavors, the creation, in the wake of European expansion and imperialism, of the world's first multi-racial, cosmopolitan societies." Newcomers to western cities often found as many—or more—foreign languages spoken there than as in New York, Paris, or Moscow.

Historians' attitudes toward Andrew Jackson could hardly be expected to remain untouched by these currents of change. Even before the new western history came into vogue, historians had begun reevaluating Jackson's career. For historian Michael Rogin, who wrote about Jackson during the tumultuous seventies, Old Hickory was the "embodiment" of the West for reasons entirely different from Turner's. Jackson embodied the West simply because he was instrumental in driving the Indians from their lands. "Historians have failed to place Indians at the center of Jackson's life," Rogin argued. "They have interpreted the Age of Jackson from every perspective but Indian destruction, the one from which it actually developed historically."

Robert Remini made a similar case in his biography of Jackson, the first volume of which appeared in 1977. Time after time, Jackson led efforts to force Indians to sign treaties ceding millions of acres. While he served as major general of the Tennessee militia and later as major general in the U.S. army, Jackson consistently exceeded his instructions on such matters. At the conclusion of his war against the Creek Indians, the remnants of the Creek Red Stick faction (whom Jackson had been fighting) retreated to Florida in hopes of continuing their war. Since the general could not compel his enemies to cede land, he turned around and demanded 23 million acres from his Indian allies, signing the treaty instead with them! Fearing that the government might revoke such a brazen action, he called for the new boundary lines to be run and land sold to settlers as quickly as possible. "The sooner this country is brought in the market the better," he advised President-Elect James Monroe, on yet another occasion. Over the years, Jackson's negotiations led to the acquisition by the United States of Indian lands amounting to one-third of Tennessee, three-quarters of Alabama and Florida, one-fifth of Georgia and Mississippi, and one-tenth of Kentucky and North Carolina.

Of course, Jackson's involvement in land acquisition did not end with his military career. As president, he championed the movement to force the remaining 125,000 Indians east of the Mississippi onto much less valuable lands west of the river, freeing up additional millions of prime acres in the midst of the booming cotton kingdom. At the president's urging, Congress set the policy of Indian removal into motion in 1830. "In terms of acquisition," commented Remini, "it is not too farfetched to say that the physical shape of the United States today looks pretty much like it does largely because of the intentions and efforts of Andrew Jackson."

Perhaps ironically, none of the new western historians has yet stepped forward to recast Jackson in light of recent scholarship. In part, the lack of attention arises because many younger scholars have preferred to focus on the trans-Mississippi West, well beyond the territory Andrew Jackson roamed. Yet there is more at work here than a different geographic focus. In many ways, the questions posed by the new western historians cannot be answered by making Jackson the center of attention. Focusing on the actions of the Anglo conquerors like Jackson tells us little about the intermixture of cultures that arose before removal began, during an era when both whites and Indians held significant power along the frontier.

By adopting the metaphor of a "middle ground," Richard White proposed a situation in which "whites could neither dictate to Indians nor ignore them."

One of the new western historians, Richard White, examined the frontier of the seventeenth and eighteenth century along the Great Lakes in a book suggestively titled *The Middle Ground*. White argued that older discussions of the frontier portrayed the contrasting cultures as essentially and always in opposition. In contrast, White preferred to highlight a process of accommodation at work. By adopting the metaphor of a "middle ground," he highlighted a situation in which "whites could neither dictate to Indians nor ignore them. Whites needed Indians as allies, as partners in exchange, as sexual partners, as friendly neighbors." Only with the passing of this frontier did the middle ground break down, accompanied by a hardening of attitudes among whites, a "re-creation of the Indians as alien, as exotic, as other."

From this perspective, Jackson and his policies of Indian removal seem only the depressing endgame of what is the more interesting and neglected territory of the middle ground. Indeed, the Old Southwest from about 1780 to 1820—the middle ground Jackson traveled—was a region rich in cultural accommodation. For two hundred years the land had witnessed a remarkable intermingling of Indian, French, Spanish, and English cultures. From its base in Florida, Spain actively courted trade with Indians, many of whom had intermarried with whites. The trader Alexander McGillivray, for example, was not the white European his name conjures up, but an influential Indian leader of the Creeks who concluded a treaty of alliance between his people and the Spanish in 1784. His parentage reflected the mixed heritage of the middle ground: a mother of French-Creek descent and a father who was a Scots trader.

Adding to the regional mixture of the Old Southwest were African Americans. White traders who intermarried with Indians were the first among the Cherokees, Creeks, and other tribes to clear cotton plantations and use slaves to work them. Often these slaves were runaways whose skills the Indians drew upon in their attempt to emulate white plantation owners. African Americans knew how to spin and weave, shoe horses, and repair guns. Often they served as translators. Ironically, as a minority of Cherokees adopted a frame of government similar to the U.S. Constitution, they also set up slave codes similar to those in the white antebellum South.

This Chickasaw Indian girl's elegant hair and fashionable dress suggest the complexity of cultural relations in the middle ground of the Old Southwestern frontier in Andrew Jackson's time. The girl was among the thousands of Indians removed to territory west of the Mississippi.

Seminole Indians also held slaves, although they gave more autonomy to these "black Seminoles," as the slaves were known. When runaways fled Spanish or American plantations for Seminole lands, the Seminoles allowed the newcomers to live in separate villages, often far from their Indian owners. In return for being allowed to raise crops, black Seminoles paid a portion of the harvest to their masters—in effect, sharecropping. If, as Donald Worster suggested, the lure of the new western history involved tracing a process of multiracial, multicultural mixing along the frontier, topics such as the middle ground held a greater attraction than did rehashing the traditional stories of Andrew Jackson as Indian fighter.

After such a procession of grand historical theories, what may be said of the "real" Andrew Jackson? Skeptics may be tempted to conclude that there was not one but four Old Hickories roaming the landscape of Jacksonian

America: Jackson the frontier democrat; Jackson the aristocratic planter and speculator; Jackson, friend of labor; and Jackson, taker of Indian lands. The use of historical theory seems to have led the reader into a kind of boggy historical relativism where there is no real Jackson, only men conjured up to fit the formulas of particular historical theories or the fashionable currents of the day.

But that viewpoint is overly pessimistic. It arises from the necessary emphasis of this chapter, where our concern has been to point out the general effects of grand theory rather than to evaluate the merits of each case. Theory, we have stressed, provides a vantage point that directs a researcher's attention to significant areas of inquiry. But the initial theorizing is only the beginning. Theories can be and are continually tested. Sometimes old theories are thrown out, replaced by new ones. In such fashion did Copernicus replace Ptolemy. On the other hand, some theories stand up to testing or are merely refined to fit the facts more closely. In yet other instances, old theories are incorporated into more encompassing frameworks. Newtonian mechanics are still as valid as ever for the everyday world, but they have been found to be only a special case of the broader theories of relativity proposed by Einstein.

Historical theory will probably never attain the precision of its counterparts among the natural sciences. In part, such precision remains beyond our reach because historical narrative seeks to account for specific, unique chains of events—events that can never be replicated in the way scientists replicate experiments in the lab. The complexity of the task will no doubt ensure that our explanations will remain subject, for better and for worse, to contemporary concerns. Of all people, historians should be the first to acknowledge that they are shaped by the currents of their own times.

But that does not mean historians must give up on the possibility of describing and explaining an objective reality. In the present example, we may argue that far from having four different Jacksons roaming the historical landscape, we are seeing various aspects of Jackson's personality and career that need to be incorporated into a more comprehensive framework. It is the old tale of the blind men describing the different parts of an elephant: the elephant is real enough, but the descriptions are partial and fragmentary. Frederick Jackson Turner was writing about a nebulous Jacksonian style. Indeed, one may as well come out with it—"democracy" and "individualism" were, for Turner, little more than styles. Abernethy, on the other hand, focusing on the material interests and class alliances that Jackson developed during his Tennessee career, paid almost no attention to the presidential years. Schlesinger did precisely the opposite: he picked up Jackson's story only after 1824 and in the end was more concerned with the Jacksonian movement than with its nominal leader. The historians who came of age in the 1960s and 1970s have replaced Turner's imaginary frontier line with a contested cultural space whose middle grounds are populated with a Jacksonian "common people" more multiracial and diverse than Turner was ever able to conceive.

A unified field theory for Jacksonian America? Perhaps the outlines are there, but the task of deciding must be left to some future Turner of the discipline. What remains clear is that though particular theories continue to be revised or rejected, theory itself will accompany historians always. Without it, researchers cannot begin to select from among an infinite number of facts; they cannot separate the important from the incidental; they cannot focus on a manageable problem. Albert Einstein put the proposition succinctly. "It is the theory," he concluded, "which decides what we can observe."

Additional Reading

Frederick Jackson Turner's key essays are reprinted in *The Frontier in American History* (New York, 1920). He also wrote *The Rise of the New West* (New York, 1906). The best accounts of Turner's life and work are by Ray Billington, the last major Turnerian; see *Frederick Jackson Turner: Historian, Scholar, Teacher* (New York, 1973) and *The Genesis of the Frontier Thesis* (San Marino, CA, 1971). A contrasting view may be found in Richard Hofstadter, *The Progressive Historians: Turner, Beard, Parrington* (New York, 1968). In addition to Thomas Abernethy's *From Frontier to Plantation in Tennessee* (Chapel Hill, NC, 1932), see his brief biography of Jackson in the *Dictionary of American Biography*. Arthur Schlesinger Jr.'s *Age of Jackson* (Boston, 1945) generated much discussion among historians, discussion that is summarized well in the bibliographical essay of Edward Pessen, *Jacksonian America: Society, Personality, and Politics*, Rev. ed. (Homewood, IL, 1978). For a balanced portrait of Jackson's place in the political landscape, see Harry L. Watson, *Liberty and Power* (New York, 1990).

The views of the new western history are expounded in Patricia Limerick, *The Legacy of Conquest: The Unbroken Past of the American West* (New York, 1987); Donald Worster, *Under Western Skies: Nature and History in the American West* (New York, 1992); and William Cronon, George Miles, and Jay Gitlin, eds., *Under an Open Sky: Rethinking America's Western Past* (New York, 1992). Richard White's *The Middle Ground: Indians, Empires, and the Republics in the Great Lakes Region, 1650–1815* (New York, 1991) provides one of the best models of the new approaches. Finally, to understand the role of theory in both science and history, readers will profit from Thomas Kuhn, *The Structure of Scientific Revolutions*, Rev. ed. (Chicago, 1970).

CHAPTER 7
The Madness of John Brown

Was John Brown a heroic martyr—a white man in a racist society willing to lay down his life on behalf of slaves? Or was he a madman whose taste for wanton violence propelled the nation toward avoidable tragedy?

Now that the trial was over, Virginia's governor, Henry Wise, worried what he would do about John Brown. A state court had recently convicted Brown of treason, murder, and inciting a slave insurrection, after he led an attack on Harpers Ferry and its federal arsenal. Now held captive in the Charles Town jail, Brown faced death by hanging. In the early weeks of November 1859, mail poured into Wise's office. Some abolitionists swore they had gathered armies to liberate the great abolitionist. Proslavery writers threatened to lynch the man who had invaded Virginia with a plan to trigger a slave insurrection. Like many southerners, Wise worried that Brown was just the first of many abolitionist fanatics prepared to wage war against the South and the institution of slavery. He had warned Virginians to take up arms to defend their state.

Yet among the thousands of correspondents, many northerners condemned Brown for his violence and dismissed him as an aberration. Fernando Wood, mayor of New York City, urged Wise to grant clemency lest Brown become a martyr whose execution would deepen passions over the issue of slavery. Other writers appealed to Wise to show mercy. Among them were a considerable number who argued that Brown was simply insane. Wise placed the letters he received into one of two piles: *Governor Wise recognized that to declare Brown insane promised certain political advantages.* "Consider" and "Contemptible Nonsense." The insanity letters went into the "Consider" pile. Wise recognized that to declare Brown insane promised certain political advantages. Rather than stand as a hero or a martyr, Brown would become an object for pity or even scorn.

Certainly the sheer folly of what Brown attempted at Harpers Ferry gave people reason to question his sanity. For some two months his band of twenty-one men had hidden in a farmhouse outside the town. They were idealists, bound together during the tedious waiting by their faith in Brown and a common hatred of slavery. The group comprised five blacks and sixteen whites, including three of Brown's sons, Owen, Oliver, and Watson. Only on the eve of the raid had their leader revealed to them his final plan. For years Brown had nurtured the idea of striking a blow against slavery. He planned to move into Harpers Ferry to capture the town and its federal arsenal. As his men gathered arms, slaves would pour in from the surrounding countryside to join their army. Before the local militia had time to organize, Brown's forces would escape to the nearby hills. From there, they would fight a guerilla war until the curse of slavery had been exorcised and all slaves freed from bondage.

An autumn chill filled the air and a light rain fell as the war party made its way down the dark road toward Harpers Ferry. Three men had remained behind to handle supplies and arm slaves who took up the fight. A sleepy stillness covered the small town nestled in the hills where the Shenandoah joined the Potomac, sixty miles from Washington, D.C. It was a region of small farms and relatively few slaves. Most likely, the presence of the arsenal and an armory explains why Brown chose to begin his campaign there.

The attack began without a hitch. Two raiders cut telegraph lines running east and west from the town. The others seized a rifle works, the armory, and hostages, including Lewis Washington, the first president's grandson. Along with Washington's slaves, the raiders appropriated a ceremonial sword given to George Washington by Frederick the Great of Prussia. For Brown, a black man brandishing this sword would become a potent symbol of his crusade for liberation and racial equality. Soon the sounds of gunfire drew the townspeople from their beds. Amid the confusion, the church bell pealed the alarm dreaded by whites throughout the South—slave insurrection! By late morning the hastily joined militia and armed farmers had trapped Brown and his men in the engine house of the Baltimore and Ohio Railroad. One of Brown's sons had been killed, and another lay dying at his father's side. Drunken crowds thronged the streets, crying for blood and revenge. When news of the raid reached Washington, President Buchanan dispatched federal troops under Colonel Robert E. Lee to put down the insurrection.

Thirty-six hours after the first shot, John Brown's war on slavery ended. By any calculation the raid had been a total failure. Not a single slave had risen to join Brown's army. Ten of the raiders lay dead or dying; the rest had been scattered or captured. Although wounded, Brown had miraculously escaped death. The commander of the assault force had mistakenly put on his dress sword, which bent double when he struck Brown, leaving painful but insubstantial wounds. Seven other people had been killed and nine more wounded during the raid.

Most historians would agree that the Harpers Ferry raid was to the Civil War what the Boston Massacre had been to the American Revolution: an incendiary event. In an atmosphere of aroused passions, profound suspicions, and irreconcilable differences between abolitionist and proslavery factions,

John Brown, man of action: After leading the Pottawatomie Massacre in Kansas in 1856, Brown grew a beard to disguise his appearance. His eastern abolitionist backers were impressed with the aura he radiated as a western man of action. The image was not hurt by the fact that Brown carried a bowie knife in his boot and regularly barricaded himself nights in his hotel rooms as a precaution against proslavery agents.

Brown and his men put a match to the fuse. Once they did their deed and shed blood, there seemed to be no drawing back for either North or South. The shouts of angry men overwhelmed the voices of compromise. Across the North, defenders of national union and of law and order generally condemned Brown and his violent tactics. Such northern political leaders as Abraham Lincoln, Stephen Douglas, and William Seward spoke out against him. The Republican Party in 1860 went so far as to adopt a platform censuring the Harpers Ferry raid. At the same time, a group of transcendental philosophers cast Brown in a noble light. His dignity during his trial and the force of his convictions inspired Henry David Thoreau to defend him as a heroic man of action. Ralph Waldo Emerson pronounced the raider a "saint . . . whose martyrdom, if it shall be perfected, will make the gallows as glorious as the cross." Newspaper editor Horace Greeley called the raid "the work of a madman," for which he had nothing but the highest admiration.

Moderate northern voices were lost, however, on southern fire-eaters, to whom all abolitionists and Republicans were potential John Browns. Across the South angry mobs attacked northerners, regardless of their views on the slave question. Everywhere the specter of slave insurrection fed fears, and the uproar strengthened the hand of secessionists, who argued that the South's salvation lay in expunging all traces of northern influence.

THE MOTIVES OF A FANATIC

And what was Governor Wise to make of the man who triggered all those passions? Had John Brown foreseen that his quixotic crusade would reap such a whirlwind of violence? On that issue both his contemporaries and historians have been sharply divided. Brown himself left a confusing and often contradictory record of his objectives. To his men, and to Frederick Douglass, the former slave and black abolitionist, Brown made clear he intended nothing less than to provoke a general slave insurrection. His preparations all pointed to that goal. He went to Harpers Ferry armed for such a task, and the choice of the armory as the raid's target left little doubt he intended to equip a slave army. But throughout the months of preparation, Brown had consistently warned the coconspirators financing his scheme that the raid might fail. In that event, he told them, he still hoped the gesture would so divide the nation that a sectional crisis would ensue, leading to the destruction of slavery.

From his jail cell and at his trial, Brown offered a decidedly contradictory explanation. Ignoring the weapons he had accumulated, he suggested that the raid was intended as an extension of the Underground Railroad work he had previously done. He repeatedly denied any intention to commit violence or instigate a slave rebellion. "I claim to be here in carrying out a measure I believe perfectly justifiable," he told a skeptical newspaper reporter, "and not to act the part of an incendiary or ruffian, but to aid those [slaves] suffering great wrong." To Congressman Clement Vallandigham of Ohio, who asked Brown if he expected a slave uprising, the old man replied, "No sir; nor did I wish it. I expected to gather them up from time to time and set them free." In court, with his life hanging in the balance, Brown once again denied any violent intent. He sought only to expand his campaign for the liberation of slaves.

Brown's contradictory testimony has provoked much speculation over the man and his motives. Was he being quite rational and calculating in abruptly changing his story after capture? Certainly Brown knew how much his martyrdom would enhance the abolitionist movement. His execution, he wrote his wife, would "do vastly more toward advancing the cause I have earnestly endeavored to promote, than all I have done in my life before." On the other hand, perhaps Brown was so imbued with his own

John Brown, the impractical idealist: "The old idiot—the quicker they hang him and get him out of the way, the better." So wrote the editor of a Chicago paper to Abraham Lincoln. Many contemporaries shared the view of the cartoon reprinted here, that Brown was a foolish dreamer. Yet Brown had other ideas. "I think you are fanatical!" exclaimed one southern bystander after Brown had been captured. "And I think you are fanatical," Brown retorted. "'Whom the Gods would destroy they first made mad,' and you are mad."

righteousness that he deceived himself into believing he had not acted the part of "incendiary or ruffian" but only meant to aid those slaves "suffering great wrong." "Poor old man!" commented Republican presidential hopeful Salmon Chase. "How sadly misled by his own imaginations!"

Yet for every American who saw Brown as either a calculating insurrectionist or a genuine, if self-deluded, martyr, there were those who thought him insane. How else could they explain the hopeless assault of eighteen men against a federal arsenal and the state of Virginia—where slaves were "not abundant" and where "no Abolitionists were ever known to peep"? Who but a "madman" (to quote Greeley) could have concocted, much less attempted, such a wild scheme?

Nor was the issue of John Brown's sanity laid to rest by his execution on December 2, 1859. Brown had become a symbol, for both North and South, of the dimensions of the sectional struggle. Inevitably, the question of personal motivation becomes bound up in historians' interpretations of the root causes of sectional and social conflict. Was Brown a heroic martyr—a white man in a racist society with the courage to lay down his life on behalf of his black brothers and the principles of the Declaration of Independence? Or was he an emotionally unbalanced fanatic whose taste for wanton violence propelled the nation toward avoidable tragedy?

During the middle years of the twentieth century, the view of Brown as an emotional fanatic gained ground. John Garraty, in a popular college survey text, described Brown as so "deranged" that rather than hang him for his "dreadful act . . . It would have been far wiser and more just to have committed him to an asylum." Allen Nevins defined a middle ground when he argued that on all questions except slavery, Brown could act coherently and rationally. "But on this special question of the readiness of slavery to crumble at a blow," Nevins thought, "his monomania . . . or his paranoia as a modern alienist [psychoanalyst] would define it, rendered him irresponsible."

> *For every American who saw Brown as a genuine, if self-deluded, martyr, there were those who thought him insane.*

In 1970 Brown biographer Stephen Oates agreed that in many ways his subject was not "normal." Yet Oates rejected the idea that insanity could either be adequately demonstrated or used in any substantive way to explain Brown's actions. That Brown had an "excitable temperament" and a single-minded obsession with slavery Oates conceded. He concluded, too, that Brown was egotistical, an overbearing father, an often-inept man worn down by disease and suffering, and a revolutionary who believed himself called to his mission by God.

But having said that, Oates argued that before dismissing Brown as insane, historians must consider the context of Brown's actions. To call him insane, Oates argued, "is to ignore the tremendous sympathy he felt for the black man in America." And, he added, "to label him a 'maniac' out of touch with 'reality' is to ignore the piercing insight he had into what his raid—whether it succeeded or whether it failed—would do to sectional tensions." More recently David Reynolds, like Oates, argued persuasively that Brown was sane. Reynolds viewed the "monomania" some associated with insanity as a "burning desire to topple slavery in the name of God and American democracy." What made Brown different was not his vehemence about slavery—most abolitionists shared that passion. But they were almost all racists, whereas Brown believed in the absolute equality of the races. In the 1850s, even abolitionists thought that idea was mad.

Given such conflicting views on the question of John Brown's sanity, it makes sense to examine more closely the evidence of his mental state. As a last-minute stratagem, Lawson Botts, Brown's attorney, submitted nineteen affidavits from Brown's friends and acquaintances, purporting to demonstrate Brown's mental instability. This evidence would seem the most obvious place to start our inquiry.

John Brown, martyr of freedom:

John Brown of Ossawatomie, they led him out to die;

And lo! a poor slave-mother with her little child pressed nigh,

Then the bold, blue eye grew tender, and the harsh face grew mild,

And he stooped between the jeering ranks and kissed the Negro's child!

John Greenleaf Whittier based this incident in his poem "Brown of Ossawatomie" (December 1859), on an erroneous newspaper report. Apparently Brown did kiss the child of a white jailor he had befriended. Brown also remarked to the same jailer that "he would prefer to be surrounded in his last moments by a poor weeping slave mother with her children," noting that this "would make the picture at the gallows complete."

Two major themes appear in those affidavits. First, a number of people testified to a pronounced pattern of insanity in the Brown family, particularly on his mother's side. In addition to his maternal grandmother and numerous uncles, aunts, and cousins, Brown's sister, his brother Salmon, his first wife,

John Brown, the terrorist: Mahala Doyle, the wife of James P. Doyle, one of the men Brown killed at Pottawatomie, testified of Brown, "He said if a man stood between him and what he considered right, he would take his life as cooly as he would eat his breakfast. His actions show what he is. Always restless, he seems never to sleep. With an eye like a snake, he looks like a demon."

Dianthe, and his sons Frederick and John Jr. were all said to have shown evidence of mental disorders. Second, some respondents described certain patterns of instability they saw in Brown himself. Almost everyone agreed he was profoundly religious and that he became agitated over the slavery question. A few traced Brown's insanity back through his years of repeated business failures. The "wild and desperate" nature of those business schemes and the rigidity with which he pursued them persuaded several friends of his "unsound" mind and "monomania."

Many old acquaintances thought that Brown's controversial experiences in Kansas had unhinged the man. There, in May 1856, proslavery forces had attacked the antislavery town of Lawrence. In retaliation, Brown led a band of seven men (including four of his sons) in a midnight raid on some proslavery settlers at Pottawatomie Creek. Although the Pottawatomie residents had taken no part in the Lawrence attack, Brown's men, under his orders, took their broadswords and hacked five of them to death. "Pottawatomie" Brown, as many people called him after that night of horror, became a figure both vilified for his violence and venerated for his courageous stand against murderous proslave forces. But for Brown, Kansas was only a prelude to his grander scheme to destroy slavery in the South.

Many old acquaintances thought that Brown's controversial experiences in Kansas had unhinged the man.

A number of acquaintances testified in 1859 that from the time of the Pottawatomie killings onward, Brown had been mentally deranged. E. N. Sill, an acquaintance of both Brown and his father, admitted that he had once had considerable sympathy for Brown's plan to defend antislavery families in Kansas. "But from his peculiarities," Sill recalled, "I thought Brown an unsafe man to be commissioned with such a matter." It was Sill who suggested the idea, which Allen Nevins later adopted, that on the slavery question alone Brown was insane. "I have no confidence in his judgment in matters appertaining to slavery," he asserted. "I have no doubt that, upon this subject . . . he is surely as monomaniac as any inmate in any lunatic asylum in the country." David King, who talked to Brown after his Kansas experience, observed that "on the subject of slavery he was crazy" and that Brown saw himself as "an instrument in the hands of God to free slaves."

Such testimony seems to support the view that Harpers Ferry was the outcome of insanity. Yet even then, and ever since, many people have rejected that conclusion. Confronted with the affidavits, Governor Wise thought to have Brown examined by the head of the state's insane asylums. Upon reflection he changed his mind. Wise believed Brown perfectly sane and had even come to admire begrudgingly the old man's "indomitable" spirit. The governor once described Brown as "the gamest man I ever saw," and for him that settled the sanity question. "He is," Wise concluded, "a man of clear head, of courage, fortitude and simple ingenuousness." That did not prevent the governor from viewing Brown and his band as "wanton, malicious, unprovoked felons" deserving of the gallows.

For what it is worth, Brown himself rejected any intimation that he was anything but sane. He admitted the presence of insanity in his family but dismissed the issue as "a miserable artifice and pretext." Insane people, he asserted, "have but little ability to judge of their own sanity." As for himself, he was "perfectly unconscious of insanity" and therefore refused "any attempt to intervene in my behalf on that score." For him, the matter was both moral and spiritual. Slavery constituted an unethical and unconstitutional assault of one class of citizens against another. Under that assault, acts that society deemed unlawful—dishonesty, murder, theft, or treason—could be justified in the name of a higher morality.

Historians have ample reason to doubt the reliability of the Botts evidence. Among those signing the affidavits were friends and relatives who hoped Governor Wise would spare Brown's life. Might they not have exaggerated the instances of mental disorders in his family to make their case more convincing? Most had not taken Brown's fanaticism seriously until his raid on Harpers Ferry. Just as important, none of them had any medical training or experience that would qualify them to determine with any expertise whether Brown or any member of his family could be judged insane. Only one affidavit came from a doctor, and like most physicians of the day, he had no particular competence in psychological observation. The "preponderance" of insanity in Brown's family could have been nothing more than a series of unrelated disorders.

As Governor Wise understood, the question of Brown's sanity was as much a political and legal issue as a medical issue. Moderates from both North and South, seeking to preserve the Union, hoped to soften the divisive impact of Harpers Ferry. If Brown was ruled insane, people would view him as an aberration rather than the martyr some northerners applauded or the precursor of abolitionist attacks that southern slaveholders feared. Their argument that the South would be safe only outside the Union would have far less force. Even antislavery Republicans tried to dissociate themselves from Brown's more radical tactics. During the 1859 congressional elections, the Democrats tried to persuade voters that Harpers Ferry resulted inevitably from the Republicans' appeal to the doctrine of "irresistible conflict" and "higher law" abolitionism. To blunt such attacks, leading Republicans regularly attributed the raid to Brown's insanity.

Clearly the affidavits provide no convincing basis for judging the condition of Brown's mental health. But some historians have argued that the larger pattern of Brown's life demonstrated his imbalance. Indeed, even the most generous biographers must admit that Brown botched miserably much that he attempted to do. In the years before moving to Kansas, Brown had tried his hand at tanning, sheepherding, surveying, cattle driving, and wool merchandising—all with unfortunate financial results. By 1852 he had suffered fifteen business failures in four different states. Creditors were continually hounding him. "Over the years before his Kansas escapade," John Garraty concluded, "Brown had been a drifter, horse thief and swindler, several times a bankrupt, a failure in everything he attempted."

But this evidence, too, must be considered with circumspection. During the period Brown applied himself in business, the American economy went through repeated cycles of boom and bust. Many hardworking entrepreneurs lost their shirts in business despite their best efforts. Brown's failures over the years may only suggest that he did not have an aptitude for business. His schemes were usually ill-conceived, and he was too inflexible to adapt to the rapidly changing business climate. But to show that Brown was a poor businessman and that much of his life he made foolish decisions hardly proves him insane. Under those terms, much of the adult population in the United States would belong in asylums.

Insanity has been widely used as a defense in criminal cases. By demonstrating that at the time of the crime a client could not distinguish right from wrong or was incapable of determining the nature of the act committed, a lawyer can protect the accused from some of the legal consequences of the act. To find Brown insane, as attorney Botts asked the court, would have been to assert Brown's inability to understand the consequences of his actions at Harpers Ferry. The court, much like Governor Wise, determined that in the legal sense, Brown was fit to stand trial. He may have been unrealistic in estimating his chance of success at Harpers Ferry, but he repeatedly demonstrated that he knew the consequences of his actions: that he would be arrested and punished if caught; that large portions of American society would condemn him; that, nevertheless, he believed himself in the right. In the legal sense, Brown was quite sane and clearheaded about his actions. Indeed the passion and power of his words in the courtroom won him admirers across the North.

MADNESS OR GENIUS?

Yet the court's judgment, accurate as it may have been, leaves us uneasy. To have Brown pronounced sane or insane, in addition to guilty or not guilty, does little to explain, deep down, why the man acted as he did. What drove John Brown to crusade against slavery? To execute in cold blood five men along a Kansas creek? To lead twenty-one men to Harpers Ferry? To fail to escape before the militia trapped him? Many abolitionists, though they abhorred the institution of slavery, were pacifists who rejected violence. John Brown was one of the few who acted with such vehemence. In that sense he was far from being a normal American—far, even, from being a normal abolitionist. How can we begin to understand the intensity of his convictions?

Here we approach the limits of explanations based on rational motives. To describe John Brown simply by referring to his professed and undoubtedly sincere antislavery ideology is to leave unexplored the fire in the man. Such an approach assumes too easily that consciously expressed motives can be taken at face value. Yet we have already seen, in the case of the bewitched at Salem, that unconscious motivations often play important roles in human behavior. If we are willing to grant that apparently "normal" people sometimes act for reasons beyond those they consciously express, how much more likely is it that we must go beyond rational motives in understanding Brown? It seems only logical that historians should bring to bear the tools of modern psychology to assess the man's personality.

Indeed, a subbranch of history has applied such methods to a wide variety of historical problems. Known as psychohistory, this approach at first drew on the discipline of psychoanalysis pioneered by Sigmund Freud, an Austrian physician who propounded his theories during the early twentieth century. Psychoanalysts and the historians who followed them located states of mind in their subjects' life experiences and the circumstances that shaped them. They ignored the extent to which mental disorders are biologically rooted and inheritable. As psychologist Kenneth Carroll put it, mental health experts now generally agree, "experience plays a far smaller role in the development of major mental illness than does biology."

"Experience plays a far smaller role in the development of major mental illness than does biology."

Although John Brown never underwent a psychological examination, sufficient evidence exists to provide us, as it happens, with the means of conducting one ourselves. In that light, the affidavits take on a new significance. Rather than wonder if they reveal a pattern of insanity, we can ask if they reveal patterns of behavior that reflect a clinically recognized mental disorder. Psychiatrists and psychologists have codified their rules for evaluating behavior in what is known as the *Diagnostic and Statistical Manual of Mental Disorders* (4th ed.), commonly known as the DSM-IV. The DSM-IV provides a means to distinguish between behaviors that are normal and those that are symptoms of a mental illness.

Here *illness* is a critical term, because it denotes a medical condition. In that sense, psychologists recognize that what they deem as pathological behaviors are symptoms of a disease. They do not base their diagnoses on personal interpretation or belief. Through research, clinical experience, and observations, they have reached a consensus that certain symptoms are associated with widely recognized mental disorders. The DSM-IV reflects that consensus. Unlike psychoanalysis, with its complex theories of personality, the medical model does not seek to explain why pathological symptoms exist; it only asks whether they do exist.

Psychologist Kenneth Carroll undertook just such an examination of the affidavits. While Carroll recognized the presence of bias and subjectivity among those testifying to Brown's insanity, he discovered a consistent pattern in their observations. First, they identified the widespread mental disorders among Brown's immediate family and relatives. Carroll understood that the presence of those disorders in no way indicated that Brown, himself, suffered from them. All the same, it does make it more likely that commonly recurring symptoms over the course of his life did in fact indicate a mental disorder.

Almost all the affidavits describe a man subject to mood swings, easily excited on more issues than slavery, persuaded of the rightness and rectitude of his own opinions, inflexible, and given to unrealistic expectations. His brother-in-law, Milton Lusk, for example, described Brown as "disposed to enter on wild and desperate projects and adventures, and incapable of deliberation or reasoning." His cousin, Gideon Mills, suggested Brown had been "subject to periods of insanity especially when from any cause his mind has been fixed for any length of time on any subject." George Leach, a lifelong friend who first met Brown as a young boy, commented that on "any subject and from any cause his mind was brought to dwell upon," Brown became "greatly excited" and "liable to attacks of mania." Another friend reported that "on the subject of slavery he [Brown] was crazy—he was armed to the teeth and remarked among other things that he was 'an instrument in the hands of God to free the slaves.'"

Had these various people exaggerated their impressions in order to persuade the court of Brown's unfitness to stand trial? Carroll thought not. None of those who signed affidavits mentioned bizarre behaviors, mad episodes, or lunacy to embellish their impressions. Indeed, Carroll found reference to no symptoms that contradict accepted psychological diagnosis. Further, the affidavits offer no evidence that Brown suffered from any mental retardation, dementia, hallucinations, or thought disorders. Carroll thus concluded that Brown was not schizophrenic, nor did he manifest the compulsive and repetitive behaviors associated with obsessive-compulsives. Several affiants did use the term "mania," and that is the diagnosis Carroll chose. Brown was manic or manic-depressive, hence suffering from what psychologists call a bipolar disorder.

The DSM-IV provides useful criteria for judging this condition, among them:

A. A distinct period of abnormality and abnormally elevated, expansive, or elevated mood, lasting at least one week.

B. During the period of mood disturbance three (or more) of the following symptoms . . . have been present to a significant degree:

1. inflated self-esteem or grandiosity
2. decreased need for sleep
3. more talkative than usual, or pressure to keep talking
4. flight of ideas or subjective experience that thoughts are racing
5. distractibility (i.e., attention too often drawn to unimportant or irrelevant external stimuli)
6. increase in goal-directed activities . . . or psychomotor agitation
7. excessive involvement in pleasurable activities that have a high potential for painful consequences (e.g., engaging in unrestrained buying sprees, sexual indiscretions, or foolish investments)

From what we know so far of Brown, most, if not all, of these symptoms were evident in his behavior. His many business failures, his refusal to consider advice from friends who challenged his plans, his deep sense of a God-ordained mission, and his ability to go for long periods without much sleep are all elements of a manic personality.

Often, too, are bouts of depression, and we have available a remarkable document to explore in order to learn if Brown did experience intermittent depressive moods. Better yet, unlike the affidavits that express the views of others, this document comes from Brown's own hand. At the age of fifty-seven, he wrote a long letter to a thirteen-year-old boy named Harry Stearns. Harry was the son of one of Brown's wealthiest financial patrons. In the letter, Brown told the story of "a certain boy of my acquaintance" who, "for convenience," he called John. This name was especially convenient, because the boy was none other than Brown himself. The letter is one of the few surviving sources of information about Brown's childhood. It is reprinted here with only a few omissions of routine biographical data.

I can not tell you of anything in the first Four years of John's life worth mentioning save that at that *early age* he was tempted by Three large Brass Pins belonging to a girl who lived in the family & *stole them*. In this he was detected by his Mother; & after having a full day to think of the wrong; received from her a thorough whipping. When he was Five years old his Father moved to Ohio; then a wilderness filled with wild beasts, & Indians. During the long journey, which was performed in part or mostly with an *ox-team*; he was called on by turns to assist a boy Five years older (who had been adopted by his

Father & Mother) & learned to think he could accomplish *smart things* by driving the Cows; & riding the horses. Sometimes he met with Rattle Snakes which were very large; & which some of the company generally managed to kill. After getting to Ohio in 1805 he was for some time rather afraid of the Indians, & of their Rifles; but this soon wore off: & he used to hang about them quite as much as was consistent with good manners; & learned a trifle of their talk. His father learned to dress Deer Skins, & at 6 years old John was installed a young Buck Skin. He was perhaps rather observing as he ever after remembered the entire process of Deer Skin *dressing;* so that he could at any time dress his own leather such as Squirel, Raccoon, Cat, Wolf and Dog Skins, and also learned to make Whip Lashes, which brought him some change at times, & was of considerable service in many ways. At Six years old he began to be a rambler in the wild new country finding birds and squirrels and sometimes a wild Turkey's nest. But about this period he was placed in the school of *adversity;* which my young friend was a most necessary part of his early training. You may *laugh* when you come to read about it; but these were *sore trials* to John: whose earthly treasures were very *few & small.* These were the beginning of a severe but *much needed course* of discipline which he afterwards was to pass through; & which it is to be hoped has learned him before this time that the Heavenly Father sees it best to take all the little things out of his hands which he has ever placed in them. When John was in his Sixth year a poor *Indian boy* gave him a Yellow Marble the first he had ever seen. This he thought a great deal of; & kept it a good while; but at last *he lost* it beyond recovery. *It took years to heal the wound* & I *think* he cried at times about it. About Five months after this he caught a young Squirrel tearing off his tail in doing it; & getting severely bitten at the same time himself. He however held on *to the little bob tail Squirrel;* & finally got him perfectly tamed, so that he almost idolized his pet. *This too he lost;* by its wandering away; or by getting killed; & for a year or two John was *in mourning;* and looking at all the Squirrels he could see to try & discover Bobtail, *if possible.* I must not neglect to tell you of a very *bad and foolish* habit to which John was somewhat addicted. I mean *telling lies;* generally to screen himself from blame; or from punishment. He could not well endure to be reproached; & I now think had he been oftener encouraged to be entirely frank; *by making frankness a kind of atonement* for some of his faults; he would not have been so often guilty of this fault; nor have been (in after life) obliged to struggle *so long* with *so mean* a habit.

John was never *quarelsome;* but was *excessively* fond of the *hardest & roughest* kind of plays; & could *never get enough* [of] them. Indeed when for a short time he was sometimes sent to School the opportunity it afforded to wrestle & Snow ball & run & jump & knock off old seedy Wool hats; offered to him almost the only compensation for the confinement, & restraints of school. I need not tell you that with such a feeling & but little chance of going to school *at all:* he did not become much of a schollar. He would always choose to stay at home & work hard rather than be sent to school; & during the warm season might generally be seen *barefooted & bareheaded:* with Buck skin Breeches suspended often with one leather strap over his shoulder but sometimes with

Two. To be sent off through the wilderness alone to very considerable distances was particularly his delight; & in this he was often indulged so that by the time he was Twelve years old he was sent off more than a Hundred Miles with companies of cattle; & he would have thought his character much injured had he been obliged to be helped in any such job. This was a boyish kind of feeling but characteristic however.

At Eight years old, John was left a Motherless boy which loss was complete and pearmanent for notwithstanding his Father again married to a sensible, intelligent, and on many accounts a very estimable woman; yet he never *adopted her in feeling;* but continued to pine after his own Mother for years. This opperated very unfavorably upon him; as he was both naturally fond of females; &, withall, extremely diffident; & deprived him of a suitable connecting link between the different sexes; the want of which might under some circumstances, have proved his ruin. . . .

During the war with England [in 1812] a circumstance occured that in the end made him a most determined *Abolitionist:* & led him to declare, or *Swear: Eternal war* with Slavery. He was staying for a short time with a very gentlemanly landlord since a United States Marshall who held a slave boy near his own age very active, inteligent and good feeling; & to whom John was under considerable obligation for numerous little acts of kindness. *The master* made a great pet of John: brought him to table with his first company; & friends; called their attention to every little smart thing *he said or did:* & to the fact of his being more than a hundred miles from home with a company of cattle alone; while the *negro boy* (who was fully if not more than his equal) was badly clothed, poorly fed; *& lodged in cold weather;* & beaten before his eyes with Iron Shovels or any other thing that came first to hand. This brought John to reflect on the wretched, hopeless condition, of *Fatherless & Motherless* slave *children:* for such children have neither Fathers or Mothers to protect, & provide for them. He sometimes would raise the question *is God their Father?* . . .

I had like to have forgotten to tell you of one of John's misfortunes which set rather hard on him while a young boy. He had by some means *perhaps* by gift of his father become the owner of a little Ewe Lamb which did finely till it was about Two Thirds grown; & then sickened & died. This brought another protracted *mourning season:* not that he felt the pecuniary loss so much: for that was never his disposition; but so strong & earnest were his attachments.

John had been taught from earliest childhood to "fear God and keep his commandments;" & though quite skeptical he had always by turns felt much serious doubt as to his future well being; & about this time became to some extent a convert to Christianity & ever after a firm believer in the divine authenticity of the Bible. With this book he became very familiar, & possessed a most unusual memory of its entire contents.

Now some of the things I have been *telling of;* were just such as I would recommend to you: & I would like to know that you had selected these out; & adopted them as part of your own plan of life; & I wish you to have some *deffinite plan.* Many seem to have none; & others never stick to any that they do form. This was not the case with John. He followed up with *tenacity* whatever he set about so long as it answered his general purpose; & hence he rarely failed in some good degree to effect the things he undertook. This was so much the case that he *habitually expected to succeed* in his undertakings. With this feeling *should be coupled;* the consciousness that our plans are right in themselves.

During the period I have named, John had acquired a kind of ownership to certain animals of some little value but as he had come to understand that the *title of minors* might be a little imperfect: he had recourse to various means in order to secure a more *independent;* & perfect right of property. One of those means was to exchange with his Father for something of far less value. Another was by trading with others persons for something his Father had never owned. Older persons have some times found difficulty with *titles.*

From Fifteen to Twenty years old, he spent most of his time working at the Tanner & Currier's trade keeping Bachelors hall; & he officiating as Cook; & for most of the time as foreman of the establishment under his Father. During this period he found much trouble with some of the bad habits I have mentioned & with some that I have not told you off: his conscience urging him forward with great power in this matter: but his close attention to *business;* & success in its management, together with the way he got along with a company of men, & boys; made him quite a favorite with the serious & more inteligent portion of older persons. This was so much the case; & secured for him so many little notices from those he esteemed; that his vanity was very much fed by it: & he came forward to manhood quite full of self-conceit; & self-confident; notwithstanding his *extreme* bashfulness. A younger brother used sometimes to remind him of this: & to repeat to him *this expression* which you may somewhere find, "A King against whom there is no rising up." The habit so early formed of being obeyed rendered him in after life too much disposed to speak in an imperious or dictating way. From Fifteen years & upward he felt a good deal of anxiety to learn; but could only read & studdy a little; both for want of time; & on account of inflammation of the eyes. He however managed by the help of books to make himself tolerably well acquainted with common arithmetic; & Surveying; which he practiced more or less after he was Twenty years old.

Before exploring the letter's psychological clues, it may be worth reminding ourselves what a straightforward reading of the document provides. Attention would first center on Brown's religious nature. His writing style is much influenced by the Bible. He was all his life a fervent Puritan who as a child "learned to fear God and his commandments" and accepted the "divine authenticity of the Bible" whose contents he had committed to memory. Such religiosity was certainly common in Brown's day. We should note, however, his intense and unquestioning faith. He refers to the loss of some precious objects in his youth as "the beginning of a severe but much needed course of discipline." And to what did Brown attribute his string of

John Brown, the kindly father: Brown's daughter Ruth remembered the following incident from her childhood: "When I first began to go to school, I found a piece of calico one day behind one of the benches,—it was not large, but seemed quite a treasure to me, and I did not show it to any one until I got home. Father heard me then telling about it, and said, 'Don't you know what girl lost it?' I told him I did not. 'Well, when you go to school tomorrow take it with you, and find out if you can who lost it. It is a trifling thing, but always remember that if you should lose anything you valued, no matter how small, *you* would want the person that found it to give it back to you.'"

misfortune? To God, "the Heavenly Father [who] sees it best to take all the little things out of his hands which he has ever placed in them." Those who do not share Brown's harsh Calvinist faith might find his religious fundamentalism a form of mental disorder. Most of Brown's contemporaries, even those who worshipped a gentler God, would have respected his beliefs, even if they did not fully share them.

A second, even more striking element of the letter naturally centers on Brown's tale of how, as a twelve-year-old, he was first roused to oppose slavery. Shocked by the cruel treatment of his young black friend, John was further incensed by the unfair and contrasting treatment from which he benefited simply because he was white. This vivid, emotional experience seems to go a good way toward explaining why the evil of slavery weighed so heavily on Brown's mind. In an essay on the motivations behind the raid at Harpers Ferry, this anecdote is quite clearly the major piece of evidence in the letter. The additional material on Brown's childhood, which often seems to ramble incoherently, might be included in a book-length biography of Brown but hardly seems relevant to an article that must quickly get to the heart of the man's involvement with abolition.

Yet when we look more closely, Brown's story of the mistreated young slave does not explain much about Brown's motives. In a land where slavery was central to the culture, hundreds, even thousands, of young white boys must have had experiences in which black playmates were unfairly whipped, degraded, and treated as inferiors. Nonetheless, many of those boys went on to become slaveholders. Furthermore, although some undoubtedly developed a strong dislike of slavery (Abraham Lincoln among them*), none felt compelled to mount the kinds of campaigns Brown did in Kansas and at Harpers Ferry. Why did Brown's rather commonplace experience make such a strong impression on him?

The answer to that question may be learned if we do not dismiss the other portions of Brown's childhood experiences as irrelevant but instead examine them for clues to his psychological development. So let us turn, for a moment, from a direct examination of Brown's abolitionism to the other elements of the letter to Harry Stearns. In doing so we must consider each of Brown's stories, illustrations, and comments with care, keeping in mind the characteristics of bipolar disorders outlined in the DSM-IV. In previous chapters we have seen that historians must always treat primary sources skeptically, identifying the personal perspectives and biases that may influence the writer. Psychological theory requires us to take that skepticism one step further, assuming not only that the evidence may be influenced by unstated motivations (such as Brown's wishing to impress Harry Stearns's father with his virtue) but also that some, even the most powerful of Brown's motivations, may be unconscious—hidden even from Brown himself.

At first glance the narrative appears to recount to his reader a life full of pioneering adventure. Brown faced rattlesnakes, befriended Indians, and learned to tan deerskins. Other details address fairly ordinary events in a child's life. Who, after all, has not cried one time or another at the loss of a pet, or has not been proud of accomplishments like driving cows and riding horses? Yet we must remember that these events are only a few selected from among thousands in Brown's childhood, events meaningful enough to him that he remembered and related them more than fifty years later. Why did Brown retain these memories rather than others? What suggestive images and themes recur? Because Brown remembered them so vividly later in life, we may assume that these were for him life-defining experiences.

One overriding theme is a recurring sense of loss. Brown recalls the yellow marble he valued so much, his pet squirrel, and the ewe lamb he raised with great affection. All of these he lost, but none pained him so much as the death of his mother. Of his two parents, she is the more visible in this letter, and it is clear that Brown loved her dearly. Notice the language describing his mother's death. "John was left a Motherless boy," he writes—not the simpler and less revealing, "John's mother died," which places the emphasis on the mother rather than on the loss incurred by the "Motherless boy."

> *One overriding theme is a recurring sense of loss.*

Periods of mourning followed all these events. Of his prize marble he recalls, "It took years to heal the wound & I think he cried at times about it." The disappearance of his pet squirrel led to a similar period of mourning.

---

* As a young man, Lincoln was reputed to have been strongly moved by the sight of slaves being auctioned in New Orleans.

What strikes the reader is not Brown's feelings. Almost everyone has had similar feelings at some time. Rather, in Brown's case, it is the duration and intensity of these periods of grieving. They strike the reader as a potential sign of depression. Especially in the case of his mother, the loss was "complete and pearmanent." Brown admits he never grew to love his new mother and "continued to pine after his own Mother for years." As Kenneth Carroll noted, where mania is often publicly expressed, depression is more likely a private matter in which a person withdraws into himself or herself. As a consequence, friends and acquaintances may be less aware of its presence. Brown, in other instances, expressed a "steady strong desire to die" and certainly made no attempt to save his life when he faced execution. Whether or not he did suffer from depression is not essential to a diagnosis of bipolar disorder. Nonetheless, it expands our understanding of the man and his motives for attacking Harpers Ferry.

The letter to Stearns does suggest other elements of the DSM-IV diagnosis for mania. One key symptom is "inflated self-esteem or grandiosity." Brown admits to an "imperious or dictating way" that a younger brother summed up as "A King against whom there is no rising up." According to his brother, Brown could be a tyrant. Brown speaks also of being a "favorite" among older persons he esteemed so much so "that his vanity was very much fed by it: & he came forward to manhood quite full of self-conceit; & self-confident; notwithstanding his extreme bashfulness." What he meant by his "bashfulness" is difficult to determine. Yet he goes on to say that he "followed up with tenacity whatever he set about" and then concludes, "he rarely failed in some good degree to effect the things he undertook." That must strike us as a rather remarkable claim from a person whose life was beset by endless business failures and personal loss. It certainly smacks of "inflated self-esteem." So, too, does the following assertion, "This was so much the case that he habitually expected to succeed in his undertakings." As we have seen, even the event that defined his life's great success, Harpers Ferry, began as a fiasco.

Recall as well that many of those signing affidavits mentioned Brown's unwillingness to alter his views or change his plans when confronted with contradictory advice. He asserts that his expectations for success "should be coupled" with "the consciousness that our plans are right in themselves." This sense of carrying out a divinely ordained mission is consistent with Brown's deep religious convictions, but it also suggests rigidity in his behavior and the grandiosity of one who assumes he has a monopoly on the truth. So strong were these feelings that Brown admitted that as a youth he frequently told lies, "generally to screen himself from blame; or from punishment." Why? Because "He could not well endure to be reproached." Brown, in short, admits that he could not stand to be criticized.

One final criterion from the DSM-IV seems to be present. Brown describes himself as "excessively fond of the hardest & roughest kind of plays; & could never get enough [of] them." Rather than seize the opportunity school afforded to improve himself, Brown preferred "to wrestle & Snow

John Brown, the stern father: Brown was influenced in his harsh discipline by his father, Owen (*left*), and in turn influenced his own son, John Jr. (*right*). Father John kept a detailed account book of young John's sinful acts, along with the number of whiplashes each sin deserved. Even sins, it seemed, were carefully enumerated as property.

ball & run & jump & knock off old seedy Wool hats; [that] offered to him almost the only compensation for the confinement, & restraints of school." The DSM-IV mentions psychomotor agitation and "excessive involvement in pleasurable activities that have a high potential for painful consequences." Brown's hyperactivity might have meant physical injury to himself or others, expulsion from school, or academic failure.

Does all this evidence thus prove that Brown was bipolar? It certainly suggests that might have been the case. Still, we cannot be convinced our diagnosis is correct. The evidence is simply too fragmentary to lead us to a certain conclusion. We can only say with confidence that all the evidence is consistent with a diagnosis of a bipolar disorder. But that in turn forces us to ask a more important question: How does that diagnosis better help us explain John Brown and his motives? Many historians, such as Brown biographer Stephen Oates, would argue that to label Brown as mentally ill does a grave disservice to the man and his cause. It demeans the extraordinary sympathy he felt for African Americans as either slaves or human beings. John Brown, for Oates as well as David Reynolds, was a rare American who rejected the racism of both northern abolitionists and southern slaveholders.

Psychologists might answer that the righteousness of his cause and his mental health are two different matters. Mental illnesses, they insist, are "well-known, well-described, clinically significant, and scientifically legitimate entities that have maintained their integrity over time, place, and culture." A bipolar disorder manifests similar symptoms, whether in the Virginia of the 1850s or of the twenty-first century. As a result, the more important question is not whether Brown was or wasn't mentally ill but whether Brown would have attacked Harpers Ferry had he not been bipolar. The answer Carroll suggests is "probably not." A mentally healthy person would have been less likely to fail so often in business, to travel so widely seeking success, or to launch a grand scheme to liberate slaves. As Carroll concludes, "In short, he might have been an ordinary man." Brown, we know, whether a success or a failure, a madman or a saint, was in no sense ordinary. Many of history's heroes, inventors, and artists have shared Brown's mental condition. To label them bipolar in no way diminishes the record of their achievements. Rather, we recognize that at critical moments they poured their manic energy into creative channels. In the process, they forced us to revise our reality and move in new directions. The consequences have not always been positive or constructive, as the Adolf Hitlers of the world remind us. Nor do periods of creative success protect these geniuses from painful episodes of psychosis that often follow manic outbursts. F. Scott Fitzgerald, the great American author, seldom drank when he was writing. He lost himself in alcohol when he lacked the intense energy he needed to create new work.

So it was for John Brown. At the moment he transcended his life of failure, he forced his generation to identify either positively or negatively with the action he took to liberate black Americans. His act of violence was appropriate to what Oates described as "the violent, irrational, and paradoxical times in which he lived." Given Brown's bipolar condition,

Brown forced his generation to identify either positively or negatively with the action he took to liberate black Americans.

expressed through his profoundly religious nature and passionate commitment to human liberty and equality, he could not be at peace so long as his society refused to recognize the contradiction between its religious and political ideals and the existence of slavery.

In the end, John Brown turned the tables on society. The man who struck so many friends and acquaintances as simply mad and out of control forced society to confront his view of the historical moment. After Harpers Ferry, his fellow Americans had to consider whether it was not actually their values, and society's, that were immoral and "abnormal." The outbreak of civil war, after all, demonstrated that American society was so maladjusted and so divided that it could not remain a "normal," integrated whole without violently purging itself. If Brown's raid was an isolated act of a disturbed man, why did it drive an entire generation to the brink of war? Why did Brown's generation find it impossible to agree about the meaning of Harpers Ferry? As C. Vann Woodward concluded, the importance lay not so much in the man or the event, but in the use made of them by northern and southern partisans. For every Emerson or Thoreau who pronounced the raid the work of a saint, a southern fire-eater condemned the venture as the villainy of all northerners.

None of these actors in the historical drama paid much attention to evidence. A crisis mentality thwarted any attempts at understanding or reconciliation. In the fury of mutual recrimination, both sides lost sight of the man who had provoked the public outcry and propelled the nation toward war. In such times it will always be, as abolitionist Wendell Phillips remarked, "hard to tell who's mad."

Additional Reading

The current version of this chapter draws heavily on two fine works of historical analysis. The first is David S. Reynolds, *John Brown, Abolitionist* (New York, 2005). Reynolds firmly rejects any notion that Brown was insane. Peggy A. Russo and Paul Finkelman gathered a group of scholars to reconsider John Brown. Their edited collection, *Terrible Swift Sword: The Legacy of John Brown* (Athens, Ohio 2005), includes an essay by Kenneth Carroll, "A Psychological Examination of John Brown," that informed our understanding of mental disorders. Carroll deftly mixes historical evidence and psychological evidence. For additional perspectives, see Paul Finkelman, ed., *His Soul Goes Marching On: Responses to John Brown and the Harpers Ferry Raid* (Charlottesville, VA, 1995), in particular the essays by Bertram Wyatt-Brown (pp. 10–40) and Robert E. McGlone, who discusses the political considerations of contemporaries' debates about Brown's sanity (pp. 213–252). McGlone has also published *John Brown's War Against Slavery* (New York, 2009), which appeared too late to incorporate into this chapter.

A valuable earlier biography on John Brown is Stephen Oates, *To Purge This Land with Blood* (New York, 1970). Oates's treatment is evenhanded, scholarly, and stirring in its narrative. (Other modern biographies include studies by Jules C. Abels and Richard O. Boyer, both published during the 1970s.) C. Vann Woodward's "John Brown's Private War" is one of the best short interpretive essays available on the raid and can be found in his *Burden of Southern History* (Baton Rouge, LA, 1968). For a detailed account of Brown's earlier doings in Kansas, see James C. Malin, *John Brown and the Legacy of Fifty-Six* (Philadelphia, 1942). Brown's relationship with his conspirators is grippingly told in Edward J. Renehan Jr., *The Secret Six: The True Tale of the Men Who Conspired with John Brown* (New York, 1995). Franklin B. Sanborn, *The Life and Letters of John Brown* (Boston, 1891), an older biography unabashedly sympathetic to Brown, contains many valuable personal letters. The fullest collection of materials on the raid and trial is R. M. De Witt, *The Life, Trial, and Execution of John Brown* (New York, 1859).

CHAPTER 8

The View from the Bottom Rail

How can we know anything about newly freed slaves who left
behind few written records? Oral evidence provides one answer.

Thunder. From across the swamps and salt marshes of the Carolina coast came the distant, repetitive pounding. Thunder out of a clear blue sky. Down at the slave quarters, young Sam Mitchell heard the noise and wondered. In Beaufort, the nearby village, planter John Chaplin heard too, and dashed for his carriage. The drive back to his plantation was as quick as Chaplin could make it. Once home, he ordered his wife and children to pack; then he looked for his slaves. The flatboat must be made ready, he told them; the family was going to Charleston. He needed eight men at the oars. One of the slaves, Sam Mitchell's father, brought the news to his wife and son at the slave quarters. "You ain't gonna row no boat to Charleston," the wife snapped, "you go out dat back door and keep agoing." Young Sam was mystified by all the commotion. How could it thunder without a cloud in the sky? "Son, dat ain't no t'under," explained the mother, "dat Yankee come to gib you freedom."

The pounding of the guns came relatively quickly to Beaufort—November 1861, only seven months after the first hostilities at Fort Sumter. Yet it was only a matter of time before the thunder of freedom rolled across the rest of the South, from the bayous and deltas of Louisiana in 1862 to the farms around Richmond in 1865. As the guns of the Union spoke, thousands of Sam Mitchells experienced their own unforgettable moments. Freedom was coming to a nation of four million slaves.

To most slaves, the men in the blue coats were foreigners—and sometimes suspect. Many southern masters painted the prospect of northern invasion in lurid colors. Union soldiers, one Tennessee slave was told, "got long horns on their heads, and tushes [pointed teeth] in their mouths, and eyes sticking out like a cow! They're mean old things." A fearful Mississippi slave refused to come out of a tree until the Union soldier below her took off his cap and demonstrated he had no horns. Many slaves, however, scoffed at such tales. "We all hear 'bout dem Yankees," a Carolina slave told his overseer. "Folks

This slave family lived on a plantation at Beaufort, South Carolina, not far from the plantation where Sam Mitchell heard the thunder of northern guns in 1861. The photograph was taken after northern forces had occupied the Sea Islands area.

tell we they has horns and a tail. . . . Wen I see dem coming I shall run like all possess." But as soon as the overseer fled, leaving the plantation in the slaves' care, the tune changed: "Good-by, ole man, good-by. That's right. Skedaddle as fast as you kin. . . . We's gwine to run sure enough; but we knows the Yankees, an' we runs that way."

For some slaves, the bond of loyalty or the fear of alternatives led them to side with their masters. Faithful slaves hid valuable silver, persuaded Yankees that their departed masters were Union sympathizers, or pretended they had a contagious illness in order to scare off marauding soldiers. But in many cases, the conflict between loyalty and freedom caused anguish. A Georgia couple, both more than sixty years old, greeted Sherman's soldiers calmly and with apparent lack of interest. They seemed content to remain with their master instead of joining the slaves flocking along behind Union troops. As the soldiers prepared to leave, however, the old woman suddenly stood up, a "fierce, almost devilish" look in her eyes. "What you sit dar for?" she asked her husband vehemently. "You s'pose I wait sixty years for nutten? Don't yer see de door open? I'se follow my child; I not stay. Yes, anudder day I goes 'long wid dese people; yes, sar, I walks till I drop in my tracks."

Other slaves felt no hesitation about choosing freedom; indeed, they found it difficult to contain their joy. One woman, who overheard the news of emancipation just before she was to serve her master's dinner, asked to be excused to get water from a nearby spring. Once there, and out of sight, she allowed her feelings free rein.

> I jump up and scream, "Glory, glory hallelujah to Jesus! I'se free! I'se free! Glory to God, you come down an' free us; no big man could do it." An' I got sort o' scared, afeared somebody hear me, an' I takes another good look, an' fall on de goun' an' roll over, an' kiss de gound' fo' de Lord's sake, I's so full o' praise to Masser Jesus.

To newly freed slaves, it seemed the world had turned upside down. Rich and powerful masters were fleeing, while freed slaves were left with the run of the plantation. The situation was summed up by one black soldier who was surprised—and delighted—to find his former master among the prisoners he was guarding. "Hello, massa!" he said cheerfully, "bottom rail top dis time!"

RECOVERING THE FREEDPEOPLE'S POINT OF VIEW

The freeing of four million black slaves ranks as one of the major events in American history. Yet the story has not been easy to tell. To understand the personal trials and triumphs of the newly liberated slaves, or "freedpeople" as they have come to be called,* historians must draw on the personal experiences of those at the center of the drama. They must recreate the freedpeople's point of view. But slaves had occupied the lowest level of America's social and economic scale. They sat, as the black soldier correctly noted, on the bottom rail of the fence. For several reasons, that social reality has made it more difficult to recover the freedpeople's point of view.

In the first place, most traditional histories suffered from a natural "top-rail" bias, writing primarily about members of the higher social classes. Histories cannot be written without primary-source material, and by and large, those on the top rails of society have produced the most records. Having been privileged to receive an education, members of the middle and upper classes are more apt to publish memoirs, keep diaries, or write letters. As leaders of society who make decisions, they are the subjects of official minutes and records.

At the other end of the social spectrum, ordinary folk lead lives that are less documented. While political leaders involve themselves in one momentous issue after another, the work of farmers and laborers is often repetitive

---

* White contemporaries of the newly freed slaves referred to them as *freedmen*. More recently, historians have preferred the gender-neutral term *freedpeople*, which we will use here except when quoting primary sources.

Point Lookout Md.

"Git away from dat dar fence white man or I'll make Old Abe's Gun smoke at you. I can hardly hold de ball back now.—De bottom rails on top now." More than one former slave used the image of the "bottom rail on top" to define the transformation wrought by the Civil War. This watercolor sketch was made by a Confederate soldier being held prisoner by Union forces at Point Lookout, Maryland.

and appears to have little effect on the course of history. The decade of the 1970s, however, saw an increasing interest in the lives of ordinary people. In Chapter 2, for example, we saw that appreciating the social and economic position of the serving class was essential to understanding the volatile society of early Virginia. Similarly, in Chapter 3 we turned to the social tensions of ordinary farmers in order to explore the alliances behind the witchcraft controversy at Salem.

Reconstructing the perspective of enslaved African Americans has proved particularly challenging. Before the Civil War, slaves were not only discouraged from learning to read and write, southern legislatures passed slave codes that flatly forbade whites to teach them. The laws were not entirely effective. A few blacks employed as drivers on large plantations learned to read and correspond so that their absent masters might send them instructions. Some black preachers were also literate. Still, most reading remained a furtive affair, done out of sight of the master or other whites. During the war, a literate slave named Squires Jackson was eagerly scanning a newspaper for word of northern victories when his master unexpectedly entered the room and demanded to know what the slave was doing. The surprised reader deftly turned the newspaper upside down, put on a foolish grin, and said, "Confederates done won the war!" The master laughed and went about his business.

Even though most slaves never wrote letters, kept diaries, or left other written records, it might at first seem possible to learn about slave life from accounts written by white contemporaries. Any number of letters, books, travelers' accounts, and diaries survive, after all—full of descriptions of life under slavery and of the experiences of freedpeople after the war. Yet the question of perspective raises serious problems. The vantage point of white Americans observing slavery was emphatically not that of slaves who lived under the "peculiar institution."

Consider, first, the observations of those whites who associated most closely with black slaves: their masters. The relationship between master and slave was inherently unequal. Slaves could be whipped for trifling offenses; they could be sold or separated from their families and closest friends; even under "kind" masters, they were bound to labor as ordered if they wanted their ration of food and clothing. With slaves so dependent on the master's authority, they were hardly likely to reveal their true feelings; the dangerous consequences of doing so were too great.

With slaves so dependent on the master's authority, they were hardly likely to reveal their true feelings to their owners

In fact, we have already encountered an example in which a slave deceived his master: the case of Squires Jackson and his newspaper. Think for a moment about the source of that story. Even without a footnote to indicate where the information came from, readers of this chapter can deduce that it was left in the historical record by Jackson, not the planter. (The planter, after all, went away convinced Jackson could not read.) Imagine how different our impression would be if the only surviving record of the incident was the planter's diary. We might then be reading an entry something like the following:

> A humorous incident occurred today. While entering the woodshed to attend some business, I came upon my slave Squires. His eyes were fixed with intense interest upon an old copy of a newspaper he had come upon, which alarmed me some until I discovered the rascal was reading its contents upside down. "Why Squires," I said innocently. "What is the latest news?" He looked up at me with a big grin and said, "Massa, de 'Federates jes' won de war!" It made me laugh to see the darkey's simple confidence. I wish I could share his optimism.

This entry is fictional, but having Jackson's version of the story serves to cast suspicion on similar entries in real planters' diaries. One Louisiana slave owner, for instance, marveled that his field hands went on with their Christmas party apparently unaware that Yankee raiding parties had pillaged a nearby town. "We have been watching the negroes dancing for the last

"They are having a merry time, thoughtless creatures, they think not of the morrow." This scene of a Christmas party, similar to the one described by the Louisiana planter, appeared with an article written by a northern correspondent for *Frank Leslie's Illustrated Newspaper* in 1857. The picture, reflecting the popular stereotype of slaves as cheerful and ignorantly content with their lot, suggests that the social constraints of the times made it as difficult for southern African Americans to be completely candid with their northern liberators as it had been to be candid with their southern masters.

two hours. . . . They are having a merry time, thoughtless creatures, they think not of the morrow." It apparently never occurred to the planter that the "thoughtless" merriment may have been especially great because of the northern troops nearby.*

The harsh realities of the war forced many southerners to consider just how little they really knew about their slaves. Often, the very servants that masters deemed most loyal were the first to run off. Mary Chesnut, whose house was not far from Fort Sumter, sought in vain to penetrate the blank expressions of her slaves. "Not by one word or look can we detect any change in the demeanor of these Negro servants. . . . You could not tell that

---

* Readers who review the opening narrative of this chapter will discover that they have already encountered quite a few other examples of deception arising out of the social situations in which the actors found themselves. In fact, except for the black soldier's comment about the bottom rail being top, every example of white-black relationships cited in the opening section has some element of concealment or deception. It may be worth noting that we did not select the opening incidents with that fact in mind. The preponderance of deception was noted only when we reviewed the draft several days after it had been written.

they even hear the awful noise that is going on in the bay [at Fort Sumter], though it is dinning in their ears night and day. . . . Are they stolidly stupid, or wiser than we are, silent and strong, biding their time?"

It is tempting to suppose that white northerners who helped liberate slaves might have provided more accurate accounts of freedpeople's attitudes. But that assumption is dangerous. Although virtually all northern slaves had been freed by 1820, race prejudice remained strong. Antislavery forces often combined a strong dislike of slavery with an equally strong desire to keep the freedpeople of the North. Most housing and transportation facilities were segregated there, so that whites and blacks had much less close social contact than in the South.

Thus, while some Union soldiers went out of their way to be kind to slaves they encountered, many looked upon African Americans with distaste or open hostility. More than a few Yankees believed they were fighting a war to save the Union, not to free the "cursed Nigger," as one recruit put it. White officers who commanded black regiments could be remarkably unsympathetic.

Both northern and southern white accounts of black Americans need to be viewed with caution.

"Any one listening to your shouting and singing can see how grotesquely ignorant you are," one officer lectured his troops, when they refused to accept less than the pay promised on enlistment. Even missionaries and other sympathetic northerners who came to occupied territory had preconceptions to overcome. "I saw some very low-looking women who answered very intelligently, contrary to my expectations," noted Philadelphia missionary Laura Towne. So we need to be cautious even when reviewing northern accounts.

Indeed, perceptive whites recognized that just as slaves had been dependent on their southern masters before the war, freedpeople found themselves similarly vulnerable to the new class of conquerors. "One of these blacks, fresh from slavery, will most adroitly tell you precisely what you want to hear," noted northerner Charles Nordhoff.

> To cross-examine such a creature is a task of the most delicate nature; if you chance to put a leading question he will answer to its spirit as closely as the compass needle answers to the magnetic pole. Ask if the enemy had fifty thousand men, and he will be sure that they had at least that many; express your belief that they had not five thousand, and he will laugh at the idea of their having more than forty-five hundred.

Samuel Gridley Howe, a wartime commissioner investigating the freedpeople's condition, saw the situation clearly. "The negro, like other men, naturally desires to live in the light of truth," he argued, "but he hides in the shadow of falsehood, more or less deeply, according as his safety or welfare seems to require it. Other things equal, the freer a people, the more truthful; and only the perfectly free and fearless are perfectly truthful."

Furthermore, northerners found it hard to imagine the freedpeople's point of view because the culture of southern African Americans was so unfamiliar. The first hurdle was simple communication, given the wide variety of accents and dialects spoken by northerners and southerners. Charles Nordhoff noted that often he had the feeling that he was "speaking with foreigners." The slaves' phrase "I go shum" puzzled him until he discovered it to be a contraction of "I'll go see about it." Another missionary was teaching his students "what various things were for, eyes, etc. He asked what ears were made for, and when they said, 'To yer with,' he could not understand them at all."

If black dialect was difficult to understand, black culture and religion could appear even more unfathomable. Although most slaves shared with northerners a belief in Christianity, black methods of worship shocked more than one staid Unitarian. After church meetings, slaves often participated in a singing and dancing session known as a "shout," in which the leader would sing out a line of song and the chorus would respond, dancing in rhythm to the music. As the night proceeded, the music became more vocal and the dancing more vigorous. One missionary noted, "It was the most hideous and at the same time the most pitiful sight I ever witnessed."

As sympathetic as many northerners wished to be, significant obstacles prevented them from fully appreciating the freedpeople's point of view. The nature of slave society and the persistence of prejudice made it virtually impossible for blacks and whites to deal with one another candidly.

THE FREEDPEOPLE SPEAK

From the very beginning, however, some observers recognized the value of the former slaves' perspective. If few black people could write, their stories could be written down by others and made public. Oral testimony, transcribed by literate editors, would allow black Americans to speak out on issues that affected them most.

The tradition of oral evidence began even before the slaves were freed. Abolitionists recognized the value of firsthand testimony against the slave system. They took down and published the stories of fugitive slaves who escaped to the North. During the war, Congress also established the Freedman's Inquiry Commission, which collected information that might aid the government.

In the half century following Reconstruction, however, interest in preserving black history languished. An occasional journalist or historian interviewed former slaves. Educators at black schools, such as the Hampton Institute, published recollections. But most historians writing about Reconstruction ignored them, as well as the freedpeople's perspective in general. Instead they relied on white accounts, which painted a rather partial picture.

William A. Dunning, a historian at Columbia University, was perhaps the most influential advocate of the prevailing viewpoint. He painted the freedpeople as childish, happy-go-lucky creatures who failed to appreciate the responsibilities of their new status. "As the full meaning of [emancipation] was grasped by the freedmen," Dunning wrote, "great numbers of them abandoned their old homes, and, regardless of crops to be cultivated, stock to be cared for, or food to be provided, gave themselves up to testing their freedom. They wandered aimless but happy through the country." At the same time, Dunning claimed that southern whites had "devoted themselves with desperate energy to the procurement of what must sustain the life of both themselves and their former slaves." Such were the conclusions deduced without the aid of the freedpeople's perspectives.

Only in the twentieth century were systematic efforts made to question blacks about their experiences. Interest in the African American heritage rose markedly during the 1920s, spurred by the efforts of black scholars such as W. E. B. DuBois, Charles Johnson, and Carter Woodson, the editor and founder of the *Journal of Negro History*. Those scholars worked hard to overturn the stereotypes promoted by the Dunning school. Moreover, sociologists and anthropologists at American universities began to analyze southern culture, using the tools of the new social sciences. By the beginning of the 1930s, historians at Fisk University in Nashville and Southern University in Baton Rouge had instituted projects to collect oral evidence.

Ironically, the hard times of the Depression sparked the greatest single effort to gather oral testimony from the freedpeople. One of the many agencies chartered by the Roosevelt administration was the Federal Writers' Project (FWP). The project's primary goal was to compile and publish cultural guides to each of the forty-eight states, using unemployed writers and journalists. But under the direction of folklorist John Avery Lomax, the FWP also organized staffs in many states to interview former slaves.

The hard times of the Depression sparked the greatest single effort to gather oral history from former slaves.

Although Lomax's project placed greatest emphasis on collecting black folklore and songs, the FWP's directive to interviewers included a long list of historical questions that they were encouraged to ask. The following sampling gives an indication of the project's interests:

What work did you do in slavery days? Did you ever earn any money?
What did you eat and how was it cooked? Any possums? Rabbits? Fish?
Was there a jail for slaves? Did you ever see any slaves sold or auctioned off?
    How and for what causes were the slaves punished? Tell what you saw.
What do you remember about the war that brought you your freedom? When
    the Yankees came, what did they do or say?

The results of these interviews were remarkable. More than 2,300 were recorded and edited in state FWP offices and sent to Washington, assembled in 1941, and published in typescript. A facsimile edition, issued during the 1970s, takes up nineteen volumes. Supplementary materials, including hundreds of interviews never forwarded to Washington during the project's life, comprise another twenty-two volumes. Benjamin Botkin, the series' original editor, recognized the collection's importance. "These life histories, taken down as far as possible in the narrator's words, constitute an invaluable body of unconscious evidence or indirect source material," he noted. "For the first and last time, a large number of surviving slaves (many of whom have since died) have been permitted to tell their own story, in their own way."

Even Botkin, however, recognized that the narratives could not simply be taken at face value. Like all primary-source materials, they need to be viewed in terms of the context in which they originated. To begin with, even nineteen volumes packed with interviews constitute a small sampling of the original four million freedpeople. What sort of selection bias might exist? Geographic imbalance comes quickly to mind. Are the slave interviews drawn from a broad cross section of southern states? Counting the number of slaves interviewed from each state, we discover only 155 interviews from African Americans living in Virginia, Missouri, Maryland, Delaware, and Kentucky—about 6 percent of the total number of interviews published. Yet in 1860, 23 percent of the southern slave population lived in those states. Thus the upper South is underrepresented in the collection.

What about age? Because the interviews took place primarily between 1936 and 1938, former slaves were fairly old: fully two-thirds were more than eighty years of age. How sharp were the elderly informants' memories? The Civil War was already seventy years in the past. Common sense suggests that the further away from an event, the less detailed a person's memory is likely to be. In addition, age may have biased the type of recollections given. Historian John Blassingame has noted that the average life expectancy of a slave in 1850 was less than fifty years. Those who lived to a ripe old age might well have survived because they were treated better than the average slave. If so, their accounts would reflect some of the milder experiences of slaves.

Are the interviews biased because they focus on those who survived slavery, rather than those who died from harsh treatment?

Also, if those interviewed were predominantly old in 1936, they were predominantly young during the Civil War. Almost half (43 percent) were less than ten years old in 1865. Sixty-seven percent were under age fifteen, and 83 percent were under age twenty. Thus many interviewers remembered slavery as it would have been experienced by a child. If the conditions of bondage were relatively less harsh for a child than for an adult slave, once again the FWP narratives may be somewhat skewed toward an optimistic view of slavery. (On the other hand, it might be argued that because children are so impressionable, memories both good and bad might have been magnified.)

Distortions may be introduced into the slave narratives in ways more serious than sample bias. Interviewers, simply by choosing their questions, define the kinds of information a subject will volunteer. Even the most seemingly innocent questions are liable to influence the way a subject responds. Take, for example, the following questions:

Where did you hear about this job opening?
How did you hear about this job opening?
So you saw our want ad for this job?

Each question is directed at the same information, yet each suggests to the subject a different response. The first version ("Where did you hear . . .") implies that the interviewer wants a specific, limited answer ("Down at the employment center."). The second question, by substituting "how" for "where," invites the subject to offer a longer response ("Well, I'd been look-ing around for a job for several weeks, and I was over at the employment office when . . ."). The final question signals that the interviewer wants only a yes or no confirmation to a question whose answer is believed to be already known.

Interviewers, in other words, constantly communicate to their subjects the kind of evidence they want, the length of the answers, and even the manner in which answers ought to be offered. If such cues influence routine con-versations, they prove even more crucial when a subject as controversial as slavery is involved, and when relations between blacks and whites continue to be strained. In fact, the most important cue an interviewer was likely to have given was one presented before any conversation took place. Was the inter-viewer white or black? Interracial tensions remained sharp throughout the South during the 1930s. In hundreds of ways, black people were made aware that they were still considered inferior and that they were to remain within strictly segregated and subordinate bounds. From 1931 to 1935, more than seventy African Americans were lynched in the South, often for minor or non-existent crimes. Black prisoners found themselves forced to negotiate grossly unfavorable labor contracts if they wished to be released. Sharecroppers and other poor farmers were constantly in debt to white property owners.

Matters of etiquette reflected the larger state of affairs. White south-erners commonly addressed black adults by their first names, or as "boy," "auntie," or "uncle," regardless of the black person's status and even if the white person knew the black person's full name. Black people were required to address white people as "ma'am" or "mister." Such distinctions applied even on the telephone. If an African American placed a long-distance call for "Mr. Smith" in a neighboring town, the white operator would ask, "Is he colored?" The answer being yes, her reply would be, "Don't you say 'Mister' to me. He ain't 'Mister' to me." Conversely, an operator would refuse to place a call by a black caller who did not address her as "Ma'am."

Thus most African Americans were reticent about volunteering informa-tion to white FWP interviewers. "Lots of old slaves closes the door before they tell the truth about their days of slavery," noted one black Texan to an interviewer. "When the door is open, they tell how kind their masters was how rosy it all was." Samuel S. Taylor, a skilled black interviewer in Arkansas,

"I've told you too much. How come they want all this stuff from the colored people anyway? Do you take any stories from the white people? . . . They don't need me to tell it to them." This Georgia woman, like many of the subjects interviewed for the Federal Writers' Project, was still living in the 1930s on the plantation where she had grown up as a slave child. The plantation was still owned by descendants of her former master. Under such conditions, suspicion toward FWP interviewers was a predictable reaction, even if the interviewer was black; doubly so if he or she was white and a resident of the community.

found that he had to reassure informants that the information they were giving would not be used against them. "I've told you too much," one subject concluded. "How come they want all this stuff from the colored people anyway?

Do you take any stories from the white people? They know all about it. They know more about it than I do. They don't need me to tell it to them."

Often the whites who interviewed blacks lived in the same town and were long acquaintances. "I 'members when you was barefoot at de bottom," one black interviewee told his white (and balding) interviewer; "now I see you a set-tin' dere, gittin' bare at de top." Another black man revealed an even closer rela-

"I've told you too much. How come they want all this stuff from the colored people anyway? Do you take any stories from the white people?"

tionship when he noted that his wife, Ellen, "'joy herself, have a good time nussin' [nursing] white folks chil-lun. Nussed you; she tell me 'bout it many time." In such circumstances, African Americans could hardly be expected to speak frankly. One older woman summed up the situation quite cheerfully. "Oh, I know your father en your granfather en all of dem. Bless Mercy, child, I don't want to tell you nothin' but what to please you."

The methods used to set down FWP interviews raise additional problems. With only a few exceptions, voice recorders were not used. Instead, interviewers took written notes of their conversations, from which they later reconstructed their interviews. In the process, interviewers often edited their material. Sometimes changes were made simply to improve the flow, so that the interview did not jump jarringly from topic to topic. Other interviewers edited out material they believed to be irrelevant or objectionable.

Furthermore, no protocol existed for transcribing African American dialect. A few interviewers took great pains to render their accounts in correct English, so that regional accents and dialect disappeared. ("Fo" became "for," "dem" became "them," and so forth.) But most interviewers tried to provide a flavor of black dialect, with wildly varying success. In some cases the end result sounded more like the stereotypical "darky dialect" popular with whites of the period. "I wuz comin' frum de back uv de stable," an interviewer might quote his subject as saying—a colloquial approach that, to some readers, might at first seem unobjectionable. Yet few of the same interviewers would have thought it necessary to render, with similar offbeat spelling, the accents of a white "southun plantuh," whose speech might seem equally exotic to an American from another region of the United States. For that matter, consider the spellings used in "I wuz comin' frum de back uv de stable." In fact, there is no difference in pronunciation between "was" and "wuz"; or "frum" and "from"; or "uv" and "of." In effect, those transcriptions are simply cultural markers conveying the unspoken message that, in the eyes of the interviewer, the speaker comes from a less cultured and less educated social class. Eventually, the FWP sent its interviewers a list of Approved Dialect Expressions: "dem," "dose," and "gwine" were among the permitted transcriptions; "wuz," "ovah," and "uv" were not allowed.

By understanding the difficulties of gathering oral evidence, researchers are able to proceed more carefully in evaluating the slave narrative collection. Even so, readers new to this field may find it difficult to appreciate the varying responses that different interviewers might elicit. In order to bring the point home, it may be helpful to analyze material that we came across during our own research in the slave narrative collection. The interview below is with Susan Hamlin, a black woman who lived in Charleston, and we reprint it exactly as it appears in typescript.

Interview with Ex-Slave

On July 6th, I interviewed Susan Hamlin, ex-slave, at 17 Henrietta street, Charleston, S. C. She was sitting just inside of the front door, on a step leading up to the porch, and upon hearing me inquire for her she assumed that I was from the Welfare office, from which she had received aid prior to its closing. I did not correct this impression, and at no time did she suspect that the object of my visit was to get the story of her experience as a slave. During our conversation she mentioned her age. "Why that's very interesting, Susan," I told her, "If you are that old you probably remember the Civil War and slavery days." "Yes, Ma'am, I been a slave myself," she said, and told me the following story:

"I kin remember some things like it was yesterday, but I is 104 years old now, and age is starting to get me, I can't remember everything like I use to. I getting old, old. You know I is old when I been a grown woman when the Civil War broke out. I was hired out then, to a Mr. McDonald, who lived on Atlantic Street, and I remembers when de first shot was fired, and the shells went right over de city. I got seven dollars a month for looking after children, not taking them out, you understand, just minding them. I did not got the money, Mausa got it." "Don't you think that was fair?" I asked. "If you were fed and clothed by him, shouldn't he be paid for your work?" "Course it been fair," she answered, "I belong to him and he got to get something to take care of me."

"My name before I was married was Susan Calder, but I married a man named Hamlin. I belonged to Mr. Edward Fuller, he was president of the First National Bank. He was a good man to his people till de Lord took him. Mr. Fuller got his slaves by marriage. He married Miss Mikell, a lady what lived on Edisto Island, who was a slave owner, and we lived on Edisto on a plantation. I don't remember de name cause when Mr. Fuller got to be president of de bank we come to Charleston to live. He sell out the plantation and say them (the slaves) that want to come to Charleston with him could come and them what wants to stay can stay on the island with his wife's people. We had our choice. Some is come and some is stay, but my ma and us children come with Mr. Fuller.

"We lived on St. Philip street. The house still there, good as ever. I go 'round there to see it all de time; the cistern still there too, where we used to sit 'round and drink the cold water, and eat, and talk and laugh. Mr. Fuller have lots of servants and the ones he didn't need hisself he hired out. The slaves had rooms in the back, the ones with children had two rooms and them that didn't have any children had one room, not to cook in but to sleep in. They all cooked and ate downstairs in the hall that they had for the colored people. I don't know about slavery but I know all the slavery I know about, the people was good to me. Mr. Fuller was a good man and his wife's people been grand people, all good to their slaves. Seem like Mr. Fuller just git his slaves so he could be good to dem. He made all the little colored chillen love him. If you don't believe they loved him what they all cry, and scream, and holler for when dey hear he dead? 'Oh, Mausa dead my Mausa dead, what I going to do, my Mausa dead.' Dey tell dem t'aint no use to cry, dat can't bring him back, but de chillen keep on crying. We used to call him Mausa Eddie but he named Mr. Edward Fuller, and he sure was a good man.

"A man come here about a month ago, say he from de Government, and dey send him to find out 'bout slavery. I give him most a book, and what he give me? A dime. He ask me all kind of questions. He ask me dis and he ask me

> *"He ask me all kind of questions. He ask me dis and he ask me dat, didn't de white people do dis and did dey do dat but Mr. Fuller was a good man, he was sure good to me and all his people."*

dat, didn't de white people do dis and did dey do dat but Mr. Fuller was a good man, he was sure good to me and all his people, dey all like him, God bless him, he in de ground now but I ain't going to let nobody lie on him. You know he good when even the little chillen cry and holler when he dead. I tell you dey couldn't just fix us up any kind of way when we going to Sunday School. We had to be dressed nice, if you pass him and you ain't dress to suit him he send you right back and say tell your ma to see dat you dress right. Dey couldn't send you out in de cold barefoot neither. I 'member one day my ma want to send me wid some milk for her sister-in-law what lived 'round de corner. I fuss cause it cold and say 'how you going to send me out wid no shoe, and it cold?' Mausa hear how I talkin and turn he back and laugh, den he call to my ma to gone in de house and find shoe to put on my feet and don't let him see me barefoot again in cold weather.

"When de war start going good and de shell fly over Charleston he take all us up to Aiken for protection. Talk 'bout marching through Georgia, dey sure march through Aiken, soldiers was everywhere.

"My ma had six children, three boys and three girls, but I de only one left, all my white people and all de colored people gone, not a soul left but me. I ain't been sick in 25 years. I is near my church and I don't miss service any Sunday, night or morning. I kin walk wherever I please, I kin walk to de Battery if I want to. The Welfare use to help me but dey shut down now, I can't find out if dey going to open again or not. Miss (Mrs.) Buist and Miss Pringle, dey help me when I can go there but all my own dead."

"Were most of the masters kind?" I asked. "Well you know," she answered, "times den was just like dey is now, some was kind and some was mean; heaps of wickedness went on just de same as now. All my people was good people. I see some wickedness and I hear 'bout all kinds of t'ings but you don't know whether it was lie or not. Mr Fuller been a Christian man."

"Do you think it would have been better if the Negroes had never left Africa?" was the next question I asked. "No Ma'am, (emphatically) dem heathen didn't have no religion. I tell you how I t'ink it is. The Lord made t'ree nations, the white, the red and the black, and put dem in different places on de earth where dey was to stay. Dose black ignoramuses in Africa forgot God, and didn't have no religion and God blessed and prospered the white people dat did remember Him and sent dem to teach de black people even if dey have to grab dem and bring dem into bondage till dey learned some sense. The Indians forgot God and dey had to be taught better so dey land was taken away from dem. God sure bless and prosper de white people and He put de red and de black people under dem so dey could teach dem and bring dem into sense wid God. Dey had to get dere brains right, and honor God, and learn uprightness wid God cause ain't He make you, and ain't His Son redeem you and save you wid His Precious blood. You kin plan all de wickedness you want and pull hard as you choose but when the Lord mek up His mind you is to change, He can change you dat quick (snapping her fingers) and easy. You got to believe on Him if it tek bondage to bring you to your knees.

"You know I is got converted. I been in Big Bethel (church) on my knees praying under one of de preachers. I see a great, big, dark pack on my back, and it had me all bent over and my shoulders drawn down, all hunch up. I look up and I see de glory, I see a big beautiful light, a great light, and in de middle is de Sabior, hanging so (extending her arms) just like He died. Den I gone to praying good, and I can feel de sheckles (shackles) loose up and moving and de pack fall off. I don't know where it went to, I see de angels in de Heaven, and hear dem say 'Your sins are forgiven.' I scream and fell off so. (Swoon.) When I come to dey has laid me out straight and I know I is converted cause you can't see no such sight and go on like you is before. I know I is still a sinner but I believe in de power of God and I trust his Holy name. Den dey put me wid de seekers but I know I is already saved."

"Did they take good care of the slaves when their babies were born?" she was asked. "If you want chickens for fat (to fatten) you got to feed dem," she said with a smile, "and if you want people to work dey got to be strong, you got to feed dem and take care of dem too. If dey can't work it come out of your pocket. Lots of wickedness gone on in dem days, just as it do now, some good, some mean, black and white, it just dere nature, if dey good dey going to be kind to everybody, if dey mean dey going to be mean to everybody. Sometimes chillen was sold away from dey parents. De Mausa would come and say 'Where Jennie,' tell um to put clothes on dat baby, I want um. He sell de baby and de ma scream and holler, you know how dey carry on. Geneally (generally) dey sold it when de ma wasn't dere. Mr. Fuller didn't sell none of us, we stay wid our ma's till we grown, I stay wid my ma till she dead.

"You know I is mix blood, my grandfather bin a white man and my grandmother a mulatto. She been marry to a black so dat how I get fix like I is. I got both blood, so how I going to quarrel wid either side?"

SOURCE: Interview with Susan Hamlin, 17 Henrietta Street.

NOTE: Susan lives with a mulatto family of the better type. The name is Hamlin not Hamilton, and her name prior to her marriage was Calder not Collins. I paid particular attention to this and had them spell the names for me. I would judge Susan to be in the late nineties but she is wonderfully well preserved. She now claims to be 104 years old.

From the beginning, the circumstances of this conversation arouse suspicion. The white interviewer, Jessie Butler, mentions that she allowed Hamlin to think she was from the welfare office. Evidently, Butler thought Hamlin would speak more freely if the real purpose of the visit was hidden. But surely the deception had the opposite effect. Hamlin, like most of the black people interviewed, was elderly, unable to work, and dependent on charity. If Butler appeared to be from the welfare office, Hamlin would likely have done whatever she could to ingratiate herself. Many black interviewees consistently assumed that their white interviewers had influence with the welfare office. "You through wid me now, boss? I sho' is glad of dat," concluded one subject. "Help all you kin to get me dat pension befo' I die and de Lord will bless you, honey. . . . Has you got a dime to give dis old nigger, boss?"

Furthermore, Butler's questioning was hardly subtle. When Hamlin noted that she had to give her master the money she made from looking after children, Butler asked, "Don't you think that was fair?" "Course it been fair," came the quick response. Hamlin knew very well what was expected, especially since Butler had already answered the question herself: "If you were fed and clothed by him, shouldn't he be paid for your work?"

Not surprisingly, then, the interview paints slavery in relatively mild colors. Hamlin describes in great detail how good her master was and how she had shoes in the winter. When asked whether most masters were kind, Hamlin appears eminently "fair"—"some was kind and some was mean." She admits hearing "all kinds of t'ings but you don't know whether it was lie or not." She does note that slave children could be sold away from parents and that black mothers protested; but she talks as if that were only to be expected ("de ma scream and holler, you know how dey carry on").

Equally flattering is the picture Hamlin paints of relations between the races. "Black ignoramuses" in Africa had forgotten about God, she explains, just as the Indians had; but "God sure bless and prosper de white people." So Africans and the Indians are placed under white supervision, "to get dere brains right, and honor God, and learn uprightness." Those were not exactly the words proslavery apologists would have used to describe the situation, but they were the same sentiments. Defenders of slavery constantly stressed that Europeans served as benevolent models leading Africans and Indians on the slow upward road to civilization.

All these aspects of the interview led us to be suspicious about its content. Moreover, several additional clues in the document puzzled us. Hamlin had mentioned a man who visited her "about a month ago, say he from de Government, and dey send him to find out 'bout slavery." Apparently her interview with Jessie Butler was the second she had given. Butler, for her part, made a fuss at the end of the transcript over the spelling of Hamlin's name ("I paid particular attention to this."). It was "Hamlin not Hamilton," and her maiden name was "Calder not Collins." The phrasing indicates that somewhere else Butler had seen Hamlin referred to as "Susan Hamilton." If someone had interviewed Hamlin earlier, we wondered, could Hamilton have been the name on that original report?

We found the answer when we continued on through the narrative collection. The interview following Butler's was conducted by a man named Augustus Ladson, with a slave named "Susan Hamilton." When compared with Jessie Butler's interview, Augustus Ladson's makes absorbing reading. Here it is, printed exactly as it appears in the collection:

Ex-Slave 101 Years of Age

Has Never Shaken Hands Since 1863

Was on Knees Scrubbing when Freedom Gun Fired

I'm a hund'ed an' one years old now, son. De only one livin' in my crowd frum de days I wuz a slave. Mr. Fuller, my master, who was president of the Firs' National Bank, owned the fambly of us except my father. There were eight men an' women with five girls an' six boys workin' for him. Most o' them wus hired out. De house in which we stayed is still dere with de sisterns an' slave quarters. I always go to see de old home which is on St. Phillip Street.

My ma had t'ree boys an' t'ree girls who did well at their work. Hope Mikell, my eldest brodder, an' James wus de shoemaker. William Fuller, son of our Master, wus de bricklayer. Margurite an' Catharine wus de maids an' look as de children.

My pa b'long to a man on Edisto Island. Frum what he said, his master was very mean. Pa real name wus Adam Collins but he took his master' name; he wus de coachman. Pa did supin one day en his master whipped him. De next day which wus Monday, pa carry him 'bout four miles frum home in de woods an' give him de same 'mount of lickin' he wus given on Sunday. He tied him to a tree an' unhitched de horse so it couldn't git tie-up an' kill e self. Pa den gone to de landin' an' cetch a boat dat wus comin' to Charleston wood fa'm products. He (was) permitted by his master to go to town on errands, which helped him to go on de boat without bein' question'. W'en he got here he gone on de water-front an' ax for a job on a ship so he could git to de North. He got de job an' sail' wood de ship. Dey search de island up an' down for him wood houndogs en w'en it wus t'ought he wus drowned, 'cause dey track him to de river, did dey give up. One of his master' friend gone to New York en went in a store w'ere pas wus employed as a clerk. He reconize' pa is easy is pa reconize' him. He gone back home an' tell pa master who know den dat pa wusn't comin' back an' before he died he sign' papers dat pa wus free. Pa' ma wus dead an' he come down to bury her by de permission of his master' son who had promised no ha'm would come to him, but dey wus' fixin' plans to keep him, so he went to de Work House an' ax to be sold 'cause any slave could sell e self if e could git to de Work House. But it wus on record down dere so dey couldn't sell 'im an' told him his master' people couldn't hold him a slave.

People den use to do de same t'ings dey do now. Some marry an' some live together jus' like now. One t'ing, no minister nebber say in readin' de matrimony "let no man put asounder" 'cause a couple would be married tonight an' tomorrow one would be taken away en be sold. All slaves wus married in dere master house, in de livin' room where slaves an' dere missus an' mossa wus to witness de ceremony. Brides use to wear some of de finest dress an' if dey could afford it, have de best kind of furniture. Your master nor your missus objected to good t'ings.

I'll always 'member Clory, de washer. She wus very high-tempered. She was a mulatto with beautiful hair she could sit on; Clory didn't take foolishness frum anybody. One day our missus gone in de laundry an' find fault with de clothes. Clory didn't do a t'ing but pick her up bodily an' throw 'er out de door. Dey had to sen' fur a doctor 'cause she pregnant an' less than two hours de baby wus bo'n. Afta dat she begged to be sold fur she didn't [want] to kill missus, but our master ain't nebber want to sell his slaves. But dat didn't keep Clory frum gittin' a brutal whippin'. Dey whip' 'er until dere wusn't a white spot on her body. Dat wus de worst I ebber see a human bein' got such a beatin'. I t'ought she wus goin' to die, but she got well an' didn't get any better but meaner until our master decide it wus bes' to rent her out. She willingly agree' since she wusn't 'round missus. She hated an' detest' both of them an' all de fambly.

> *"Our master ain't nebber want to sell his slaves. But dat didn't keep Clory frum gittin' a brutal whippin'. Dey whip' 'er until dere wusn't a white spot on her body. Dat wus de worst I ebber see a human bein' got such a beatin'. I t'ought she wus goin' to die."*

W'en any slave wus whipped all de other slaves wus made to watch. I see women hung frum de ceilin' of buildin's an' whipped with only supin tied 'round her lower part of de body, until w'en dey wus taken down, dere wusn't breath in de body. I had some terribly bad experiences.

Yankees use to come t'rough de streets, especially de Big Market, huntin' those who want to go to de "free country" as dey call' it. Men an' women wus always missin' an' nobody could give 'count of dere disappearance. De men wus train' up North fur sojus.

De white race is so brazen. Dey come here an' run de Indians frum dere own lan', but dey couldn't make dem slaves 'cause dey wouldn't stan' for it. Indians use to git up in trees an' shoot dem with poison arrow. W'en dey couldn't make dem slaves den dey gone to Africa an' bring dere black brother an' sister. Dey say 'mong themselves, "we gwine mix dem up en make ourselves king. Dats d only way we'd git even with de Indians."

All time, night an' day, you could hear men an' women screamin' to de tip of dere voices as either ma, pa, sister, or brother wus take without any warnin' an' sell. Some time mother who had only one chile wus separated fur life. People wus always dyin' frum a broken heart.

One night a couple married an' de next mornin' de boss sell de wife. De gal ma got in in de street an' cursed de white woman fur all she could find. She said: "dat damn white, pale-face bastard sell my daughter who jus' married las' night," an' other t'ings. The white man tresten' her to call de police if she didn't stop, but de collud woman said: "hit me or call de police. I redder die dan to stan' dis any longer." De police took her to de Work House by de white woman orders an' what became of 'er, I never hear.

W'en de war began we wus taken to Aiken, South Ca'lina were we stay' until de Yankees come t'rough. We could see balls sailin' t'rough de air w'en Sherman wus comin'. Bumbs hit trees in our yard. W'en de freedom gun wus fired, I wus on my 'nees scrubbin'. Dey tell me I wus free but I didn't b'lieve it.

In de days of slavory woman wus jus' given time 'nough to deliver dere babies. Dey deliver de baby 'bout eight in de mornin' an' twelve had to be back to work.

I wus a member of Emmanuel African Methodist Episcopal Church for 67 years. Big Zion, across de street wus my church before den an' before Old Bethel w'en I lived on de other end of town.

Sence Lincoln shook hands with his assasin who at de same time shoot him, frum dat day I stop shakin' hands, even in de church, an' you know how long dat wus. I don't b'lieve in kissin' neider fur all carry dere meannesses. De Master wus betrayed by one of his bosom frien' with a kiss.

SOURCE: Interview with (Mrs.) Susan Hamilton, 17 Henrietta Street, who claims to be 101 years of age. She has never been sick for twenty years and walks as though just 40. She was hired out by her master for seven dollars a month which had to be given her master.

Susan Hamlin and Susan Hamilton are obviously one and the same, yet by the end of Ladson's interview, we are wondering if we have been listening to the same person! Kindness of the masters? We hear no tales about old Mr. Fuller, only vivid recollections of whippings so harsh "dere wusn't a white spot on her body." To Butler, Hamlin had mentioned only cruelties that she had heard about secondhand ("you don't know whether it was lie or not"); to Ladson, she recounts firsthand experiences ("I see women hung frum de ceilin' of buildin's an' whipped with only supin tied 'round her lower part of de body").

Happy family relations? Instead of tales about shoes in the winter, we hear of Hamlin's father, whipped so severely he rebels and flees. We hear of family separations, not downplayed with a "you know how dey carry on," but with all the bitterness of mothers whose children had been taken "without any warnin'." We hear of a couple married one night, then callously separated and sold the next day. In the Butler account, slave babies are fed well, treated nicely; in the Ladson account, the recollection is of mothers who were given only a few hours away from the fields in order to deliver their children.

Benevolent white paternalism? This time Hamlin's tale of three races draws a different moral. The white race is "brazen," running the Indians off

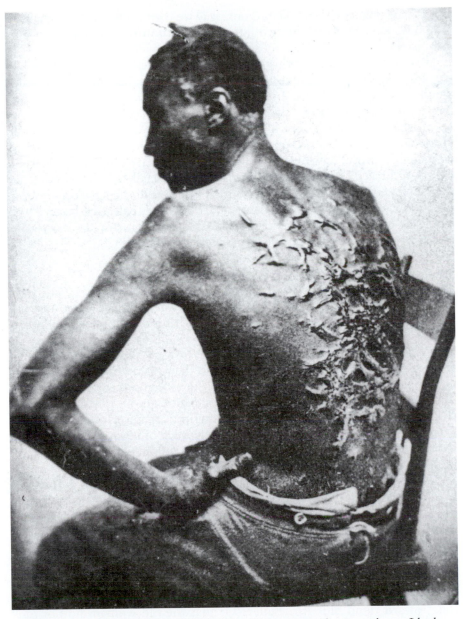

"W'en any slave wus whipped all de other slaves was made to watch. . . . I had some terribly bad experiences." The scars from whippings on this slave's back were recorded in 1863 by an unknown photographer traveling with the Union army.

their land. With a touch of admiration, she notes that the Indians "wouldn't stan' for" being made slaves. White motives are seen not as religious but as exploitative and vengeful: "Dey say 'mong themselves, 'we gwine mix dem

up en make ourselves king. Dats d only way we'd git even with de Indians.'"
The difference between the two interviews, both in tone and substance, is
astonishing.

How do we account for this difference? Nowhere in the South Carolina
narratives is the race of Augustus Ladson mentioned, but internal evidence
would indicate he is black. In a culture in which blacks usually addressed
whites respectfully with a "sir," "ma'am," or "boss," it seems doubtful that
Susan Hamlin would address a white man as "son" ("I'm a hund'ed an' one
years old now, son"). Furthermore, the content of the interview is just too
consistently critical of whites. Hamlin would never have remarked "De white
race is so brazen" if Ladson had been white, especially given the reticence
demonstrated in her interview with Butler. Nor would she have been so specific about the angry mother's curses ("damn white, pale-face bastard"). It
would be difficult to conceive of a more strikingly dramatic demonstration
of how an interviewer can affect the responses of a subject.

FREEDOM AND DECEPTION

The slave narrative collection, then, is not the unfiltered perspective it first
appears to be. In fact, interviews like Susan Hamlin's seem to suggest that
the search for the "true" perspectives of the freedpeople is bound to end in
failure and frustration. We have seen, first, that information from planters
and other white sources must be treated with extreme skepticism and, second, that northern white sources deserve similar caution. Finally, it appears
that even the oral testimony of African Americans themselves must be questioned, given the circumstances under which much of it was gathered. It is as
if a detective discovered that all the clues so carefully pieced together were
hopelessly biased, leading the investigation down the wrong path.

The seriousness of the problem should not be underestimated. It is fundamental. We can try to ease out of the dilemma by noting that differing
degrees of bias exist—that some accounts are likely to be less deceptive
than others. Susan Hamlin's interview with Ladson, for instance, surely
portrays her feelings more accurately than the interview with Butler. But
does that mean we reject all of the Butler interview? Presumably, Susan
Hamlin's master did give her a pair of shoes one cold winter day. Are we to
assume, because of Ladson's interview, that the young child felt no grati-
tude toward "kind old" Mr. Fuller? Or that the old woman did not look
back on those years with some ambivalence? For all her life, both slave
and free, Susan Hamlin lived in a world where she was required to "feel"
one set of emotions when dealing with some people and a different set
when dealing with other people. Can we be confident that the emotions
she expressed to Ladson were her "real" feelings, while the ones to Jessie
Butler were her "false" feelings? How can we arrive at an objective conclusion about "real" feelings in any social situation in which such severe
strains existed?

Putting the question in this light offers at least a partial way out of the dilemma. If so many clues in the investigation are "biased"—that is, distorted by the social situation in which they are set—then the widespread nature of the distortion may serve as a key to understanding the situation. The evidence in the case is warped precisely because it reflects a distortion in the society itself. The elements of racism and slavery determined a culture in which personal relations were grounded in mistrust, creating a kind of economy of deception, in which slaves could survive only if they remained conscious of the need to adapt their feelings to the situation.

The elements of racism and slavery determined a culture in which personal relations were grounded in mistrust, creating a kind of economy of deception.

The deception was mutual—practiced by both sides on each other. Susan Hamlin was adapting the story of her past to the needs of the moment at the same time that Jessie Butler was letting Hamlin believe her to be a welfare agent. White masters painted lurid stories of Yankee devils with horns, while slaves, playing roles they were expected to play, rolled their eyes in fear until they could run straight for Union lines.

Given this logic, it would be tempting simply to turn old historical interpretations on their heads. Whereas William Dunning took most white primary sources at face value and saw only cheerful, childlike Sambos, an enlightened history would read the documents upside down, stripping away the camouflage to reveal slaves who, quite rationally, went about the daily business of "puttin' on ole massa." We have already seen abundant evidence that slaves did consciously deceive in order to protect themselves.

But simply to replace one set of feelings with another is to drastically underestimate the strains arising out of an economy of deception. The longer that masters and slaves were compelled to live false or inauthentic lives, the easier it must have been for them to mislead themselves as well as others. Where white and black people alike engaged in daily deception, some of it was inevitably directed inward, to preserve the fiction of living in a tolerable, normally functioning society.

When the war came, shattering that fiction, whites and blacks were exposed in vivid ways to the deception that had been so much a part of their lives. For white slaveholders, the revelation usually came when Union troops entered a region and slaves deserted the plantations in droves. Especially demoralizing was the flight of slaves whom planters had believed most loyal. "He was about my age and I had always treated him more as a companion than a slave," noted one planter of the first defector from his ranks. Mary Chesnut, the woman near Fort Sumter who had tried to penetrate the blank expressions of her slaves, discovered how impossible the task had been. "Jonathan, whom we trusted, betrayed us," she lamented, while "Claiborne, that black rascal who was suspected by all the world," faithfully protected the plantation.

Many slaveholders, when faced with the truth, refused to recognize the role that deception had played in their lives, thereby deceiving themselves further. "The poor negroes don't do us any harm except when they are put up to it," concluded one Georgia woman. A Richmond newspaper editor demanded that a slave who had denounced Jefferson Davis "be whipped every day until he confesses what white man put these notions in his head." Yet the war brought painful insight to others. "We were all laboring under a delusion," confessed one South Carolina planter. "I believed that these people were content, happy, and attached to their masters. But events and reflection have caused me to change these opinions. . . . If they were content, happy and attached to their masters, why did they desert him in the moment of his need and flock to an enemy, whom they did not know?"

For slaves, news of emancipation brought an entirely different reaction, but still one conditioned by the old habits. We have already seen how one old Georgia slave couple remained impassive as Sherman's troops passed through, until finally the wife could restrain herself no longer. Even the servant who eloquently praised freedom by a secluded brook remembered the need for caution: "I got sort o' scared, afeared somebody hear me, an' I takes another good look." Although emancipation promised a society founded on equal treatment, slaves could not help wondering whether the new order would fully replace the old. That transformation would occur only if freedpeople could forge relationships that were no longer based on the customs of deception nor rooted in the central fiction of slavery: that blacks were incapable of assuming a place in free society.

As historians came to recognize the value of the slave narrative collection, they drew upon its evidence, along with other primary sources, to discover how freedpeople sought to define their new freedoms, how they distanced themselves from the old habits of bondage. The taking of new names was one step. As slaves, African Americans often had no surnames, or they took the names of their masters. Equally demeaning, given names were often casually assigned by their owners. Cicero, Pompey, and other Latin or biblical names were bestowed in jest. And whether or not slaves had surnames, they were always addressed familiarly, by their given names. Such customs were part of the symbolic language of deception, promoting the illusion that black people were helpless dependents of the planter's family.

Thus freedpeople took for themselves new names, severing the symbolic tie with their old masters. "A heap of people say they was going to name their selves over," recalled one freedman. "They named their selves big names. . . . Some of the names was Abraham an' some called their selves Lincum. Any big name 'ceptin' their master's name. It was the fashion." Even former slaves who remained loyal to their masters recognized the significance of the change. "When you'all had de power you was good to me," an older freedman told his master, "an I'll protect you now. No niggers nor Yankees shall touch you. If you want anything, call for Sambo. I mean, call for Mr. Samuel—that's my name now."

Just as freedpeople took new names to symbolize their new status, so also many husbands and wives reaffirmed their marriages in formal ceremonies. Under slavery, family ties had been ignored through the convenient fiction that Africans were morally inferior. Black affections, the planters argued, were dominated by impulse and the physical desires of the moment. Such self-deception eased many a master's conscience when slave families were separated and sold. Similarly, many planters married slaves only informally, with a few words sufficing to join the couples. "Don't mean nuthin' less you say, 'What God done jined, cain't no man pull asunder,'" noted one Virginia freedman. "But dey never would say dat. Jus' say, 'Now you married.'" For reasons of human dignity, black couples moved to solemnize their marriage vows. There were practical reasons for an official ceremony, too: it might qualify families for military pensions or the division of lands that was widely rumored to be coming.

Equally symbolic for former slaves was the freedom to travel. Historian William Dunning recognized this fact but interpreted it from the viewpoint of his southern white sources as "aimless but happy" wandering. Richard Edwards, a preacher in Florida, explicitly described how important moving or traveling was:

> You ain't, none o' you, gwinter feel rale free till you shakes de dus' ob de Old Plantashun offen yore feet an' goes ter a new place whey you kin live out o' sight o' de gret house. So long ez de shadder ob de gret house falls acrost you, you ain't gwine ter feel lak no free man, an' you ain't gwine ter feel lak no free 'oman. You mus' all move—you mus' move clar away from de ole places what you knows, ter de new places what you don't know, whey you kin raise up yore head douten no fear o' Marse Dis ur Marse Tudder.

And so, in the spring and summer of 1865, southern roads were filled with black people, hiving off "like bees trying to find a setting place," as one former slave recalled. Most freedpeople remained near family and friends, merely leaving one plantation in search of work at another. But a sizable minority traveled farther, to settle in cities, move west, or try their fortunes at new occupations.

Many former slaves traveled in order to reunite families separated through previous sales. Freedpeople "had a passion, not so much for wandering, as for getting together," a Freedman's Bureau agent observed, "and every mother's son among them seemed to be in search of his mother; every mother in search of her children." Often, relatives had only scanty information; in other cases, so much time had passed that kin could hardly recognize each other, especially when young children had grown up separated from their parents.

"Every mother's son among them seemed to be in search of his mother; every mother in search of her children."

A change of name or location, the formalization of a marriage, a reunion with relatives—all these acts demonstrated that freedpeople wanted no part of the old constraints and deceptions of slavery. But as much as these acts defined black freedom, larger issues remained. How much would emancipation broaden economic avenues open to African Americans? Would freedom provide an opportunity to rise on the social ladder? Freedpeople looked anxiously for signs of change.

Perhaps the most commonly perceived avenue to success was through education. Slavery had been rationalized, in part, through the fiction that blacks were incapable of profiting from an education. Especially where masters had energetically prevented slaves from acquiring skills in reading, writing, and arithmetic, the hunger for learning was intense. When northerners occupied the Carolina Sea Islands during the war, Yankee plantation superintendents found that the most effective way to force unwilling laborers to work was to threaten to take away their schoolbooks. "The Negroes . . . will do anything for us, if we will only teach them," noted one missionary.

After the war, when the Freedman's Bureau sent hundreds of northern schoolteachers into the South, black students flocked enthusiastically to the makeshift schoolhouses. Often, classes could be held only at night, but the freedpeople were willing. "We work all day, but we'll come to you in the evening for learning," Georgia freedpeople told their teacher. Some white plantation owners discovered that if they wished to keep their field hands, they would have to provide a schoolhouse and teacher.

Important as education was, the freedpeople were preoccupied even more with their relation to the lands they had worked for so many years. The vast majority of slaves were field hands. The agricultural life was the one they had grown up with, and as freedpeople they wanted the chance to own and cultivate their own property. Independent ownership would lay to rest the lie that black people were incapable of managing their own affairs. But without land, the idea of freedom would be just another deception. "Gib us our own land and we take care of ourselves; but widout land, de ole massas can hire us or starve us, as dey please," noted one freedman. In the heady enthusiasm at the close of the war, many former slaves were convinced that the Union would divide up confiscated Confederate plantations. Each family, so the persistent rumor went, would receive forty acres and a mule. "This was no slight error, no trifling idea," reported one white observer, "but a fixed and earnest conviction as strong as any belief a man can ever have." Slaves had worked their masters' lands for so long without significant compensation, it seemed only fair that compensation should finally be made. Further, ever since southern planters had fled from invading Union troops, some black workers had been allowed to cultivate the abandoned fields.

The largest occupied region was the Sea Islands along the Carolina coast, where young Sam Mitchell first heard the northern guns. As early as March

"My Lord, ma'am, what a great thing larning is!" a freedman exclaimed to a white teacher. Many white people were surprised by the intensity of the ex-slaves' desire for an education. To say that the freedpeople were "anxious to learn" was not strong enough, one Virginia school official noted; "they are *crazy* to learn." These schoolboys were from South Carolina.

1863, freedpeople were purchasing confiscated lands from the government. Then in January 1865, after General William Sherman completed his devastating march to the sea, he extended the area open to confiscation. In his Special Field Order No. 15, Sherman decreed that a long strip of abandoned lands, stretching from Charleston on the north to Jacksonville on the south, would be reserved for the freedpeople. The lands would be subdivided into forty-acre tracts, which could be rented for a nominal fee. After three years, the freedpeople had the option to purchase the land outright.

Sherman's order was a tactical maneuver, designed to deal with the overwhelming problem of refugees in his path. But black workers widely perceived this order and other promises by northerners as a foretaste of Reconstruction policy. Consequently, when white planters returned to their plantations, they often found blacks who no longer bowed and tipped their hats. Thomas Pinckney of South Carolina, having called his former slaves together, asked them if they would continue to work for him. "O yes, we gwi wuk! we gwi wuk all right," came the angry response. "We gwi wuk fuh ourse'ves. We ain' gwi wuk fuh no white man." Pinckney asked where they would go to work—seeing as they had no land. "We ain't gwine nowhar," they replied defiantly. "We gwi wuk right here on de lan' whar we wuz bo'n an' whar belongs tuh us."

Despite the defiance, Pinckney prevailed, as did the vast majority of southern planters. Redistribution of southern lands was an idea supported only by more radical northerners. Thaddeus Stevens introduced a confiscation bill in Congress, but it was swamped by debate and never passed. President Johnson, whose conciliatory policies pleased southern planters, determined to settle the issue as quickly as possible. He summoned General O. O. Howard, head of the Freedman's Bureau, and instructed him to reach a solution "mutually satisfactory" to both blacks and planters. Howard, though sympathetic to the freedpeople, could not mistake the true meaning of the president's order.

Sadly the general returned to the Sea Islands in October and assembled a group of freedpeople on Edisto Island. The audience, suspecting the bad news, was restless and unruly. Howard tried vainly to speak and made "no progress" until a woman in the crowd began singing, "Nobody knows the trouble I've seen." The crowd joined, then was silent while Howard told them they must give up their lands. Bitter cries of "No! No!" came from the audience. "Why, General Howard, why do you take away our lands?" called one burly man. "You take them from us who have always been true, always true to the Government! You give them to our all-time enemies! That is not right!"

Reluctantly, and sometimes only after forcible resistance, African Americans lost the lands to returning planters. Whatever else freedom might mean, it was not to signify compensation for previous labor. In the years to come, Reconstruction would offer freedom of another sort, through the political process. By the beginning of 1866 the radicals in Congress had charted a plan that gave African Americans basic civil rights and political power. Yet even that avenue of opportunity was sealed off. In the decades that followed the first thunder of emancipation, black people would look back on their early experiences almost as if they were part of another, vanished world. The traditions of racial oppression and the daily deceptions that went with them were too strong to be thoroughly overturned by the war.

"I was right smart bit by de freedom bug for awhile," Charlie Davenport of Mississippi recalled.

> It sounded pow'ful nice to be tol: "You don't have to chop cotton no more. You can th'ow dat hoe down an' go fishin' whensoever de notion strikes you. An' you can roam 'roun' at night an' court gals jus' as you please. Aint no marster gwine a-say to you, 'Charlie, you's got to be back when de clock strikes nine.'"
> I was fool 'nough to b'lieve all dat kin' o' stuff.

Both perceptions—the first flush of the "freedom bug" as well as Davenport's later disillusionment—accurately reflect the black experience. Freedom had come to a nation of four million slaves, and it changed their lives in deep and important ways. But for many years after the war put an end to human bondage, too many freedpeople still had to settle for a view from the bottom rail.

Additional Reading

Leon Litwack's superb *Been in the Storm So Long: The Aftermath of Slavery* (New York, 1979) was seminal in integrating evidence from the slave narratives into a reevaluation of the Reconstruction era. It serves as an excellent introduction to the freedpeople's experience after the war. Eric Foner's *Reconstruction: America's Unfinished Revolution* (New York, 1988) is the definitive survey of the period. Steven Hahn provides an even broader sweep in *A Nation Under Our Feet: Black Political Struggles in the Rural South from Slavery to the Great Migration* (Cambridge, MA, 2003). A selection of oral interviews from the Federal Writers' Project appears in Ira Berlin et al., *Remembering Slavery: African Americans Talk about Their Personal Experiences of Slavery and Freedom* (New York, 1998). The highlight of this collection is an audiocassette containing more than a dozen of the only known original recordings of former slaves. For the full collection of interviews, see George P. Rawick, *The American Slave: A Composite Autobiography*, 19 vols. and suppl. (Westport, CT, 1972–). Further analysis of the slave narratives may be found in John Blassingame, *Slave Testimony* (Baton Rouge, LA, 1977). Paul D. Escott, *Slavery Remembered: A Record of Twentieth-Century Slave Narratives* (Chapel Hill, NC, 1979), breaks down the percentage of interviews with field hands, house servants, and artisans; the occupations they took up as freedpeople; and the destinations of those who migrated. Heather Andrea Williams, *Self-Taught: African American Education in Slavery and Freedom* (Chapel Hill, NC, 2003), details the desire for learning.

PAST AND PRESENT
Whose Oral History?

During the 1930s, John Avery Lomax and his son Alan used state-of-the-art equipment to record the oral histories of former slaves on acetate disks. Their recorder was portable, but only barely: they had to load its 315 pounds into the trunk of a car. Given the cumbersome technology, most slave narratives were not recorded on audio disks. Still, the voices of twenty-three former slaves are available on CD from PaperlessArchives.com for those who wish to listen to them today.

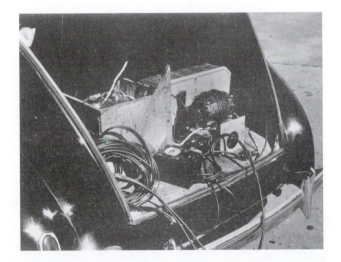

Historians now face a different problem—too much material. Almost anyone can record recollections of the past. Through StoryCorps, for example, the Library of Congress and National Public Radio have created both permanent booths and mobile facilities where ordinary people can record their memories. But anyone with a digital voice recorder can undertake his or her own independent project. These devices, smaller than a pack of cigarettes,

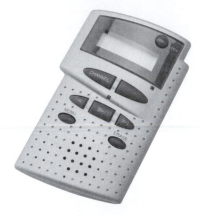

have the capability of capturing well over 100 hours of material. Think what the Lomaxes could have done with such portable equipment.

Who, then, is a proper subject for an oral-history interview? The Federal Writers' Project chose slaves because the survivors were dying out. Now we are losing the recollections of those who experienced World War II and the Korean War. Quickly enough we will face the loss of veterans from Vietnam and the civil rights movement. Obviously, the older the subject being interviewed, the greater the chronological reach. A 90-year-old recalling his or her childhood can provide personal recollections of the 1920s, while memories passed along by *their* parents and grandparents might contain stories reaching back to the Civil War.

But oral history is equally useful in preserving recent experiences, to be recalled by family or historians decades from now. "Our parents forced us to read the Korean bible every night," recalled one Korean American in an oral history from the 1990s. "If we couldn't finish reading it, we sometimes had to stay up until two in the morning on school nights. . . . My younger sister, who's at Barnard College in New York, doesn't go to church now; she despises the dogma and sees the ideology as male chauvinist. Lately, I'm a little in line with her. I went to a Korean church here in L.A. for a while, but some of the things they said really bothered me. In the pulpit, the minister would say something about Hillary Clinton or make snide remarks about 'feminazis.'" Such contemporary stories bid fair to create a mosaic as engrossing as those recorded by the Lomaxes eight decades ago.

Credits

Prologue
p. xix: Library of Congress, Prints and Photographs Division; p. xxviii: The Art Archive/Bibliothèque des Arts Décoratifs Paris/Gianni Dagli Orti.

Chapter 1
p. 2: © Blue Lantern Studio/Corbis; p. 4: Courtesy of the author; p. 10: © Dorling Kindersley/Getty Images; p. 13: Courtesy of Dr. Jeffrey M. Mitchem, Arkansas Archeological Survey; p. 14: Courtesy of the John Carter Brown Library at Brown University.; p. 16: South Carolina State Museum; p. 24: The National Library of Medicine/Visual Image Presentations; p. 27: The Granger Collection, New York.

Chapter 2
p. 34: Library of Congress, Prints and Photographs Division; p. 42: Neimeyer Tabaksmuseum, Groningen, The Netherlands; p. 47: Library of Congress, Prints and Photographs Division.

Chapter 3
p. 62: Yale University, Sterling Memorial Library; p. 72: By permission of The British Library (Add. 32496 f. 51).

Chapter 4
p. 76: Library of Congress Prints and Photographs Division [LC-USZC62-3736]; p. 80L: Library of Congress, Prints & Photographs Division, LC-USZ62-49950; p. 80R: Library of Congress, Prints & Photographs Division, LC-USZ62-128740; p. 88: Library of Congress, Prints & Photographs Division, LC-USZ62-8549; p. 95: Public Domain.

Chapter 5
p. 98: Photograph courtesy of the Pocumtuck Valley Memorial Association, Memorial Hall Museum, Deerfield, MA. All rights reserved. (Acc. no. 1960.17); p. 99L: Rare Books Division, The New York Public Library, Astor, Lenox and Tilden Foundations; p. 99R: Rare Books Division, The New York Public Library, Astor, Lenox and Tilden Foundations; p. 100: Photograph courtesy of the Pocumtuck Valley Memorial Association, Memorial Hall Museum, Deerfield, MA. (Acc. no. 1897.09); p. 103: Photograph courtesy of the Pocumtuck Valley Memorial Association, Memorial Hall Museum, Deerfield, MA. (Acc. no. 1999.13.507); p. 104: John Lewis Krimmel, "Quilting Frolic," 1813. Courtesy, Winterthur Museum,

DE. (Acc. no. 1953.0178.002);
p. 105: Old Sturbridge Village, MA
(Acc. no. B29098); p. 106: John Lewis
Krimmel, "Quilting Frolic" (detail),
1813. Courtesy, Winterthur Museum,
DE. (Acc. no. 1953.0178.002); p. 107:
Courtesy of Historic Deerfield,
Photograph by Amanda Merullo. (Acc.
no. 1998.35); p. 108: Hannah Barnard.
Press Cupboard, c. 1710. The Henry
Ford, Dearborn, MI. (36.178.1);
p. 110: Courtesy of Historic Deerfield.
Photograph by Amanda Merullo. (Acc.
no. 56.140); p. 116: Old Sturbridge
Village, MA; p. 117: Old Sturbridge
Village, MA; p. 118: "There Is No
School Like the Family School," from
The Mother's Assistant and Young
Lady's Friend.

Chapter 6

p. 126L: Collection of The University
of Wisconsin-Madison Archives;
p. 126R: The Huntington Library,
San Marino, CA (Box 58 #16);
p. 132: Library of Congress, Prints
and Photographs Division; p. 136:
Thomas Scully, "Andrew Jackson,"
c. 1857. Library of Congress,
Prints and Photographs Division;
p. 139: Library of Congress, Prints
and Photographs Division; p. 144:

Photo courtesy of Edward E. Ayer
Collection, The Newberry Library,
Chicago.

Chapter 7

p. 150: Library of Congress, Prints
and Photographs Division; p. 152:
Library of Congress, Prints and
Photographs Division; p. 154: Library
of Congress, Prints and Photographs
Division; p. 155: Library of Congress,
Prints and Photographs Division;
p. 164: Library of Congress, Prints
and Photographs Division; p. 167L:
Library of Congress, Prints and
Photographs Division; p. 167R:
Library of Congress, Prints and
Photographs Division.

Chapter 8

p. 172: Library of Congress, Prints and
Photographs Division; p. 174: John Jacob
Omenhausser, "Guard Challenging
Prisoner," 1864. © Collection
of the New York Historical Society.
(ae00045); p. 176: Library of Congress,
Prints and Photographs Division;
p. 182: National Archives; p. 191:
National Archives; p. 197: Public
Domain; p. 201: American Folklife
Center, Library of Congress; p. 202:
© TRBfoto/Getty Images/PhotoDisc.

Index